XIX
XX
XXI
XXII
XXIII
XXIIII
I
II
III
IIII
V

# 100,000 YEARS OF DAILY LIFE

## A VISUAL HISTORY

# 100,000 YEARS OF DAILY LIFE

## A VISUAL HISTORY

by Jacques Brosse

Paul Chaland and Jacques Ostier

UNDER THE GENERAL EDITORSHIP OF

Robert Laffont

TRANSLATED BY

Anne Carter

GOLDEN PRESS · NEW YORK

Other Editions of this Book

In French by
EDITIONS DU PONT ROYAL, PARIS

In English by
THE BODLEY HEAD LTD, LONDON
(for the United Kingdom)

In German by
ALFRED SCHERZ VERLAG, BERNE—STUTTGART

In Italian by
VALENTINO BOMPIANI & C., MILAN

In Spanish by
PLAZA & JANES S.A., BARCELONA

In Portuguese by
LIVRARIA BERTRAND, LISBON

In Dutch by
J. M. MEULENHOFF UITGEVER, AMSTERDAM

In Finnish by
WERNER SÖDERSTRÖM OSAKEYHTIÖ, HELSINKI

49510


Library of Congress Catalog Card Number: 61-14411
Printed and bound in France for
GOLDEN PRESS, INC.
New York, N.Y.
by Editions du Pont Royal
*First published 1961*

# EDITOR'S FOREWORD

A hundred thousand years of daily life: the history of the changes in men's lives through three thousand generations to the point in time which is our own civilisation. The story we have tried to tell is a fabulous one, a complex of ideas and experience, of sudden leaps and slow, infinitesimal change, of bitter conflicts and new discoveries.

It is a story that would have been meaningless had we tried to confine it within the limits of a single country or a single continent, for we of today have learned much of what we know from the wisdom and experience of people all over the earth. Man's constant struggle towards a better life is as a relay race in which humanity is a single team, passing the torch from hand to hand down the centuries and across the globe. If we are to gain any clear impression of how this evolution has come about we must look for the time and place where each new age has started, watching the fresh discoveries as they are made, and this is why we have turned our attention especially to the highlights of the world's great civilisations.

The form of the Visual History series lends itself more readily than any other to this investigation. Its combination of text and pictures creates an appearance of actual life and gives the best possible illustration of how across the divides of time and space the essentials of life remain the same, though the surface alters. We have dispensed altogether with arbitrary chapter headings, which in our view only serve to create divisions where none exist, and have allowed the whole panorama of mankind to unroll itself before the reader at its own pace.

We have followed, sometimes for a single day and sometimes for a whole lifetime, the day-to-day activities of a single representative individual in preference to simply cataloguing the achievements of each country in turn.

Among the characters whose lives are briefly illumined by our spotlight are Akurgal, a schoolboy in Ur, two thousand years before Christ; Neferhotep, Lord of the Secrets of the Morning Apartment, in the realm of the Pharaohs; Callicles, an Athenian citizen; Lucius Marcus, a Roman knight; Abu-l-Hasan al Hahshab who lived in twelfth-century Cairo; Fong Tch'ang, a civil servant of Imperial China; John Wyndham, a clerk of Oxford; Messer Francesco di Marco, merchant of Prato and many others of all nationalities, French, German, Dutch, Russian, Norwegian, American, Japanese and Indian, as well as Mayas, Mongols, Africans, Australians and Polynesians.

In this book the reader, or perhaps we should call him the spectator, can enter into every detail of their private lives and eavesdrop on each moment of their day. All doors open before him and he can explore palaces, cottages and even harems at will. Text and pictures are always substantiated by direct, factual evidence and never rest solely on imagination or conjecture. But in *100,000 Years of Daily Life* the reader will find not only the living shades of the past but also those permanent features of the landscape in all parts of the world which outlive many generations of men: the paddy fields of China, Flemish convents, Japanese paper houses, the costumes of Peruvian Indians and the peasant dresses of Europe.

To trace the beginnings of this development we have to go far back into prehistory, to those earliest ancestors of ours who, long before any written texts, took the first initiatives and passed on to their descendants the rudiments of the art of living. They have left us all too few ways of making their acquaintance but there are still tribes in certain remote parts of the globe who lead lives hardly different from theirs. By capturing some incidents of their day-to-day existence we are able to catch a glimpse of the life of the first men on earth.

The history of daily life is more than a story of growth of technical knowledge and the multiplication of ways in which we can procure our comfort and safety; it also concerns the increase in the number of people able to enjoy these benefits. After the relative equality of all prehistoric men in face of constant hardship, famine and danger, the gradual improvements brought by the birth of civilisation benefited only a minority. For many centuries civilisation was the privilege of a select aristocracy and we still know little of the life of the great mass of the people. Yet changes, however slow, were approaching. They began with the decline of slavery and the rise of the middle classes and in recent history have spread among the masses the sort of advantages to which they had previously had no claim. Yet even today standards of living throughout the world vary beyond belief. A new era is in the making and, in the already foreseeable future, the time may come when all nations of the world can share in a common prosperity brought about by united effort.

In these pages, the man of the 1960's will find the origins of the million varied and complex elements which go to make up his own daily life. He will realise, much more vividly than from a straightforward history book, that in this vast treasure house of countless generations of all races and colours he shares an inheritance in common with all mankind.

What makes *100,000 Years of Daily Life* unique among history books is the fact that only in recent years have men consciously recorded the details of their daily life or started to piece together that of former ages. This is a pioneer work involving years of patient research and it has meant combing through literally thousands of books and documents and entailed a rigorous process of selection to present this panorama of world history in domestic terms, from Neanderthal Man to our own day.

In the beginning there was only the earth.

## Then came man.

When hundreds of thousands of years ago the first man appeared on the earth his existence was fraught with danger and difficulty. Every living creature was better equipped, for even those without fangs, claws, horns or venom to attack him possessed wings or armour plating or could run and climb with a speed and agility denied to the heavier, bulkier man. He was naked and clumsy in a hostile world; yet with nothing to rely on but his bare hands he learned to survive and prosper. It was a long struggle, and for a space of time a hundred times longer than the entire history of civilisation mankind served his lonely apprenticeship to the cruel master of necessity. Slowly and painfully, with many stumbles and errors, he learned to feed and clothe himself, to find protection against wild beasts and tame the terrifying god of fire. There was no going back. Today we can reconstruct, piece by piece through clues such as the flint tools unearthed by archaeologists, and cave paintings of the type found at Lascaux in Southern France, the incredible miracle of prehistory, and can do nothing but wonder at the tenacity and endurance with which early man clung to life for which he was so ill-equipped.

To begin with there were only small groups of human beings snatching a precarious existence deep in the heart of primeval forests, on open plains or frozen steppes. These were all mankind, and though we should hardly recognise them for our own ancestors they were the creators of our own daily life. They took the first steps without which our complex civilisation with its ideas and inventions could never have existed, for even our most basic and instinctive actions, habits and reflexes had to be discovered by somebody, once, for the first time.

# Neanderthal Man's first cradle: a segment of eucalyptus bark strippe

2

3

More than a hundred thousand years ago a creature already existed on earth who was very nearly a human being. He has been called *Neanderthal Man* after the small district near Düsseldorf, in Germany, where his remains were first found in 1856. Traces of him were later discovered in many parts of Europe, including Gibraltar, Belgium, France, Italy, Yugoslavia and the Crimea, and even further afield in South Africa, Palestine and Java. But Neanderthalers were not the direct ancestors of modern man, only one link in a chain whose beginnings are buried far back in the mists of time—with Pithecanthropus and Sinanthropus—and whose other end is *Homo sapiens*, the type of man as we now know him. All we know of these early forerunners of mankind is that they possessed fire and carved the flint clubs and axe heads* which are found in Africa and south Asia as well as in Europe. We do not know what these early men looked like; they had not yet learned how to draw and left behind no portraits of themselves, and we can only make rough, approximate guesses from reconstructed skeletons. Did they walk crouching, like animals? Or are we placing too much emphasis on the features which seem to make them more apelike than human? All we can tell for certain is that *Neanderthal Man* was not very tall (round about 5 ft.) and had a large head with very prominent features, and his legs were short and bowed.

The Neanderthaler lived in a climate generally rather warmer than our own and his needs were few and simple; a rough shelter made of branches was all he wanted to live in, and he could do without clothes altogether. From his predecessors on earth he inherited the art of making flint tools. The flint axe used by Australian aborigines to this day served him both as tool and weapon, but it was a clumsy implement and only suitable for the roughest work. The man in the picture* is using one to chip an oval-shaped segment of bark from a eucalyptus tree to make a dish, or perhaps a cradle for his baby*. The dishes and cradles used by

# slowly and painfully from the living tree with a crude flint axe.

*Neanderthal Man* were very much the same as these, though they have long since crumbled into dust.

What did these primitive men eat? Examination of their teeth suggests that their diet was mainly vegetarian, consisting of fruit, berries and roots. Finding these must certainly have been an easier and less hazardous enterprise than hunting.

Fire, the greatest single domestic asset known to man, they did possess. Such primitive people must have had to overcome their instinctive fear of it. Probably one day after a storm some man, bolder and more intelligent than the rest, must have snatched a brand from a forest blaze and used it, but who this Promethean hero was we shall never know. Yet it is thanks to him that humanity has developed at all, since fire has been man's constant companion throughout the ages. Since the earliest mythologies of the Ancient World fire has been a symbol, and among many different races, from the Carthaginians to the American Indians of the eighteenth century, it has been worshipped as a god. Were fire to vanish from the world, the whole structure of human civilisation would perish.

If his ability to rise above the sheer animal terror of the unknown is one reason for man's superiority, another, and even more important, is the power of speech. He can communicate facts and ideas. It is through a common language that men are able to work together and live together in mutual understanding.

However far back into the past we delve, there is no real evidence for the existence of the 'primitive hordes' which some have suggested is the oldest form of human society. There is on the contrary ample proof that clearly defined social groups have existed since the very earliest times. *Neanderthal Man* wore ornaments. He did not leave his dead to rot but painted their bodies with red ochre, blood-coloured. He bound them to ensure their resurrection, and then buried them. Hunting also had its ritual significance, and we know something about this from the bears' skulls, neatly laid out or hidden in caches in the rocks, which have come to light in caves in eastern Switzerland and Franconia.

The Neanderthaler was helpless against the earthquakes and climatic changes resulting from succeeding geological eras. The ice ages came and the animals he depended on for food moved south. Man had to follow them or perish. Then the cold swept further south bringing to all living things alike the menace of annihilation.

Western Europe became tundra, and men and beasts sought shelter in the caves where their remains, hunters and hunted, can still be found*. 5 For a while they survived; but the struggle could have only one end and *Neanderthal Man* disappeared, to be succeeded by a new race, stronger perhaps, certainly more intelligent, in a word, more human. This was *Homo sapiens*, the real ancestor of all modern men, whatever their race or the colour of their skin. Yet although their brief life ended finally in the damp darkness of the caves, the Neanderthalers were a vital link in the chain towards modern man. *Homo sapiens* was to go much further along the road, but its beginnings had been already trodden for him.

4

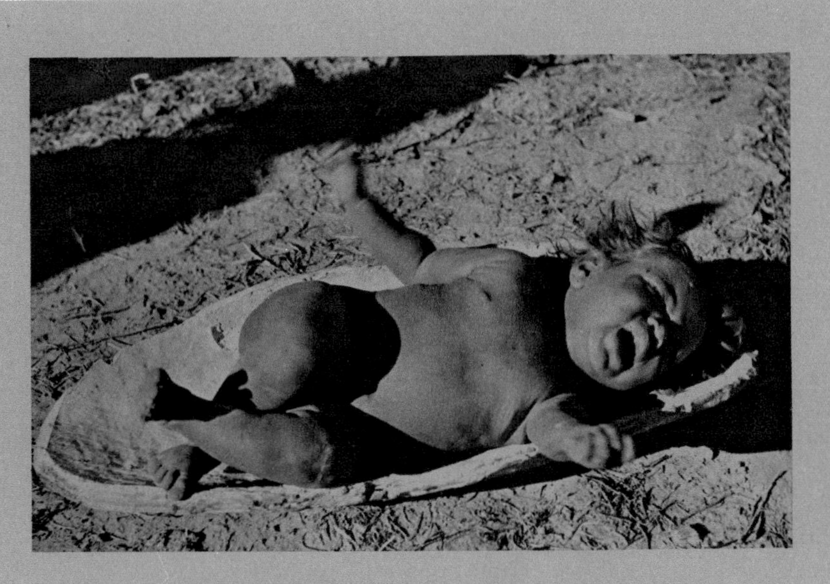

5

6

Two sticks are rubbed together and the first spark springs into flame.

7

8

9

Explorers in recent times have discovered tribes in the deserts of central Australia still living very much in the same way as the earliest human beings must have done. This aborigine*, patiently 6 rubbing his stick against a sliver of bark until the heat ignites the tinder underneath it, owns only the most primitive tools: flint axes, slings, boomerangs for hunting small game, and a few wooden dishes.

His main business in life is the quest for food. 7 The man hunts kangaroo* and emu, a bird a little smaller than an ostrich, and his kill is cooked in its skin over a fire of logs laid in a shallow trench and afterwards divided up among the whole 8 tribe*. When the hunter comes home empty-handed his wife must provide, and she will make use of anything within reach. Snakes, rats, lizards and caterpillars are all good for food, and there are eggs and berries to be found besides. A stick hardened in the fire makes her a spade to dig for roots. When the resources of one place give out the whole tribe moves on and does not return until the land has had time to recover, so their homes are no more than temporary screens of branches to keep off the wind*. At night everyone sleeps on 9 the ground round the fire.

It is a life in which only the strong and cunning stand a chance of survival and in which man's needs are reduced to their simplest and most basic essentials of food and self-protection.

But there are times when for a short while men can forget their hand-to-hand struggle with starvation, and one of these is the *corroborree*, when they paint their bodies and dance to propitiate the mysterious powers who rule the universe and to ensure their protection. The sight of the *churinga*, a carved stone amulet*, usually kept 10 hidden, imbues initiates with its own magic strength and power.

10

## This is life at its starkest: man wrests his living from the wide earth.

*Homo sapiens* emerged during the last ice age, when he reached a comparatively high standard of development. There were three distinct races of *Homo sapiens* in Europe: Grimaldi, a negroid type of medium build; Chancelade, a type closely resembling the Eskimoes of today; and Cro-Magnon. Cro-Magnon was the tallest of the three, often as much as 6 ft. and even more, and probably the most advanced, as it is this race which has left the most interesting relics. Human life also existed in other parts of the world at about the same period, notably in the southern parts of Africa, China and Java, but we know very little about it.

Early European man has left us some indication of what he looked like. There is the strangely lovely head of a woman from Brassempouy, with her stiffly braided hair*, and the 'Venus' of Laussel*, her opulent figure swollen fantastically to symbolise fertility, who holds a horn from which she is on the point of pouring a libation. There are other figures, possibly male, but none of them is an actual portrait, and in all probability there was a strong taboo against making a likeness of any person for fear it could be used to exert an evil influence on him.

11 12

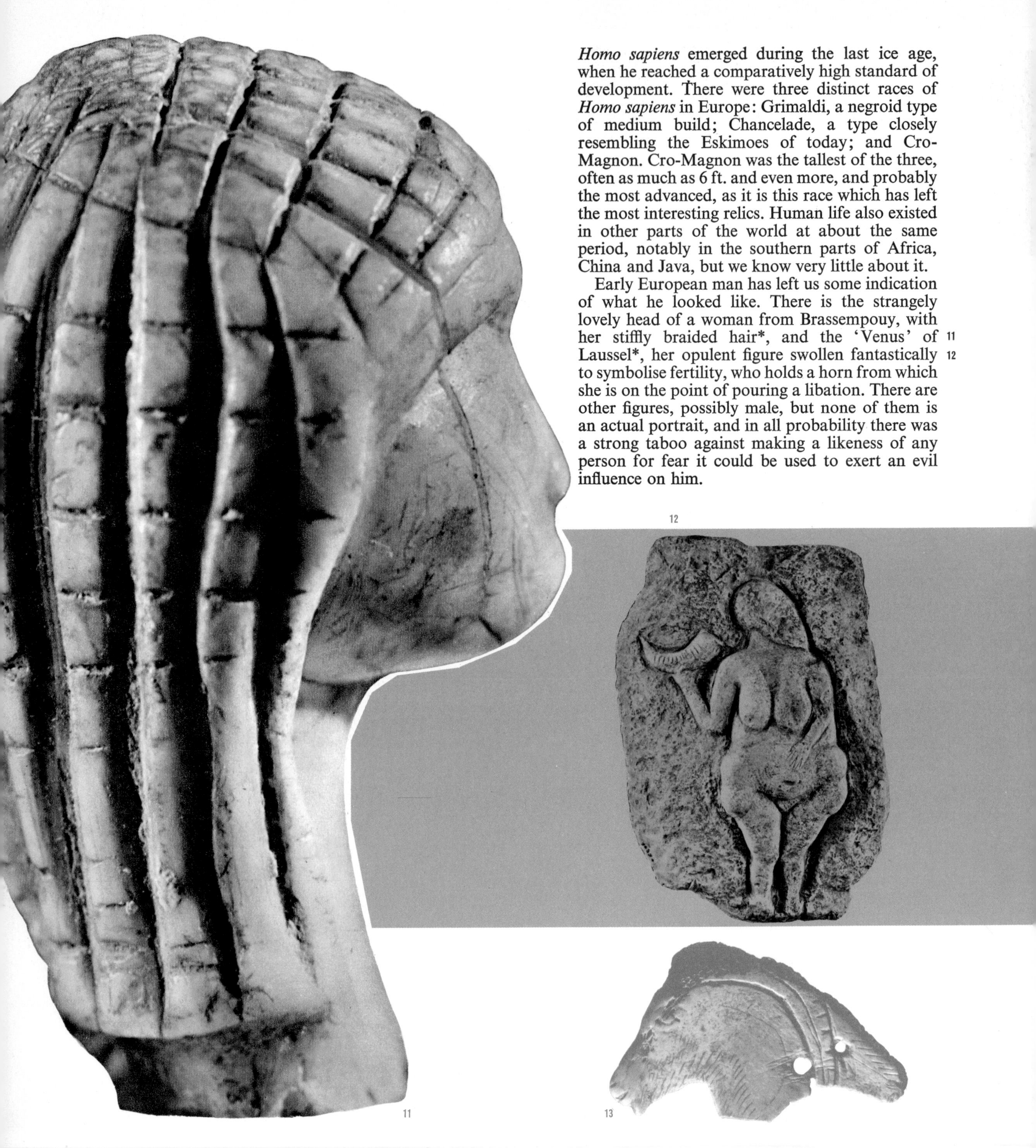

12

11

13

Grimaldi, Chancelade and Cro-Magnon, the three types of *Homo sapiens*.

14

13 The belief in magic was a fundamental part of these peoples' lives. Before setting out to hunt for deer, chamois or horses*—which were still regarded solely as potential food—they would court success by acting out the chase in mime, and in so doing they made an important discovery. By learning to imitate the world he saw around him man felt his control over it enormously increased. All art was probably strictly utilitarian in its origins, since by drawing and carving replicas of animals early man believed he acquired power

could tackle larger victims, such as the bison in the picture, which would provide food for several days; and once they were no longer preoccupied with the frantic search for food men had time to spare for other things. They could begin to think in terms of comfort as well as survival. Some became craftsmen who did not take part in the hunt themselves but were expert at making the flint weapons the huntsmen were learning to use with increasing skill.

This is a vanished world, but even today there are still some parts of the globe, untouched by civilisation, where something very similar survives, although its days are numbered. If we look at these tribes, it takes very little imagination to see in them a living image of what the lives of our remote ancestors must have been like. In Borneo this Punan* returns from hunting to be given a shower by his wife, poured from a piece of hollowed-out bamboo. In the evening he will dance with the rest of the tribe in thanksgiving for success and a safe return. The Dayaks also live in Borneo and are rather more advanced than the Punans. They are as fond of ornaments as the Cro-Magnon men, many of whose necklaces made 15

15

16

17

14 over them at a distance. On this bone tablet* a bison can be seen beating its outstretched forefeet against a palisade while round it moves a procession of men carrying spears. They are probably taking part in a ceremony of propitiation intended to pacify the angry spirit of the slaughtered beast. We know that hunting was already a highly developed skill. Men were able to set traps and organise drives. Better weapons meant that they

of seeds, fishbones and stones with holes in them have come to light, and this Dayak couple* dress in little besides bright-coloured beads. The Dayak woman, like her prehistoric sister, is the one who does all the hard work of the village. While the man is away hunting she must chop wood and tend the fire, yet she is still perfectly capable of breast feeding* her children in some cases until they are two or three years old. 16 17

## A social order is born and with it family life. The beginnings of art.

18

20

19

The people who inhabited Europe between the Aurignacian and the Solutrian ages, that is some thirty to forty thousand years ago, must have looked very like this bushwoman*, belonging to a tribe which roams the Kalahari desert to this day. They were dependent on hunting for their livelihood, and as the game moved the men had to follow, so that their life was divided between a number of camps, like this bushman village*, set up for a few days in the open, and permanent cave dwellings to which they retreated in winter. Life changed only gradually over thousands of years. Men discovered how to boil water by dropping hot stones into a bowl made of bark or hide. Cooking methods improved: they learned how to simmer meat to make stews as well as roasting it directly over the fire, and they discovered that certain vegetables tasted good to eat if they were boiled in water. Animal skins must have given them protection from the cold for a long time, but now men learned to cure the skins by patient scratching with a stone.

As the art of stone-carving grew and developed it brought a valuable wave of commerce to the people of Europe, from the south of France to as far away as Czechoslovakia and Russia. In certain places where flint was to be found centres of craftsmen grew up whose work often travelled immense distances. There was a demand for tiny carved figurines, amulets and pendants, and these too

40,000 years ago. The tribes lived by hunting and learned much from the

have been found far away from their place of origin. It is the earliest factual evidence we possess of any kind of trade or barter.

In the long hours they spent stalking their prey the prehistoric hunters had ample time to observe 20 the lives of animals* and learn from their behaviour. Watching a bear rob a hive of wild bees may have first taught man to gather honey. It was natural for him to see their highly developed instincts as proof of supernatural powers and worship the beasts accordingly, but at the same time he was trying to domesticate them. Even at this early date men probably kept reindeer near their villages for the sake of the food provided by their milk and their young in time of need. Yet famine and hardship of all kinds was still a constant threat. Infant mortality must have been appallingly high, and a quarter of those who survived would die before the age of twenty. Very few can have lived beyond forty.

22

21

23

These scenes from the life of primitive tribes today give a vivid picture of what went on in an Aurignacian settlement. The men preparing a meal on a journey, using leaves and split bamboo for 21 dishes*, and the old man carving a wooden top to 22 amuse his grand-daughter* might have stepped straight out of prehistory. Since time immemorial 23 men have mimicked bird calls on bone pipes* and studied the curious properties of plants to make 24 medicines, and also, perhaps, like this Dayak*, poisons to put on the tips of their spears. Even now in some parts of the world there still exists a strange relationship between man and the dark forces of nature, the mysterious gods and spirits to which he must sacrifice or die.

24

# nimals—but death came early.

# Cave paintings depict the bloody struggle between men and beasts.

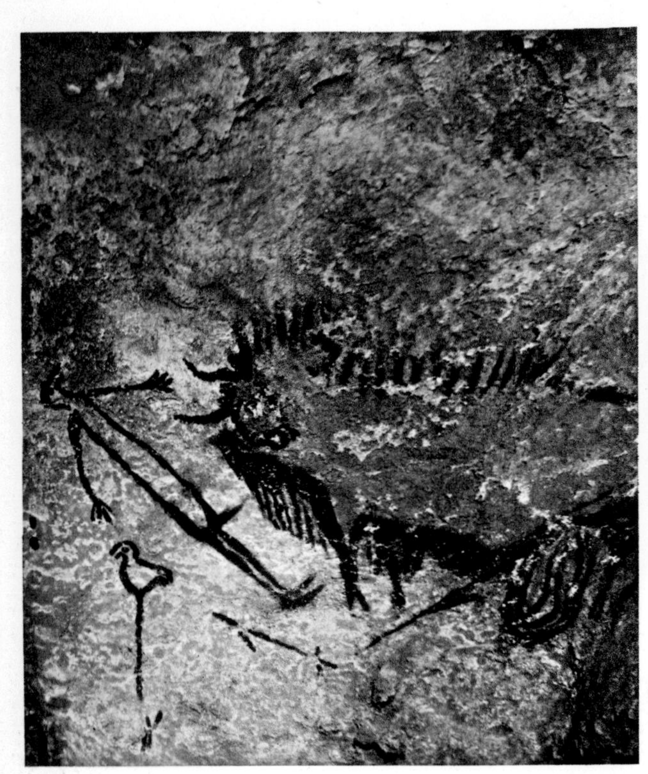

25

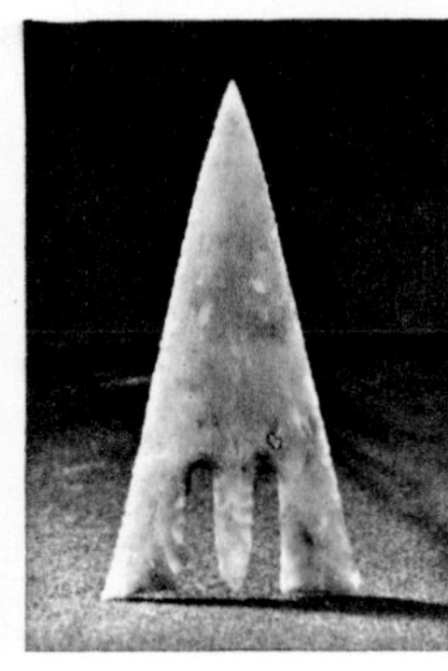

27

26

In winter the tribes withdrew to the caves, which served them both as a refuge and a holy place. Outside, the temperature might drop below freezing, but once inside it was quite warm, though the air would be thick with the smoke of fires and torches. If you had entered the narrow tunnel opening out of the rear wall of the cave and squirmed a few painful yards with the sound of harsh chanting growing louder in your ears, you would have emerged into a low chamber with stalactites hanging from its roof. On the walls might be depicted a scene that must have been an all too familiar reality: a man has been charged by a bison*, he lies on the ground wearing a bird mask, and the totem appears again beside him. The man is dead, but his attacker has received a spear thrust in the guts that leaves his entrails dragging in the dust. In the centre of the floor stand a pair of clay bison*, and the dancers, their faces masked and their bodies painted with symbols, move round them, waving their spears threateningly in imitation of the kill. Their weapons were made with great skill: the spearheads notched so as to fit more securely onto the wooden haft*, and the javelin-throwers, which augmented the thrust of the human arm, were decorated with stylised chamois, wild goats and horses*. Horses are seen again in this prehistoric fresco* along with impressions of hands, and there are others which show reindeer, stags and, most frequent of all, huge bison. All of them are caught to the life, drawn with unsurpassed vigour and simplicity and with a purity of line and intuitive understanding of proportion that amazes artists to this day.

28

29 →

30

31

In the later Palaeolithic period, about twenty thousand years before Christ, a way of life began to emerge that was much more highly developed than the Aurignacian civilisation. This was the Magdalenian, centred in the south-west of France (from the Dordogne to the Pyrenees) and eastern Spain, where there are many magnificent cave paintings of the period.

By this time the physical comforts of life had improved considerably. When the hunter returned to his camp* with a large kill* the women dried it in the smoke from the fire to make it keep longer*, so that what could not be eaten at once was no longer wasted. Man had taught himself to make stronger, more pliant tools out of bone, and learnt to use a harpoon to spear salmon as they swam up river to spawn and then cure the flesh in the sun, to be eaten later. He made bone needles for his womenfolk so that they could sew skins together to make garments hardly different from those worn by Eskimoes today.

30 31 32

Stone lamps filled with animal fat replaced the dim, smoky torches once used to light their caves, and an elementary form of barter already existed, as the shells made into knives and ornaments which have been found at places far inland go to show. They even invented a way of weaving rush-baskets.

32

Man creates comfort—cooks his food, clothes himself, makes ornaments.

33

34

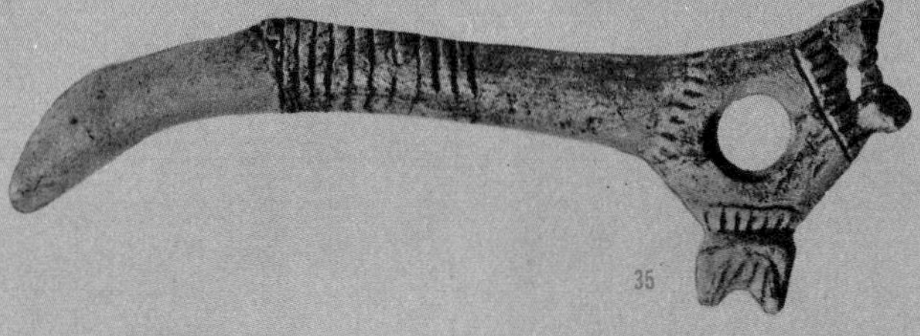

35

36

The side of these people's life we know most about is their religion. They buried their dead with great care beneath the floors of their caves, and all the dead man's personal possessions were buried with him. A fire was kept alight on a flat stone above the grave to keep him warm, so that his spirit would not desert the tribe, and from this we learn that the Magdalenians believed in survival after death. They worshipped the spirits of their ancestors, believing that the dead possessed mystical powers denied to the living, and preserved the skull, apart from the rest of the body, for a totem to protect and inspire them. This custom is still widespread among primitive tribes today*, and on certain ceremonial occasions the skulls are even supposed to speak. Their voices are made by men twirling rhombs* at great speed until they emit a humming noise. Sacred dances were performed in caves decorated with murals where the uninitiated were forbidden to enter. The dances were led by the witch doctor, wearing a head-dress of stag's horns and holding a magic wand* to represent the god who was to be propitiated. At the ceremony of initiation the young men about to attain their manhood spun dizzily in the centre of a circle of onlookers, each imitating the life of the animal whose mask he wore*.

33 34 35 36

## The souls of the dead keep watch over the hearths of the living.

37

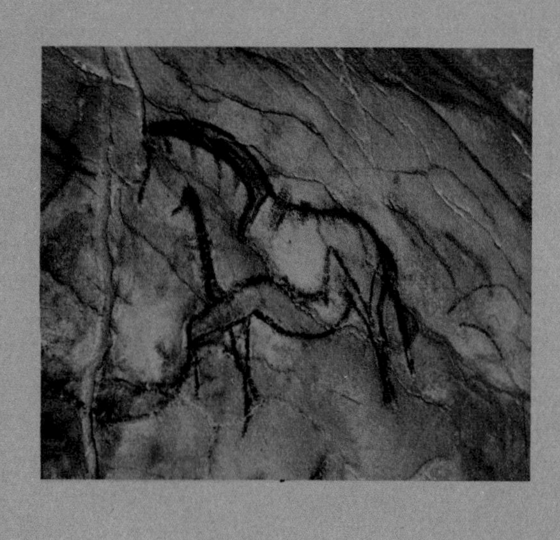

38

The witch doctor was the most important member of the tribe, on whom its prosperity depended. He alone possessed superhuman powers and could act as intermediary between men and the spirit world. It was most probably the witch doctor, using a brush made of hair or simply a finger dipped in red ochre, manganese or charcoal*, who drew the first rough outlines of figures which became drawings capturing all the essential life of the animals*. He cared for the sick, drawing the poison from the patient's body* and spitting it out, then administering magic potions and massaging him with weird ointments to exorcise the evil spirits; but he also understood the use of medicinal herbs and sufficient anatomy to perform rudimentary operations. Finally it was the witch doctor who saw to the complicated tattooing of the body, in which every detail had a specific ritual significance*.

In the midst of its relative prosperity the Magdalenian civilisation was faced with the possibility of imminent extinction. The danger which threatened mankind was the opposite of that which had annihilated *Neanderthal Man*, for the climate at this period was growing steadily warmer and the animals they depended on for food began to move northwards again. A few of the people, possibly distant ancestors of the Basques, stayed where they were, but their civilisation declined and they no longer produced works of art. Others followed the great herds of reindeer north to the Baltic and maybe even further into the Arctic circle, where the tools used by the Eskimoes are still of the same type as those common among the Magdalenians.

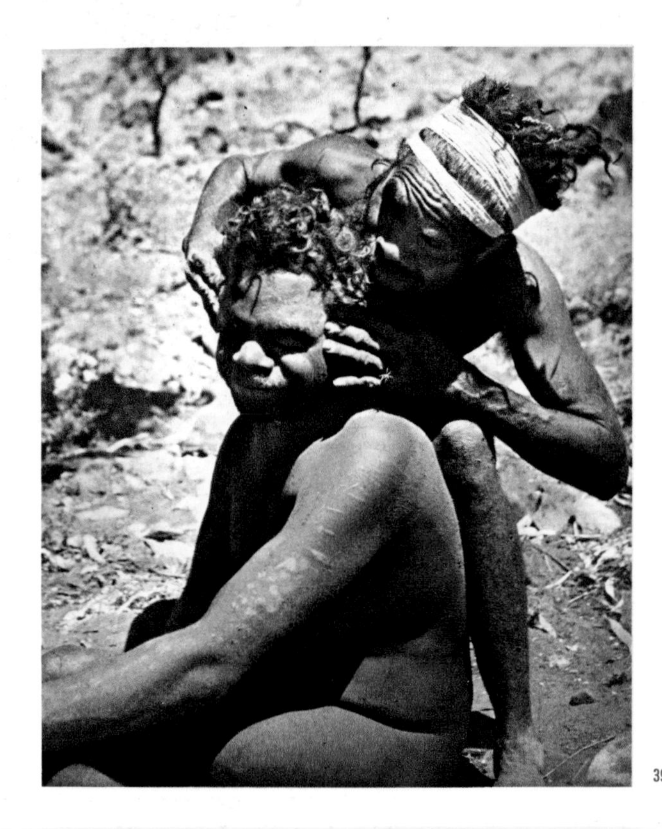

39

40

The witch doctor—repository of the tribe's collective wisdom and fear.

# Only a sealskin coat and a harpoon protect some from cold and hunger.

42

41

43 44

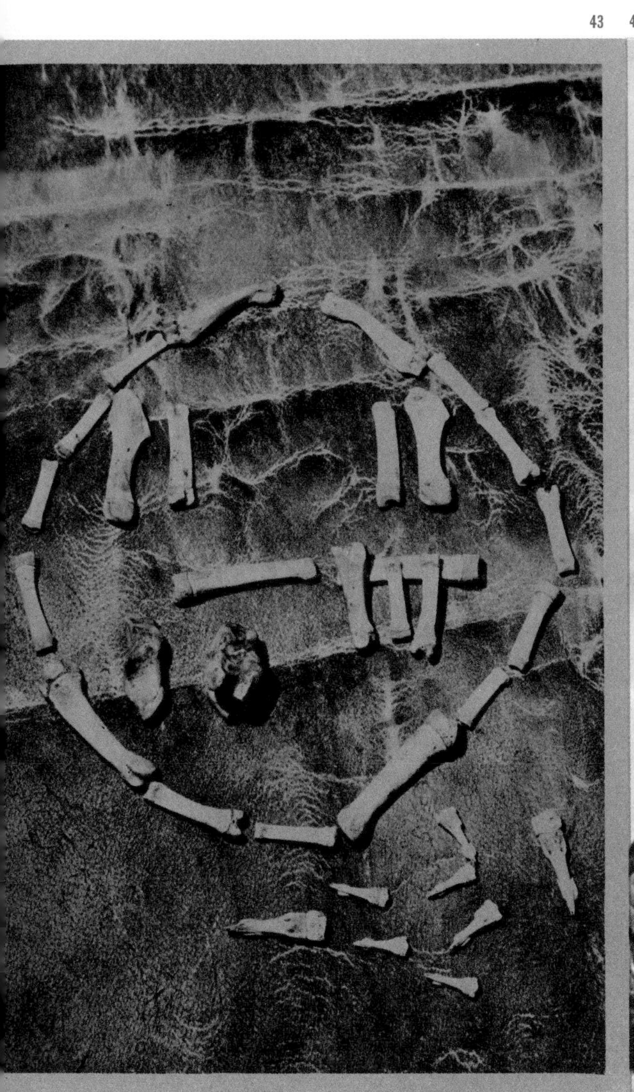

The Eskimo way of life constitutes a miracle of adaptability, for these small communities living well within the Arctic circle have to contend with conditions among the most difficult on earth. They live in total darkness for weeks at a time during their almost unending winter; whalebone needles* and harpoons* are almost their sole tools, yet they have learned to use even the snow as a protection against the intense cold. 42 41

If we were to enter a typical igloo, like the one in this diagram of small bones laid on a sealskin*, 43 we should find a winter home very similar to the summer building of turves laid over a wooden framework, in which both heat and light come from a soapstone lamp filled with oil. Food is cooked in a pot over this lamp and served in bowls and platters made of wood, decorated with attractive bone patterns. Near the lamp is a single raised couch covered with polar bear skins where the whole family sleeps together.

This Eskimo woman is watching her cooking pot and softening a piece of hide with her teeth at the same time*. 44 She keeps her children close by her and carries the youngest on her back. The hide will be used to make clothes for the family; a double thickness which allows the air to circulate in between makes an effective barrier against the cold. On top of this men and women alike wear a hooded anorak and wide trousers tucked into soft boots. Stockings and mittens complete an outfit which, with its bright coloured embroidery and fur trimmings, is as pretty as it is practical.

# Summer and winter, whatever the conditions, man must hunt in order to live

45

Seals and whales are the only game found in any quantity close to the North Pole, and they supply almost all the Eskimo's needs. He depends on them not only for meat, blubber and oil for his lamps but for the skins to cover his kayak, as well as to clothe himself and for the tendons and bones which are turned into thongs and all kinds of domestic implements.

Seal hunting is therefore the Eskimo's main business, and it is one demanding endless skill and patience. They reach their hunting grounds on sledges drawn by the dogs* (45), which are their only domestic animal, and they use the same vehicle, which travels at great speed over the frozen seas, whenever they move house. When the hunter reaches a place where he hopes to find seals, he looks for the holes through which the creatures rise to breathe. These are usually half covered by the ice re-forming, and the Eskimo clears the hole gently with his knife, then waits, often for many hours, until his quarry returns. At last his float tells him a seal is there, and he creeps up silently* (46), raising his harpoon* (47). He hurls it, keeping tight hold of the cord fastened to the shaft, so that if it strikes he can haul the seal out on to the ice. And for one more day his family will be safe from starvation.

Life in these frozen wastes is as hard and uncertain today as in prehistoric times, and as hard and uncertain as it remained in Western Europe for tens of thousands of years until one day a light dawned in the East which grew and spread its glow throughout the whole world.

46

47

48

until one day he coaxes new life from the earth: corn . . .

## To sow, to reap, to grow, to cultivate

49

50

The preceding picture shows a man, dressed in a woollen skirt, holding aloft two ears of corn like a 48 talisman*. The corn is the symbol of man's greatest discovery since he learned the use of fire: the beginnings of agriculture. At some time, about 6000 B.C., civilisation took two great steps forward: people learned to cultivate crops and to rear animals for their own use, this development occurring in two places in the Middle East: in Mesopotamia and in Egypt. From there probably farming methods spread over the whole world, bringing a new way of life to the tribes of hunters, until within a few thousand years most of the continent of Europe itself was under cultivation. In recent years 49 the head* of a cultivator was recovered almost intact from a bog where the peat had preserved his remains. He was a chief of a neolithic tribe living in Denmark, and his people believed their gods did not grant fertility to the land for nothing: they demanded offerings in exchange, and those they liked best were human sacrifices. The Tollund Man, as he is called, must have been one of these. His tribe lived in thatched stone houses*, early 50 examples of a type of peasant dwelling which has scarcely changed over the centuries in many parts of the world. The great transformation which was to revolutionise man's relations with the world around him began with an alteration in his use of stone. Prehistoric man knew that if a stone implement was polished instead of chipped, the cutting edge would preserve its original sharpness indefinitely, like this Danish axe*, but almost unbeliev- 51 able patience was needed to polish the hard stone. It appears that the same sort of patient observation led to other discoveries. Men had long ago realised that plants and seeds would take root and

—a harvest of new verbs to describe man's new activities.

spring up wherever they were thrown down, and that the vegetation always throve best on the site of an old settlement. There must have been some with a taste for experimenting and the patience to wait for results. One day their experiments bore fruit, and with time men learned to control them. They discovered how to burn a patch of scrubland and clear away stumps in order to plant and sow seeds, and then, the next summer, there was the world's first harvest. Agriculture was born, and with it a security man had never known before.

At about the same period neolithic man succeeded in taming sheep, goats, cows and pigs for domestic use. This meant not only that they could depend on a permanent supply of meat, milk and its by-products, butter and cheese, but also of other things such as leather and, especially valuable, wool. People began to hold new ideas about the life-giving gods, the sun, the father of all things and the earth-mother in whose honour they raised huge blocks of stone called *menhirs**, and their ideas of death were changing too. They believed new life would spring from the corpse buried under a *dolmen** like a fresh shoot from a seed. With their *dolmens*, *menhirs*, *cromlechs* and lines of standing stones the cultivators from the East have left a permanent mark on the lands where they settled, and many other traces of them can still be found in these places in objects such as pottery vases*, polished knives with horn handles* and little terracotta stoves*.

52 53 54 55 56

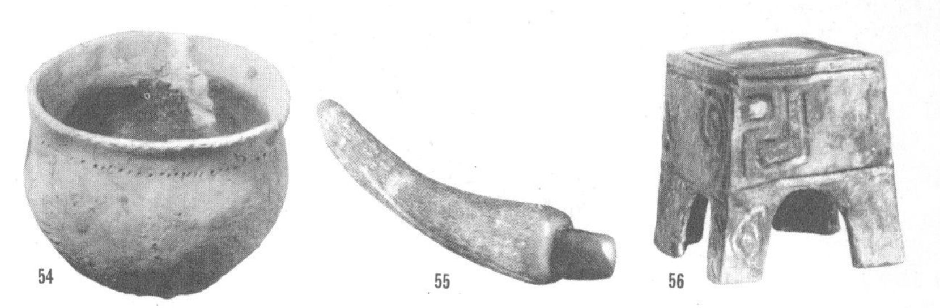

54 55 56

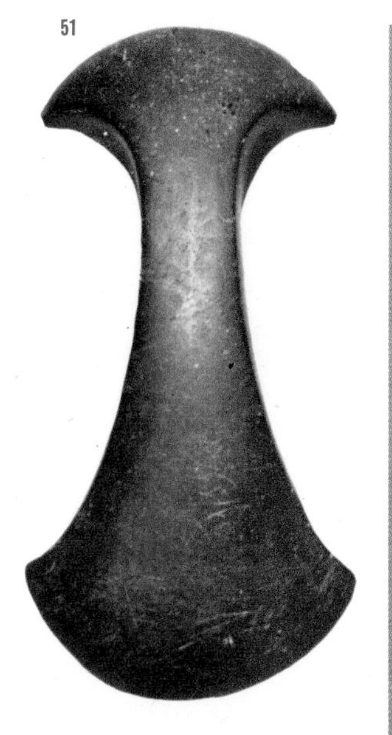

51

52

53

# Women cultivate the crops and weave colourful garments.

57

To get an idea of the sort of life lived in the earliest agricultural communities we have only to look in parts of South America today. It was only some twenty thousand years ago that men first arrived on the American continent, by crossing the Bering straits, and the new invaders moved slowly southwards from Alaska to Tierra del Fuego, some of them establishing highly developed civilisations, and others, like the tribes inhabiting the region of the Amazon and its tributaries, adhering to this day to an ancient and primitive way of life. Here the great virgin forests stretch over thousands of miles, with a brown stain in the vast, green land marking the line of the river. Villages are made up of a couple of dozen square huts with walls of split bamboo and roofs of palm branches intricately plaited together to form a watertight surface* (57). In the clear space between the huts which serves as a dance floor there is one building much larger than the rest, and here the men* (58) of the village meet to talk, passing a pot of tobacco from hand to hand round the circle. They each in turn dip a stick in the pot, for here they suck tobacco instead of smoking it, or else chew a little ball of crushed coca, which enables them to do without food, drink or sleep for many days at a time.

The whole village rises at daybreak, when everyone goes to bathe in the river, and the women carry back big jars of water on their heads. For breakfast they eat cassava, a kind of bread made from manioc flour, seasoned with pepper and an infusion of herbs. Afterwards the women work in the plantation, a patch of cleared land which they dig with the aid of sticks hardened in the fire. In it the Indians grow the manioc which is their staple diet. This is a plant with large tuberous roots, weighing up to seven or eight pounds apiece but containing a poison which has to be extracted before the plant can be used. They do this by grating the tubers into pulp, which is pressed inside a long cylinder of palm bark. The poisonous juice runs out leaving a paste which is then dried, and cassava bread is made from the flour. Other kinds of fruit and vegetable the women grow in their gardens include yams, peas, sweet potatoes and pineapples, of which the last two were first found in South America.

Besides working on the land the Indian woman makes clay pots and dries them in the sun before baking them in the hot ashes of the fire, and weaves on a rough loom the fabric for her family's clothes, which she dyes with plant juices and decorates with beautiful, symbolic patterns* (59).

58

59 →

60 61

While his wife works in the fields the man goes hunting, taking with him his young son who is just learning to bear arms*. Both carry the silent, deadly blow-pipes whose tiny darts, poisoned with curare, can kill birds and monkeys at incredible distances among the trees. Their victims will help to fill the spicy pot of meat and dried fish which is always kept simmering* and never quite emptied. This stew and cassava forms the evening meal, which is eaten after bathing again in the river. The men are served first, on large leaves which do duty as plates, and then they retire to their hammocks—yet another example of Indian ingenuity—while the women squat round the fire and finish whatever is left over. Soon the Southern Cross rises into the night sky, dimming the faint glow of the dying fires, and the only sound is the strident cry of a parrot in the jungle.

This kind of life is still primitive, but it has undoubtedly gained in stability, security and even in comfort. Man is no longer at the mercy of the elements; he has learned to use his surroundings to much better advantage and has invented numerous contrivances to make life easier for himself. Two of the most important of these discoveries made in the neolithic period were pottery and weaving, which developed all over the world at the same time as the art of farming spread to fresh lands, and tribes which had formerly lived by hunting alone took up the new accessories of life.

The Indians' daily tasks are hard and exhausting in the steamy heat of the jungle, but when these are done there are still a few hours a day left for dancing and dressing up. In a country where vermin spread with alarming speed personal cleanliness is a necessity, but their shaven chins, dyed hair and the brilliant materials and variety of decorative flowers and feathers they wear, all go to show how conscious the Indians are of their personal appearance.

Father and son go hunting. Jungle children soon learn to use a blow-pipe.

# The whole tribe dances to bring the life-giving rain from heaven.

Although the Negroes who inhabit the wide plains of West Africa have a much more advanced state of civilisation than the Amazonian Indians, there are still some aspects of their life which allow us a glimpse of what life must have been like before those early farmers and herdsmen had begun to live in cities. Let us take a brief look at their way of life before it vanishes altogether.

Theirs is a universe ordered down to the last detail; the worlds of gods and men, of superstition and everyday reality are closely interwoven and make a pattern in which everything has its purpose. This simple Dogon sanctuary, with its design of squares and diamonds, at the top of which traces of blood from sacrifices can still be 62 seen*, is an expression of the order of the world, and so is the plan of their villages, the division of the fields and the relationship between all the members of a family. There is a strict order of importance in the arrangement of their huts, and the villages no longer grow up at random.

These pictures show something of the enduring communion existing between man and the universe. The crowd of people, shuffling in a circle to represent the march of the stars across the heavens, are moving in time to a rhythm of small stones shaken in calabashes and bells attached to their 63 ankles*. The men waving assegais, and the chief in his elaborate costume of feathers for the war dance, and this girl, whirling herself into an isolated frenzy, intoxicated by her own movement*, 64 take us into the heart of one of the basic features of

63

African life: the liberation, through rhythm and movement, of subconscious forces in each individual which are suppressed in normal life, so that the energy released can be placed at the service of the entire community, and of life itself. The dances are more than simple recreation. They have a ritual significance, for through them each person renews contact with the springs of all life, and the feast ensures that the harvest will be good, the flocks will increase and the tribe prosper.

65

When the celebrations are over, life returns to its normal pattern and once again the most urgent problem is food. The god they invoke is millet, and the people try to ensure by songs and incantations that the harvest will grow and the life-giving rain, which also has its proper ceremonies, will fall.

Theirs is an arid country where, for mile upon mile, nothing grows but scattered baobabs and thorn-bushes. The men burn a patch of scrub and clear the tough roots and stumps* (65), then the women dig the stony ground with a hoe* (66) which is little more than the prehistoric axe adapted for farming. They stoop patiently for hours at a time in the strange position they seem to find comfortable. This primitive form of hoe, which is still a great advance on an ordinary stick, was the only digging implement man possessed until the invention of the plough. The millet seed is sown by hand, and,

66

When the harvest is gathered and stored people know that

where conditions are suitable, cotton is grown in the same way.

In addition, each family owns a small plantation where they grow a few vegetables and herbs to add a little variety to their food. The great co-operative effort comes at harvest time when all the women of the village combine to gather the downy cotton fibres* (67 68) and store the millet* in clay-walled granaries, like giant flower-pots. The lives of the whole family depend on the grain, and when the day's ration is removed the remainder is carefully measured* (69).

The storehouses beside each group of huts are characteristic of these villages* (70); they are generally egg-shaped, perhaps as a reminder that they contain man's nourishment, and large enough to hold several men at a time. The granary has been a fundamental part of life ever since men first

68

69

70

67

began to grow cereals for grain.

Preserving the roots of the cereals from one year to the next used to be a risky business, in spite of the silos which were then nothing more than a simple covered trench, but corn of all kinds, like wheat, barley, millet, rice or maize, keeps very well under easily fulfilled conditions.

The women in these villages take turns in pounding the millet until it is reduced to flour, from which they make a sort of porridge, flavoured with a sauce of meat, fish, peppers, powdered baobab flowers, groundnuts or palm oil, according to the resources of the moment. This is the staple dish of their main meal, which they eat at mid-day. They drink a great deal of water, especially after eating, and, although they have other drinks, millet beer and palm wine in particular, these are usually reserved for special occasions when they are drunk in enormous quantities.

another year will be free from the threat of starvation.

# Every man his own builder—mud walls, a rush door, cooking in the open.

71

There are no housing problems in tropical Africa, for the clayey soil provides a permanent supply of building material and each man is his own builder and house repairer. The walls of the houses are made of wet clay, moulded underfoot, and laid on in slabs which are patted down by hand as they dry*. Afterwards the surface is smoothed 71 down and the whole thing finished with a coat of liquid mud containing a vegetable adhesive which gives the house a whitish colour. With the addition of a thatched roof, a door made of basketwork* or 72 wood with bolts and bars*, and carved or painted 73 decorations, according to the owner's taste, the house is ready to be lived in.

Inside there are only the bare necessities. Weapons, tools and skin bottles hang from the rafters; there are some pots* on shelves against the 74 wall, a few cooking utensils and a painted wooden chest holding amulets. A raised dais of beaten earth or a plaited bamboo bed, which is the family sleeping place, and a few mats make up the rest of

72

73

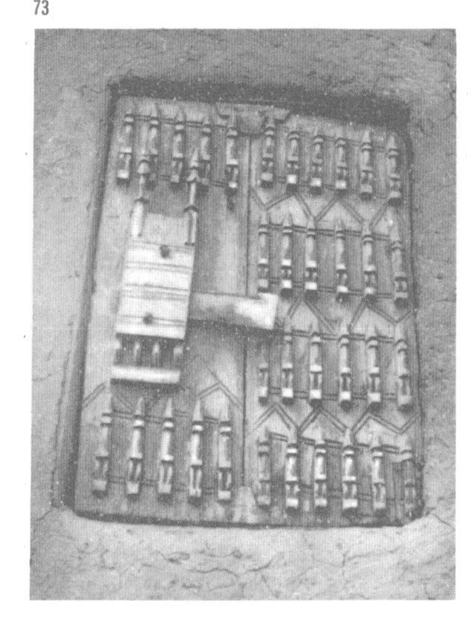

74

# The day's catch might include fish, or much larger game—a hippopotamus.

the furniture. Where polygamy is the custom, as it often is among tribal people, each wife has her own home where she lives with her children. But this is only a basic shelter for sleeping and protection against the rain; life for the most part is lived out of doors. Cooking is done in the compound* and, close by, fish are hung up to dry in the sun*. Here too the women set up their primitive looms and weave long strips of gaily coloured cloth which are afterwards made into the long, majestically flowing robes worn by the men of the tribes. The style of these garments varies from one tribe to the next all over the continent of Africa. The ample folds of brightly coloured cloth greatly enhance the natural elegance and the graceful movements of the women-folk.

The men do the heavy work, and it is their task to keep the family supplied with meat. Possibly because of unfavourable natural conditions many farming tribes indigenous to tropical Africa do not breed their own herds, but in places where game is plentiful hunting can amply satisfy their needs. An elephant or hippopotamus can provide an entire village with meat for several days. In villages near rivers or lakes, fishing is a principal occupation. These villages are not usually very well protected against attack from outside; their only defence is often a wooden palisade or a mud wall, but sometimes a tribe that is threatened by warlike neighbours will choose a site they can defend easily. The Dogons of the Sudan, who live on a rocky spur called Sangha, chose the site for this reason. Their terraced roofs crowd up the hillside*, a huddle of square houses with the round, thatched granaries peppered among them.

76

75

77

78 80

A man is dead, the spirit of life has gone out of his body and must find a new home. Perhaps it will not be satisfied by the rites which are performed over the corpse; the mourners* may not have wailed enough or the widow* failed to observe the innumerable taboos which compel her to shave her head and live apart, like one impure, until the spirit is appeased, or the traditional sacrifices and libations may not have been made on the dead man's altar stone* and then he will return and haunt the living with bad luck. But if everything has been done to please him, the mystical powers he has acquired by entering the world of the tribe's ancestors will be used to benefit his people. For the dead man lives on elsewhere, but he also stays close to his family until the day when he is reincarnated in the person of one of his descendants. The dead have their place in the village as well as the living, and each person's status depends on the degree of kinship within the tribe as also on age. As a boy grows up, every stage in his development is marked by its ritual celebration.

79

The widow mourns so that her husband's spirit may live again in a child.

# Herdsmen wander to find pastures for their flocks.

83

81

Between the grasslands inhabited by these agricultural tribes and the desert lie vast, arid plains where nomadic shepherds lead a life in which everything is reduced to its simplest possible form. They are always on the move, driving their herds of goats, or the magnificent oxen* which are sometimes beasts of burden but are also sacred animals. Nomads cannot afford to carry many household goods. Their life is hazardous, for little rain falls on the plains and they have often to travel many miles before finding pasture for their herds, but there is a certain nobility about these pastoral wanderers whose traditions have scarcely altered for thousands of years and who wrest a living from land where no crops will grow. The Peuls of West Africa, like the Bedouin Arabs, live very much as the patriarchs of biblical times, and the boy David, pasturing his flocks in long ago Palestine cannot have looked very different from this Peul shepherd boy*.

In the evening they stop at a well and unload their few belongings* while they water the thirsty goats*. Their evening meal does not take long to prepare, as it consists mostly of curds. They eat meat only occasionally: at funerals or when a beast has grown too old to be useful. Among all shepherd peoples since prehistoric times the herds have belonged to the gods, and are never slaughtered except for sacrifice, but once an animal is dead no part of it is wasted, and goat-skins are especially valuable for making their precious water-bottles. Even these wanderers take a pride in their appearance; the women's plaited hair shines with butter and the young people hold beauty contests to show off their most gorgeous clothes.

82

84

85 86

Further north is the desert. Life here is hardly less precarious than it is among the arctic snows, and the most desolate region of all, the mountainous area of Hoggar, which the Arabs call the 'place of fear', is the home of the Touareg, known as the 'blue men' because they dye their robes with indigo which, as it fades, gives this strange colour to their skin. Their dress consists of baggy trousers and a wide shirt caught in at the waist, and their faces are almost completely hidden behind a veil, called a *litham*.

Mounted high on the back of his *mehari*, his robes billowing about him, the Touareg* rides among the dunes like the lord of the desert he is. He drives his little flock of sheep, goats and donkeys from one meagre, uncertain grazing ground to the next, but he is first and foremost a warrior and even, when he cannot eke a livelihood from the land, a robber. From the earliest times the desert nomads, living on the edge of the agricultural societies of Mesopotamia and Egypt, like those of China in later periods, depended for much of their living on swift, efficient raids on undefended settlements or sudden attacks on the caravans of merchants who formed the link between the great centres of trade. They left a trail of ruin and pillage behind them, and the terror they inspired was increased by their extreme mobility. They were the first people in history to tame horses and, later, camels, and it was they who invented the saddle and bridle. On more than one occasion in different parts of the globe war-like races such as these have succeeded in establishing a lasting dominion over peaceful peasant farmers.

Today the desert dwellers are still nomads, but circumstances have forced them to live more peacefully; their visits to the South are only to barter rock salt for the millet, dates, cotton and camel-saddles they need. The Touareg's home is always on the move and it is as simple as possible. When a camping ground has been chosen where there is good pasture for the animals, the women put up their tents*, made of goatskin dyed with red ochre, and surround them with a mat to keep out the *asaber*, the harsh desert wind.

The nomadic lords of the desert, half-warriors, half-brigands, wer

87

88

Among the dependents of the Touareg are a Negro tribe, the Harratin, who cultivate for them
87 their little fields of millet*. They have slaves, too, for the most part Sudanese Negroes, who watch
88 the flocks, carry wood and water* and prepare food and who live in brushwood shelters on the
89 outskirts of the camp*. The Touareg's evening meal, often the only one of the day, is *asink*, a sort of porridge seasoned with butter or curds, which is made from millet pounded on the underside of
90 the prayer mat*.

When there are several camps close together the young people of the tribes may make an *ahal*, a party held well out of sight of the older generation. Everyone wears their best clothes, the boys with heavy stone rings on their upper arms and the girls with carefully braided hair, and they crowd into a circle in the tent. There is joking and singing, a girl plays on the *amzad*, a little one-stringed violin, and boys and girls rub noses, which is the Touareg way of kissing. The party breaks up very late and each creeps away to his own tent. To-morrow perhaps they will all be on the move again.

89

e world's first tamers of horses.

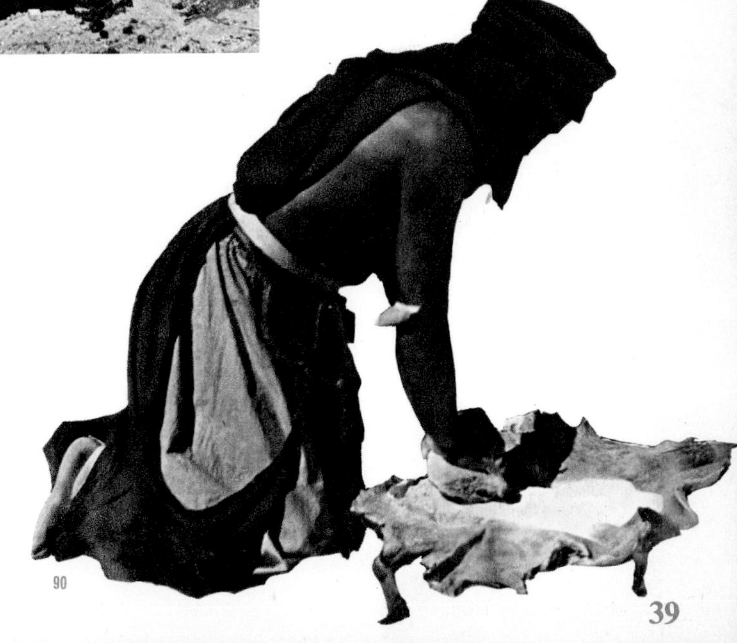

90

# Man takes stones from the ground and by infinite patience and cunnin

91

At first the number of people living on earth grew very slowly, then, about 3000 B.C., a new era began, almost overnight. What had been only villages suddenly became towns, and the reason seems to have been a number of new discoveries, of which the most important was the use of metal. Pieces of crude, meteoric metal were already in use, but hitherto they had been regarded simply as curious stones. Now, one day, someone with an enquiring mind must have resolved to examine the stones' properties, and once more we owe our development to an unknown inventor. Ever since the discovery of fire men had noticed its strange effects on certain materials, but to make use of fire to work ore into usable metal demanded a whole series of complex operations, of which the first was to obtain the consistently high temperatures necessary to melt it down. To achieve this some anonymous, primitive metallurgist invented the first blast furnace in history.

At this early date—as is still the case in parts of Africa today—men used only what metallic ore they could find above ground, and it was not until much later that they learned to dig for it beneath the earth's surface. They chipped off the matrix with a hard stone to reach the usable portions* [91] and then melted the ore in a charcoal furnace to purify it. Their furnace was a clay funnel* [92], and, as in modern smelting, it had a hearth on which the lumps of ore were placed and was then filled with charcoal and fired from the top. For two days the primitive metal-workers worked the bellows* [93], which were fitted into nozzles at the base of the oven* [94], in teams of four and kept the furnace regularly supplied with a mixture of ore and charcoal. Then at last there was a lump of metal* [95] ready for the smith to work into swords, sickles and ornaments.

At first men worked in gold and silver only; then they discovered the more common and useful copper which they learned to harden with an alloy into bronze. Last of all came iron, the most difficult to work. The new technique spread in waves across the world, and human life was transformed. For the first time man had made himself a new material that could perform miracles in providing him with strong, easily sharpened weapons and tools and, in the distant future, machines. However, metal was initially used for adornment: combs* [96], razors* [97], tweezers, necklaces and bracelets* [98]. Subsequently, the use of metal was extended: household utensils, cups, bowls and dishes would be made of metal, and the wooden agricultural implements would come to be strengthened with metal bands. The long night of prehistory was finally emerging into the dawn of civilisation.

ansforms them into gleaming lumps of precious metal.

92

93

94

95

96

97

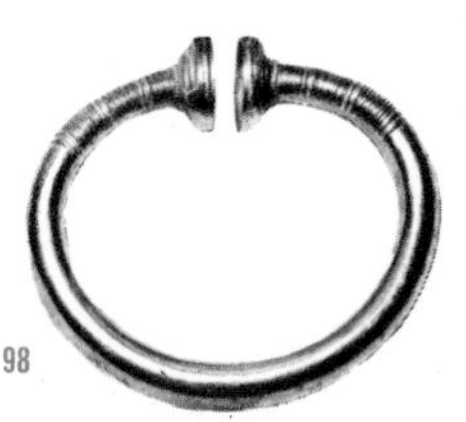
98

# The Sumerians establish the first city-states

99

The first roots of civilisation were in the great river valleys, where the silt laid down over the centuries made a rich and fertile soil. Man's next task was to learn to drain the land and control the course of the rivers so that they still rose regularly and spread their fine coat of mud over the fields, without inundating and destroying his crops. He seems to have succeeded first in Mesopotamia, where two great rivers, the Tigris and Euphrates, run parallel to one another. At some unknown date a race of people who probably came from the hills, called the Sumerians, began to reclaim the land between the rivers. They dredged the marshes, built dykes and dug canals until in time the waters began to flow where men directed them, and the

100

101

102

face of the country was transformed. Still, there came a day when the rivers broke loose; bursting the dykes, flooding over fields, villages and towns, and spreading terror in the hearts of the people. It seemed to them that the end of the world had come, and it has been recorded for all time as the great flood. Such a catastrophe only happened once in the history of the Sumerians, and every year the cultivated valley brought forth rich harvests of barley and a kind of wheat.

It was Sumerian ingenuity which produced the invention of the plough, the first agricultural implement which could be pulled by animals*, and 99 which replaced the hoe that was all earlier cultivators had possessed. The plough meant an increase in the amount of land they could keep under cultivation. They began to produce sesame oil for cooking and for use in their lamps, and stored it in huge terracotta jars*. They kept more 100 sheep and goats to provide them with meat and wool, and the reclaimed land provided excellent pasture for cows*. They had gardens where they 101 grew plants that were appetising as well as nourishing, such as onions, radishes, spinach and lettuce; and they planted orchards where the fruit they tended grew much larger and sweeter than the wild kinds, so that for the first time man had an abundance of apples, pears, dates and pomegranates.

## and master the art of writing. History is born.

Beside the simple farmers a class of artisans grew up who bartered their wares in exchange for food, and after them came merchants carrying goods from one village to the next. The tiny neolithic settlement gradually became a market, and a temple was built in honour of the gods, constructed on several different levels and called a *ziggurat*. Soon the people had to defend themselves against the incursions of robbers from the desert who were attracted by their growing wealth, and a militia was formed, the soldiers armed with hel-
102 mets and lances*. Before long the commander of the soldiers had become ruler of the city and, since political and religious power were inseparable, the high priest of the local god, whose name

104

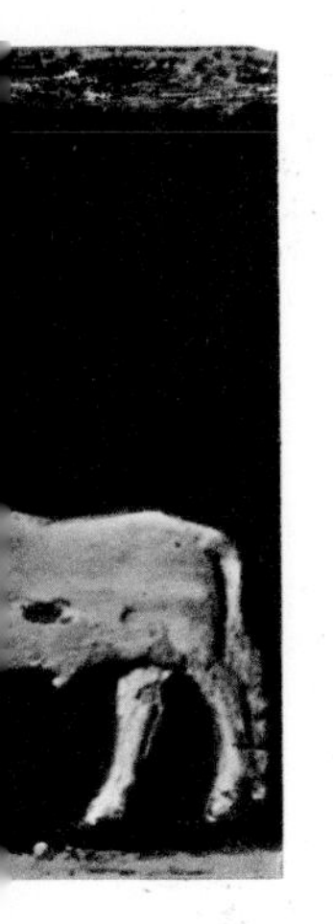

103

differed from place to place. People began to navigate the rivers in 'coracles', round baskets caulked with bitumen which can still be found in
103 remote parts of the world to this day*.

Administering the temple's wealth, keeping accounts of the harvests and of offerings made to the gods soon became too much for one man's memory, and a system of notation was developed by which records of events could be kept. Writing in its earliest form was simply pictures representing different objects, and these were slowly simplified into formal signs. Now the worshipper who came to deposit his obol in the temple court could be given a receipt by the priest to show that he had
104 paid his tribute*. People began to realise the importance of writing. They wrote down their ancestral myths, the wisdom of the sages and the deeds of their heroes so that these would never be forgotten but recorded for all time. They covered
105 their statues with inscriptions*, prayers and dedications and recitals of royal deeds, and in this way history was born. Only the scribes knew how to read and write and only they could teach others how to master the difficult art. They were the first clerks and the first historians, and it is thanks to their clay tablets that we possess a living picture of their life and thought. Lastly, it was the scribes who opened the first schools.

105

# The first sound of wheels is heard in the streets of Ur and t

106 107

Let us take a walk through the streets of Ur—the city from which Abraham set out on his wandering shepherd's life—and follow a schoolboy from his lessons. He tells us himself about his day on a tablet more than four thousand years old: 'I recited my tablet. I had my dinner. I got a fresh tablet ready and filled it up with writing. Then I was told what my lessons were for the next day and in the afternoon I had my writing lesson. After school I went home where I found my father sitting down. I told him about my writing lesson and then recited my tablet to him and my father was very pleased. . . .'

The same thing, almost word for word, might have been written by a twentieth-century schoolboy. But what this studious young man does not tell us is that instead of going straight home he hung about the streets for a little while. Looking at them through his eyes we should see square, brick-built, houses with no windows and only a single door opening on to the street because of the heat. Brick-making was a Sumerian invention, but because the houses were built of porous bricks which did not stand up very well to the rain there are few traces of houses of this period. Those used for the temples were baked, and parts of these buildings are still standing. The houses had flat roofs, forming a sort of terrace where the family slept in summer, and taken as a whole the town looked very much the same as many eastern towns of our own time, which have hardly altered their appearance in the course of four thousand years. Men warn the passers-by to stand aside, for the king is coming. He is surrounded by servants and is riding in his war chariot drawn by asses. Its solid wooden wheels are the first ever to roll on the earth and are fixed to the axle-tree by huge pegs, as in this picture of the oldest and most primitive type of vehicle*, which is still in use in parts of Asia today. As the king passes, we, like everyone else, must fall prostrate in the dust, but when we continue our walk it takes us through the bazaar, where the craftsmen's shops are crowded into a bustling pandemonium of carpenters, basket-makers, goldsmiths, potters using the newly invented wheel to make their first turned wares, cloth-makers and vendors of statuettes and ex-votos.

106

Here we are at our destination. The entrance to the house is very dark, but we soon emerge into a

:hoolboy, Akurgal, recites his lessons to please a stern father.

courtyard where Akurgal, for that is our scholar's name, greets his father who is sitting on a chair made of plaited rushes looking extremely digni-
107 fied*. Akurgal sits at his father's feet and recites his lesson. The boy's mother is busy in another part of the house, for she takes a long time dressing herself for the evening. After washing with a harsh soap made of a mixture of oil, fine clay and ashes she rubs her body with oil, puts on her embroidered
108 tunic* and arranges her heavy head-dress. Now she is sitting on a stool with carved feet, her legs tucked under her, as is still the way everywhere in
109 the East, and spinning while a servant fans her*. But dinner is served and the fish is on the table;
110 the family assembles in order of age*. Here the mistress of the house, like her husband and children, wears the traditional Sumerian costume of a heavy woollen skirt. The menu seems appetising: freshwater fish, cucumbers, marrow cooked in oil, grasshoppers on skewers with cheese and honey sweets to follow. When darkness falls they light the paraffin lamp, for strange as it may seem the inhabitants of Mesopotamia—present-day Iraq—were already familiar with the use of petroleum, though they had not learnt how to refine it. A servant brings in a jar of barley wine, and everyone gradually relaxes into a state of happy contentment. But beware, this wine is heady stuff, and if you have too much, it will mean sending for the doctor. He will soon put you right with a mixture of asafoetida, snakeskin and tortoiseshell—if it doesn't make you worse. In this painful event the only thing to do is go to the temple priests, who may be able to pull you round with a libation; but if they fail, then the exorcist is the last resort. He beats a drum and drives the evil spirit from your body, but since all illness is the result of wickedness the only way to be certain of a cure is to confess your sins and do penance.

109

108

110

111

By about 2000 B.C. the Nile delta already looked much as we know it today, an intricate network of fields and canals bordered by shady trees*. After the yearly floods, when the waters had been guided back to their usual channels, the peasant laboured with his wooden ploughshare just as the Egyptian fellah does today over the very same fields*. His wife followed in his wake, scattering the wheat or barley seed broadcast on the land. Lines of date palms and olives, a new addition to man's resources, marked the irrigation ditches bordering the fields*.

Texts have preserved snatches of the peasants' conversation as they passed at their work: 'Lovely weather! Cooler today! Things are going well, I think it'll keep fine. We all work for the prince!' They did indeed work for the prince, like the servant in the picture returning to the house with a basket of fresh rolls on her head and a duck in her hand*; or it may have been for a god, for every temple owned wide domains whose revenues went towards the upkeep of the sanctuary and its priests. Here they reared cattle for sacrifice, made wine for libations and oil to anoint the sacred effigies at their daily toilet. The statues were treated exactly as though they were alive in all respects, even to bathing, feeding and putting them to bed at night.

114

When the harvest was ripe the master appeared, followed by a train of surveyors and scribes carry-

112

Prosperous Egypt nourishes her many children. From the

113

ing pens, ink-pots and rolls of paper made from the papyrus reed which grew plentifully along the marshes. While women gathered the corn into baskets to the music of a flute an overseer perched on a pile of grain counted the harvest and the scribes seated behind him wrote down the figures*. The workers were given an allowance of water or beer, and every now and then the overseer would stop and call out to someone: 'Hey, you there! Have you bound your sheaf? Don't keep stopping for a drink before you've done any work.' More overseers patrolled the lines of harvesters, and the whips they carried were no idle threat. The fellah of antiquity had an unenviable lot and his complaints have come down to us on many ancient scrolls: 'Pity the poor peasant. The bosses carry whips and if the harvest's bad they take it out on the workers.'

115

On frescoes and bas-reliefs in Egyptian tombs artists have portrayed the lives of the kingdom's great ones in all their plenty and luxury, both as a reminder of past pleasures and as a promise for the future life which they believed continued almost unchanged in the world beyond the grave. The walls are covered with rich harvests of corn and grapes, and herds bursting with fatness*.

116

115

116

ıud of the Delta is coaxed a land of milk and honey.

117 →

# A great lord of Egypt—and those who serve him.

Neferhotep, 'lord of the secrets of the morning apartment', which is to say one of the Pharaoh's numerous counsellors, is one Egyptian who has 117 shown us his life in all its splendour*. Neferhotep is also a great landowner, with large estates not far from the capital city of Memphis. He sits in the shade of a colonnaded pavilion, dressed in a *shenti*, a white linen loincloth, with a light, diaphanous tunic over it. Round his neck is a magnificent collar made of rows of pearls, garnet and rock crystal and, like nearly all Egyptians, he has shaved his head and wears a full black wig, which serves, instead of a hat, as a protection against the sun. He is holding a handkerchief to

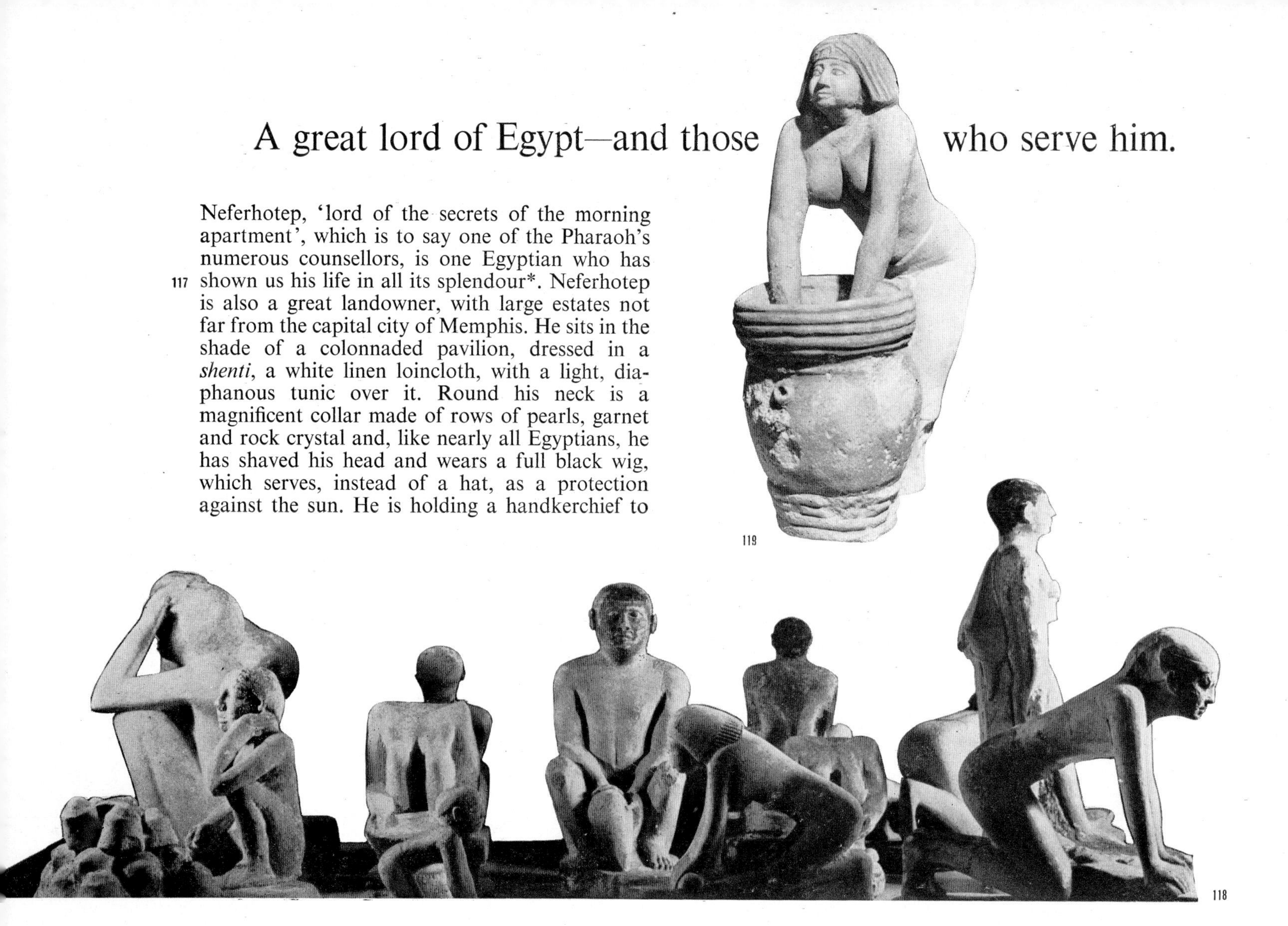

119

118

wipe the sweat from his face and a cane which is the symbol of his authority and is watching his servants at work. Offerings of all kinds of food are spread before him; sheaves of corn, quails, dishes of fruit and jugs of beer, and the steward is pointing with an imperious finger to transmit his master's orders. On the right is a group of peasants winnowing corn; the grain falls back on the heap while the chaff is carried away by the wind. On the other side men are busy gathering big bunches of grapes from the vines which, as in Italy today, are trained to grow up trellises, while others are trampling the grapes with their feet, standing upright in the press and holding on to ropes suspended from the beams to prevent them losing their balance. Wine is the drink of the rich and highly prized. Elsewhere bird-catchers have just drawn the thread of their net tight and imprisoned dozens of struggling wild duck, which cooks are seen plucking and cleaning.

Now the comptroller of Neferhotep's household enters the great courtyard, surrounded by outhouses, and the servants crouch over their work while he passes, stiff and unapproachable, watching their every movement. Maids are on their 118 knees grinding corn*, singing as they work: 'May the gods of our country grant our master health 119 and strength.' Others are kneading dough*, and a man is bringing water in wooden buckets*. 120 Further off there are brewers crumbling half-cooked barley loaves into jars and pouring on top the juice of pounded dates. When the mixture has been shaken up and filtered, it will ferment and soon the beer will be ready to drink.

The estate has to provide for the needs of all who work on it.

120

# Age-old occupations: potters and carpenters work as they did centuries ago.

121

122

123

In another part of the huge courtyard are the workshops. These are the province not of the comptroller but of the director of the household furnishings, for in the rigid hierarchy which rules here everyone has his appointed task and every object is checked and numbered. Today, after four thousand years, the potter's workshop is almost unchanged and to enter a modern potter's shop with its mud walls and roof of bamboo thatch* is to be transported back to the heart of ancient Egypt. The potter's wheel—simply the ordinary wooden cart-wheel placed horizontally on which the wet clay could be turned and shaped by hand—made possible the manufacture of smooth, even jars* and bowls which were then baked slowly in shallow trenches lined with hot embers, as is still done today*. It was not long before the same principle was adapted for glass-making.

Elsewhere launderers* are doing the washing and carpenters are using a crossbow-shaped drill which bores slowly into the wood through the horizontal movement of the bow*. Over there in the corner someone is being treated for a headache by the doctor. He puts a poultice of soothing herbs on the patient's head and holds a fish-head to his brow. The evil causing the headache will go into the fish-head which can then be thrown away*.

124

126

125

127 128

Now we will leave the kitchens and outhouses and take a look at Neferhotep's private apartments. Town houses in ancient Egypt were tall and narrow, crowded close together, with the ground floors given over to tradesmen's shops and workshops, but here in the country there is a monumental porch, similar to those still found in Upper Egypt today*, framing carved wooden doors in whose centre a pair of watchful, ever-open eyes stare outwards*. Beyond the gates are spreading gardens full of palm trees, sycamores and acacias, and if we walk down the flowering paths beside the ornamental lake covered with water lilies* we come to a shady summer-house where in hot weather the master and his family take their meals.

127

128

129

Continuing along the paved walk we come to the house itself, and we can see very much what it must have looked like from present-day Nubian houses: a whitewashed, single-storey building decorated with garlands of bright-coloured flowers and with narrow, barred windows with painted frames. Through the door, again of carved wood, is a small vestibule and then the main reception room. This is a long, narrow chamber with scarlet pillars in the centre supporting the ceiling; its walls are painted in gay colours, but little light filters through the tiny windows which are almost covered by wooden grilles to keep out the sun. Next door is the dining-room where the family meets for the two main meals of the day, usually at about noon and five o'clock. The food is served on little tables, and the adults sit on chairs while the children have leather cushions. Everyone has breakfast in his own room. The master eats a slice of meat and some bread, followed by a cake and a drink of beer as soon as he is up, and his wife has her breakfast while she dresses*.

130

Neferhotep is a rich man and his house is well

129

stocked with meat: beef, roast duck and sometimes other game such as quails or cranes or an occasional leg of gazelle. All homes, though, were plentifully supplied with fruit and vegetables: leeks, onions, garlic, chick-peas, beans, grapes, figs and dates as well as many kinds of bread and cakes. The steward, who acts as cupbearer, has put several sealed flagons of wine on the table, and there are finger-bowls and towels beside each place, for Neferhotep and Enti eat with their fingers. The dishes are numerous and include painted pottery plates, gold and silver cups, delicate vessels of jasper and alabaster* and even some glass vases, though these are still new and comparatively rare.

131 132

After the meal Neferhotep retires to his room

The great doors with their ever-open eyes lead to a hou

131

132

130

which is to the left of the communal apartments. Here the walls and floor are covered with mats of many colours. Neferhotep takes off his diaphanous tunic and lays it on a chair beside which are 133 the sandals made of papyrus* which he only wears out of doors, then lies down on the bed in an 134 alcove. The hard head-rest*, made with ebony and ivory, has a pillow to make it more comfortable and Neferhotep keeps his indispensable fly-whisk in his hand.

Opening off the room is a shower where a servant concealed behind a partition pours buckets of water over his master, then rubs him with a deodorising lotion with a base of terebinth and incense. Next door is a lavatory with a wooden seat resting on a brick base filled with sand.

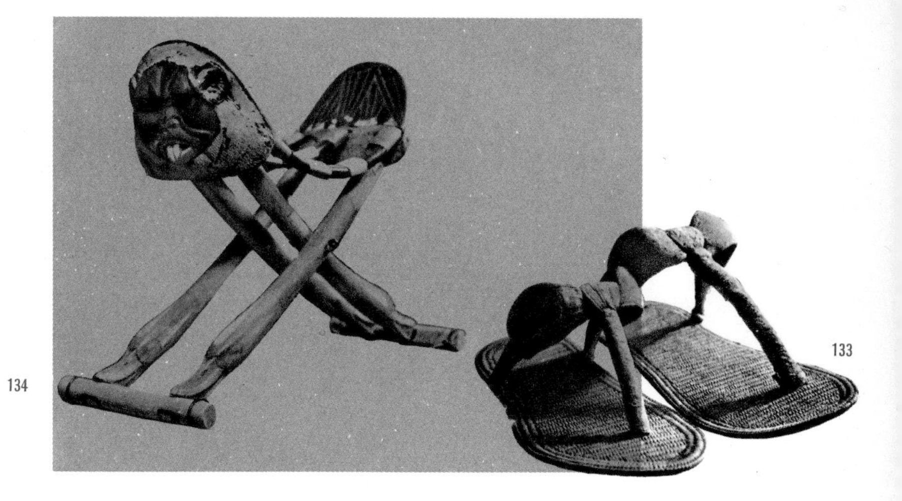

134

133

nd garden where everything is arranged for the comfort of the rich.

135 137 136

The women's apartments are on the right of the main living-rooms. Egyptian married life seems to have been very harmonious, although surviving texts show there were severe penalties for wives who were careless, or unfaithful. Women certainly enjoyed a degree of liberty unknown among the Babylonians or even, later, among the Greeks, and while polygamy was not forbidden it rarely seems to have occurred. The Egyptians married very young, boys at about fifteen and girls at thirteen, and large families were popular.

Neferhotep's wife, Enti, may not have all the faults traditionally blamed on her countrywomen but she is, nevertheless, extremely vain. She has good reason to be, for she is very lovely. Tall, slender and high-breasted with full lips and eyes

138

For the first time in history woman comes into her ow

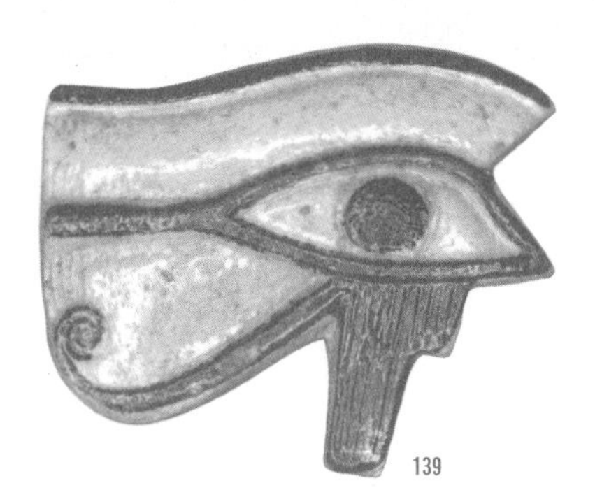

139

like a gazelle's, she has a grace and dignity that are infinitely appealing, and uses every known artifice to enhance her beauty. Here* she sits in an armchair holding the burnished silver disc which serves her as a mirror in one hand and in the other a cup that a servant has just filled for her while another handmaid sets her hair. This is done in tight curls held in place with ivory pins. A later type of Egyptian wig was much fuller*: sometimes decorated with lotus flowers or gaily-coloured ribbons. Next Enti turns to the alabaster pots of make-up, often in the shape of animals* which are set out before her, and draws a line of green on her lids and adds black to her eyelashes to make the eyes look larger. Her maid helps her to slip on the fine linen chemise and over it the diaphanous white pleated dress, which is fastened on the left breast, leaving the right one bare, and falls to her feet, hanging open from the waist down. Handmaids bring her jewel box* and Enti hesitates over her choice. At last she decides on a necklace of beaten gold leaves and a crown made of vivid blue lapis lazuli, with the eye of Osiris* to ward off evil spirits.

Satisfied with her appearance, she joins Neferhotep and their children who are waiting in the hall. Neither boys nor girls wear any clothes and they will continue to run about naked until they are old enough to receive a robe or a loincloth

140

from their parents*. This evening there is to be an entertainment by some Nubian dancers and singers who accompany themselves on the harp*. Afterwards, when the children are in bed, Neferhotep and Enti will stroll in the garden to enjoy the cool night breeze and rest in a summerhouse, where light refreshments and a game of draughts have been set out for them*, with the household cat stalking solemnly behind them. The Egyptians were the first people to keep cats as domestic animals, and they also had tame cheetahs and gazelles.

141

142

eautiful . . . . . . sophisticated, loved and pampered.

# Death comes at the end, but for the Egyptians death

143

144

145

It was a pleasant and gracious life, at least for the rich, and it is no wonder that the Egyptians were reluctant to leave it. Their belief in a life after death dates from very early times, and with the years they erected an increasingly detailed and complicated system of ideas around the subject which made the prospect of death ever more comforting. They believed that man was composed of body and soul and *Ka*. In life the *Ka* brought health and happiness, and it was the part which became immortal after death. But in order to attain immortality the deceased had to pass through a series of tests which culminated in the weighing of his deeds before a divine tribunal. The dead man's heart was placed on one side of the balance and on the other a statuette representing truth. If they balanced, the dead man could enter the kingdom of Osiris. If the *Ka* were to gain immortality there were other precautions which must be taken, the most important of them being the preservation of the corpse in a coffin made in 143 the dead man's image* and the erection of a statue to represent him*. 144

The dead also had to be supplied with all the food and household goods they could possibly need in their future life, and it is to these beliefs that we owe the number and variety of Egyptian tombs and the assortment of things they contain. It is from their preparations for death that we can learn most about the lives of the ancient Egyptians. They built tombs containing rooms where the occupant was shown in his new life and where offerings could be left; their design is reproduced in tombs in Upper Egypt today*. 145 A chamber was dug at the foot of a shaft, which could afterwards be walled in, and in this was placed the sarcophagus consisting of several coffins, one inside the other, in the last of which was the mummy.

The hour has come and Neferhotep has breathed his last. His wife, his children and his entire household stay indoors in silent grief for a period of mourning lasting a minimum of seventy days. Meanwhile the body has been sent straight to the embalmers—represented in the picture by

148

continuation in the grave of the pleasures of life.

146

146 the dog-headed god, Anubis*—who remove the brain and other organs which they place in four 147 covered vases bearing images of the gods*. The body is then treated with natron and after seventy days it is washed, anointed with balm and wax and wrapped in bandages. Only now is it ready to be placed on the bier, the Book of the Dead, a guide

147

book for the journey beyond the grave, beside it, so that the funeral can take place.

On the appointed day the funeral cortège moves off. It is led by mourners, wailing and tearing their hair, and they are followed by an impressive file of servants bearing all kinds of offerings* 148 such as cakes, flowers, vases and statuettes. Next comes the dead man's furniture, his bed, his coffers and personal possessions like his cane, sunshade and his jewels on large trays. All these things will be walled up with him in the tomb. Last of all comes the catafalque, which must be ferried across the Nile on a barge.

When the dead man's relations have said their last farewells at the tomb the priest takes an adze and a sharp knife and magically restores the dead man to the use of his organs. He opens the mouth and eyes and makes the limbs supple again. The ceremony ends with a funeral feast. The widow and children will often visit his tomb* and take 149 him all the necessities of life to sustain him in the invisible world to which he has gone.

149

We have travelled a comparatively short distance in time and space yet the picture is utterly changed. The date is 1600 B.C. and the place Crete—a few hours' sail from Egypt—but the buildings* look as though they belonged to modern times and the women have no longer anything oriental about them; one of them was even nicknamed *La Parisienne* by the archaeologists who set eyes on her for the first time. The whole face of civilisation, and perhaps its spirit too, changed when it touched this island, already a part of Europe. Since this is

151

150

152

Knossos we can take the opportunity of visiting the royal palace from which we can gain a fair idea of all Cretan houses, since its main difference is only in size. Inside, the ceilings are supported on broad pillars, painted purple. The walls are stucco with fields of lilies and saffron or huge abstract compositions* giving the rooms a feeling of coolness and peace. A soft light penetrates the wide windows, covered with oiled parchment*.

153

Civilisation comes to Europe and with it, a new spirit, nurs

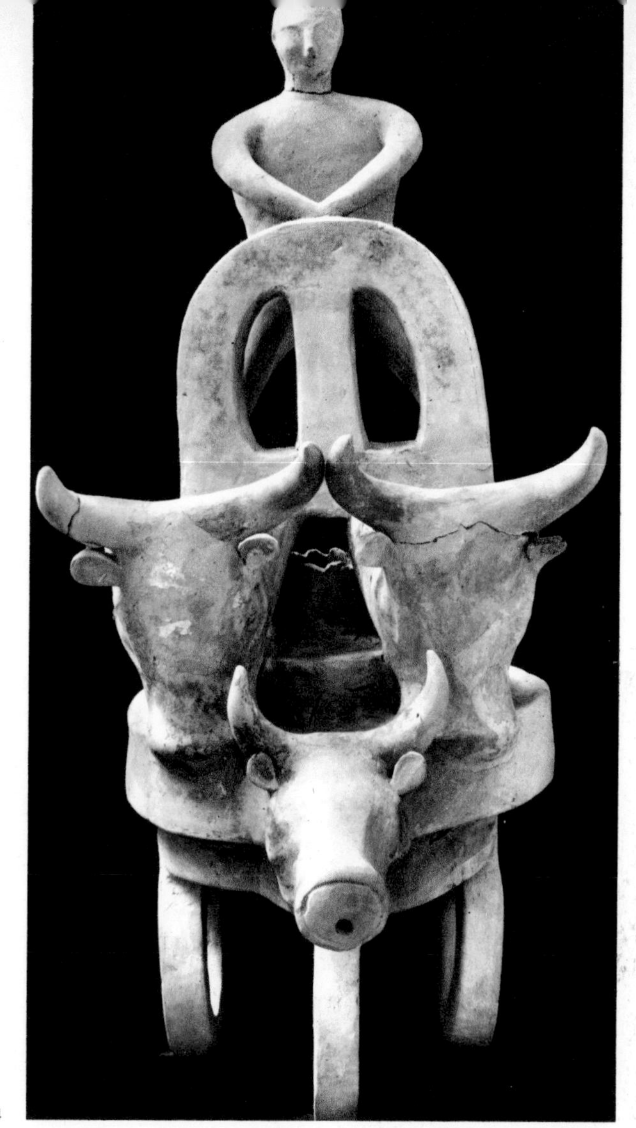

155

If we pursue our investigations a little further 153 we shall find a bathroom, with a proper bath*, and, more surprising still, a real water closet, with a wooden seat, which may even have flushed: a system and convenience that not even the court of Versailles could boast.

Now if we walk down some cobbled streets, lined with pink and blue houses, we come to a terrace surrounded by a cheerful crowd of people. It is the day when the citizens offer thanks to the gods for a good harvest. There are simple races, run by carts drawn by teams of three oxen, such 154 as we can see in this *rhyton**—a kind of drinking

154

156

cup. The climax of the festivities is when the acrobats perform their astonishingly dangerous 155 leaps before a jury of ladies. These Cretan girls*, with their delicate features and long silken curls escaping from a head-dress fastened with gleaming gold pins, are worthy of the tribute to their beauty. They wear cut-away bodices which leave the breasts bare but for a cascade of amethyst and cornelian necklaces. A procession of men carrying olive branches* comes into view. They wear the 156 normal Cretan dress, their waists are nipped in by tight belts, legs and chest are bare, and on their heads they have a sort of flat turban. The procession moves towards a paved court surrounded by tiers of seats like an open-air theatre, and this is what it is: the oldest theatre in the world, where the young men and women join hands to dance the *geranos*, the crane dance.

the Mediterranean in the island cradle of Crete.

# Crete passes, its civilisation surpassed, albeit briefly, by the Achaeans.

Crete's extraordinary prosperity was based on the control of the seas, but meanwhile, on the mainland of Greece, a bold new race, the Achaeans, was rising to power. Long before Homer's Nausicaa and her maidens took their washing 157 down to the freshwater streams* and when the work was done played gracefully by the water's edge, Agamemnon's forebears, in their palaces at Mycenae and Tyrins, were imitating Cretan fashions and planning the overthrow of the island. At last they struck, and when the blow came it was sudden and unexpected. In the throne room at

157

158

Knossos, where a ceremony was in progress, the people fled in terror and dropped whatever they were holding, to be found by archaeologists three thousand years later in the burned-out ruins. Crete weathered the storm but it was to the Greeks of the mainland that the future belonged, and before many centuries had passed their colonies extended from the coasts of the Black Sea to Italy, Sicily and southern France.

Daily life in the Homeric age, nine centuries before Christ, presented a very different picture from what it was to be in the time of Pericles, four centuries later. It was a life centred on personalities; the only people who counted were the chiefs of aristocratic clans, and the great landowning families of which they were members also controlled the beginnings of trade which was essential to the survival of Greece, whose natural resources were generally poor. The often adventurous lives of these rulers were the themes their 158 bards sang, to the accompaniment of the lyre*, and some of their names, like Odysseus, Prince of Ithaca, or Alcinous, King of the Phaeacians, have come down to us in the only surviving poetry of the period: the *Iliad* and the *Odyssey*.

159

# Sole light of a succeeding Dark Age is the poetry of Homer.

The house of such a family would form a small town in itself where life went on almost automatically within a fortified keep. Inside the great gateway was a large court surrounded by buildings in which lived the king's married sons and sometimes his sons-in-law. One side of the court was given over to store-rooms and granaries, containing chests of cloth and precious metals and long rows of *pithoi*, the great jars holding wine and oil (both of which were regarded as essential even in the poorest household). In another inner court were the women's quarters, and here the flat round loaves that can still be seen on Greek islands were made*. 159

At the far end of the main court a pillared portico gave onto the entrance to the great hall, called the *megaron*. This might be as much as 30 ft. to 40 ft. long, with four columns supporting the roof in which there was a hole to allow the smoke from the central fire to escape. This was where the family met for all occasions, including the three daily meals. These were the *ariston*, first thing in the morning, followed by the *deipnon* at midday, and the *dorpon* or evening meal.

There was little furniture in the hall apart from chairs, ranging from the high-backed armchair with its small footstool, reserved for the master of the house, to the couches on which people reclined to eat. At meal-times servants placed a small table bearing a cup and a basket of bread in front of each guest, while a maid poured water over their hands.

Joints of meat were roasted over a brazier in the courtyard, and the carver* always reserved some for a sacrifice to the gods before the servants handed the meat round to the guests. Meanwhile cup-bearers were mixing the water and wine—wine was never drunk undiluted—in a large bowl called a *crater* and filling the cups. 160

But even in the eighth century not everyone lived like Odysseus or Alcinous. Poorer people were crowded into towns. Free but wretched artisans like smiths or potters*, who were called *demiourgoi* or petty traders, looked after their stalls in the *agora**. These were the classes of people who supported the tyrannies which in the sixth century began to undermine the aristocratic society; among these classes democracy would take root. 161 162

160

161

162

163

165

164

Three centuries later saw the glory of fifth-century Athens, when the pillars of the Parthenon rose above the Acropolis and the small trader of the *agora* had become a citizen. Each citizen had his say in all that concerned the administration of the city, the law and even the command of the army. With the advent of democracy we begin to see something of the life of the middle classes. In Mesopotamia, Egypt and archaic Greece there had been only the great lords and high officials and the servants, slaves and peasants whose poverty-stricken existence varied little from one land to another. But even in Athens not all men were citizens, perhaps less than half the population. The rest were made up of *metics*, resident foreigners who were free but possessed no political rights and were subject to certain financial burdens, and of slaves. The latter were very numerous, and probably accounted for over 100,000 of the total population of Attica, which in the fifth century was about 300,000. They were prisoners of war, slaves bought outside Greece itself and descendants of slaves; a moderately rich citizen might own about fifty. This meant that a citizen such as Callicles, son of Cleinias, need not work; his slaves did that for him in the

166

## Man's place is in public life, woman's in the home.

167 168

silver mines of Laurium in Attica, only a dozen or so remaining in the house as domestic servants. The work of his slaves enabled him to be active in the field of politics, an occupation to which the Athenians devoted most of their energies.

While Callicles is arguing among the market stalls in the *agora* let us go and visit his house. We will find it in one of the crowded, twisting streets of which Athens is full—and which still exist on small islands in the Dodecanese*— 163 whose straggling, higgledy-piggledy air makes a striking contrast with the divine harmony of the temples which glisten on the skyline of the Acropolis. The house itself, with its walls thinly plastered and whitewashed, is not very impressive to look at*. 164

Indoors we are sure to find the mistress of the house, Praxinoe, since, unlike her husband Callicles, she rarely goes out. It is early and Praxinoe has only just got up. Her bed* is covered 165 with rush matting and has a pillow and woollen blankets but no sheets. While slaves are washing the linen in big pots of hot water* Praxinoe 166 washes herself in a stone washbasin*. Then she 167 puts on her pleated linen tunic and warms her hands for an instant at a brazier*—the only means 168 of heating in the house—before doing her hair up with a band and putting on her heavy ear-rings, a necklace* and one or two bracelets. She 169 170 spends the morning overseeing the servants, the porter, the cook and the ones who do the housework and fetch water. With her women Praxinoe spins and weaves the lengths of linen or woollen cloth which are draped in various ways to make the *chiton*, a short tunic, or the woman's *peplos**, 171 or the woollen cloak called the *himation*.

The children are looked after by nurses and maids who watch their games and sing them old lullabies to keep them quiet. The eldest boy, Nicias, aged nine, has a pedagogue, an old slave whose duties include taking him to school and going over his lessons with him.

169 170

171

# An early marriage, a home of her own, and children who are to becom

Since her marriage, Praxinoe has scarcely ever left the *gynaikon*, the women's apartments of her house. She never goes out without a slave to accompany her, and then only on special occasions such as festivals or family gatherings. As a girl in her parents' house she would not have been allowed any greater freedom, and certainly would not have gone to school like her brother. Yet, unlike many girls, she has learned to read, holding the papyrus scroll well out in front of her*. 172

173 Then one day when she was sixteen* her father told her that the son of his old friend Cleinias, a young man called Callicles, had asked for her hand in marriage. This had been granted and Praxinoe was delighted. Naturally she had never met Callicles but she knew he was thirty years old, came of good family and had a little money. Now at last she would have a home of her own. On the wedding day her friends went to the spring of Callirhoe to draw water for her to bathe in and afterwards a sacrifice was made to the gods, Zeus and Hera.

During the banquet which followed Praxinoe noticed that her bridegroom looked pleased with her as she sat in her embroidered tunic and saffron veil and crown. Later the two of them left together in a mule-cart followed by their friends and relations singing the wedding hymn. Praxinoe carried the grill and gridiron which were the symbols of her new status. Her parents-in-law

172 173 175

174

were waiting outside the door of her new home to give her a slice of wedding cake. The next day was again a holiday and then life went on as it had always done. Praxinoe finds nothing to complain of; so many of her friends are neglected by their husbands who have girl friends in the town. She does not feel the need to follow Dionysos onto the slopes of Parnassus and dance there, with dishevelled hair and a thyrsus in her hand, to the honour of the god*. She thinks of herself, in 174 the fullness of time, holding a little grandson on her knee who will carry on the family name*. 175

envy of the gods and the marvel of subsequent generations.

176

When Callicles was born he was washed and then tightly swaddled and laid in a wicker cradle. An olive branch was nailed above the door of his home to show that the baby was a boy. Five days later he was carried round the hearth, in the presence of the whole family, to show that he was accepted into the household and when he was ten days old there was a feast, and a sacrifice in the course of which he was given his name. When he was old enough to sit up he was put in a baby chair* and sat there prattling to his mother. He lived in the women's apartments with her till he was seven, running about with no clothes on and playing with toys, such as a horse on wheels

177

or fivestones, or listening while his mother told him the fables of Aesop—the same stories that La Fontaine retold centuries later. At last the great day came when Callicles, followed by the pedagogue who carried his books, was sent to school. There he learned to write with a stylus on wax tablets and later was taught to use papyrus and a sharpened quill. He was expected to learn and repeat hundreds of lines of Homer from memory. In the afternoon he had lessons in music*, and learned to play the *cithara*, or lyre, and the *aulos* (flute). But Callicles was lazy and it took a good many beatings to instil the notes into his head. For physical education Callicles went to the *palaestra* where, after oiling himself all over, he practised running and jumping or wrestled with his friends under the supervision of a master called the *paidotribe*. When he was eighteen Callicles became an ephebe and could prance about the streets of Athens with his friends wearing greaves called *cnemides* on his legs and with the *chlamys*, a short cloak fastened on one shoulder by a gold brooch, floating behind him*. He did two years' military training, part of it spent on garrison duty at one of the frontier forts of Attica. Now he is free to spend his time on his civic duties: he goes to meetings of the assembly,

178

does jury duty in the courts and goes to the *agora* to hear the latest news. Sometimes he may attend lectures of the sophists or go to hear that old chatterbox Socrates talking somewhere, maybe in a goldsmith's or cobbler's shop. In the evening there are always guests in his house and the women withdraw while the men relax* on couches to eat and drink and spend the night in talk and laughter. There are dancers and flute-players, and whether the talk turns on politics, literature, the arts or philosophy, it will be very late before the party breaks up.

179

# Hit plays, brilliant festivals and games draw the first tourists.

180 181

It was not her architecture, which, with the exception of the magnificent pile of the Acropolis, was not very different from that of any other Greek city whose like can be found in all parts of Greece 180 even today*, that distinguished Athens from the rest but the splendour of her festivals, which attracted visitors from all over the Greek world.

On the occasion of the greatest religious festival of all, the *Panathenaea*, a vast procession, including representatives of all classes and guilds, magistrates and priests with an escort of young girls, wound its way up to the Parthenon carrying an embroidered *peplos* for Athene, the patron goddess of the city. Ephebes on horseback galloped and curvetted around the procession. Several times a year, too, there were dramatic festivals, in honour of Dionysos, held at the foot of the Acropolis, in a theatre similar to the 181 one in the picture, which is at Delphi*. Performances began in the morning and went on until late in the evening and four plays were acted on the same day. All work was at a standstill, for no one wanted to miss the show, which was one of 182 the few opportunities for boys and girls to meet*, since women were admitted to the theatre. Athenians also travelled to Delphi, Corinth and Olympia to take part in the games in which 183 athletes* were entered from all over Greece. The Olympic games, held every four years, were the most famous of these.

Greek women lived circumscribed lives, but their Etruscan contemporaries enjoyed a degree of freedom which a few centuries later was inherited by Roman matrons. There are charming pictures showing women sitting beside their 184 husbands at meals*.

182 183

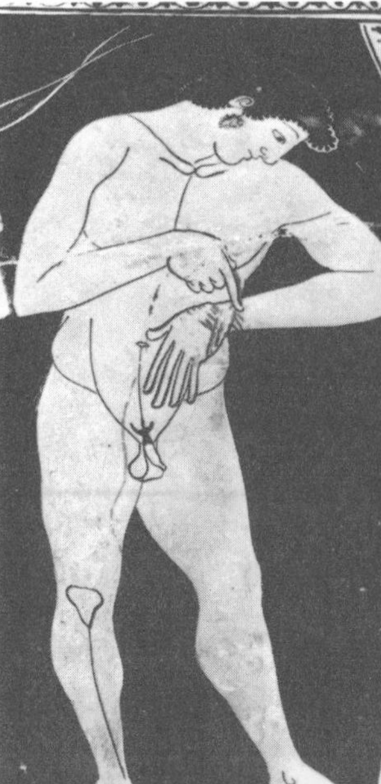

185

187

At about the same time (the first millennium) in Italy there was another race whose ideals and way of life were quite different from that of the Greeks. These were the Etruscans. Their territory spread south to meet the Greek colonies and, like the Egyptians, they lavished great care on building and furnishing their tombs. These were almost exact replicas of their houses, built of more durable material and the walls were decorated with reliefs of furniture and household utensils*. 185 The bodies were placed in niches in the walls. However, their preoccupation with death does not seem to have cast a shadow over their everyday lives, for the Etruscans show a feeling for nature that is quite foreign to the Greeks and a much more sensitive taste. The splendour of their gold jewellery with patterns in relief, the matchless elegance of their bronze mirrors, backed with engravings of mythological scenes, and the coffers* 186 in which Etruscan ladies kept their perfumes, lotions, make-up and mirrors are still wonderful to behold. Everything they made shows a heightened sense of beauty mixed with a curious fascination with the bizarre, as in this simple terracotta brazier* and this dancer who was once part of a 187 bronze candelabra*. Their skill as metal workers 188 also had one odd result in that the Etruscans were far in advance of their time in the art of dentistry, and gold fillings were not uncommon in Etruria several centuries before Christ. Another difference between the Etruscans and the Greeks was in their fashions in clothes. The men, for example, wore short-sleeved fitted tunics rather like singlets.

186

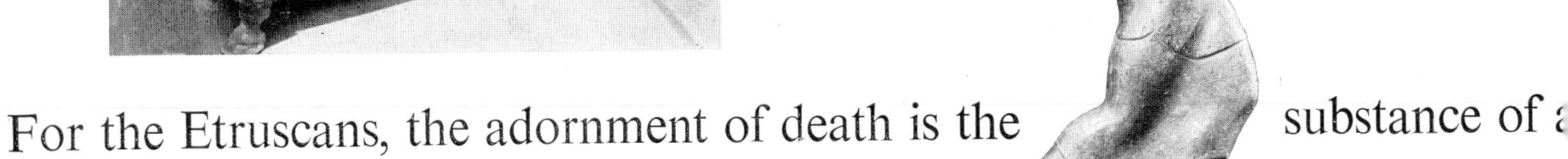

For the Etruscans, the adornment of death is the substance of a

188

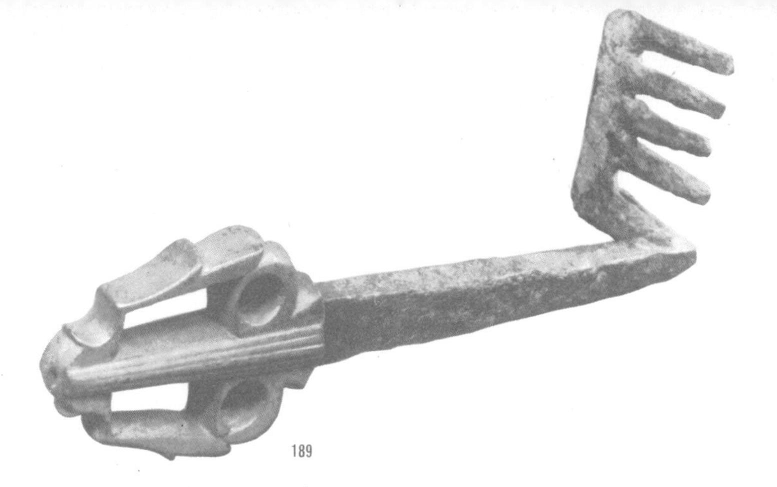

189

A few centuries later Rome, under the Emperor Hadrian, was mistress of the known world. Everywhere in the Mediterranean were garrisons defending the might of a rich and powerful empire and keeping the Roman peace. By the time of the Empire, what had become of the stern and simple life of the Republic?

189 This key* lets us into a new world. It is one of the earliest ever made, for until this time there had been only bolts and bars, and it belongs to the house of Lucius Marcus, a Roman knight, landowner and a man who by birth and fortune belongs to the powerful upper middle class. He lives with his wife and about twenty slaves in Rome and has three children, of whom the eldest is at present on garrison duty somewhere in Gaul and the two youngest at Lucius' country estate with their tutor.

191

190

If we push open the door, the first thing that we see is a mosaic threshold with the word *salve*, meaning 'welcome', and next to it a picture of a chained dog, with the well-known warning *cave* 190 *canem*. From various parts of the *vestibulum** shops open onto the street; these are rented to small traders, for the house itself does not begin until the inner courts. At the far end of the vestibule is a niche surmounted by a pediment like a miniature temple, and this is in fact the sanctuary of the *lares*, the gods of hearth and home. To reach it we have to cross the *atrium**, an open court sheltered by 191 the overhang of the tiled roof. In the centre, which is open to the sky, is a white marble basin to catch rainwater which is then stored in a cistern. Rooms open off each side of the atrium and facing the entrance is the main reception room, the *tablinum*. Another passage, running the whole length of the tablinum, leads into the *peristyle*, an open space surrounded by a colonnade*, similar to a cloister. 192

# Rome. The key to a new era.

192

193

194

195

Lucius Marcus' own room opens off the peristyle in order to be as far as possible from the noisy street, for Rome is never quiet. Carts are not allowed to move about the streets by day, but at night, after the crowds have gone home, they shake the houses with their din until first light. Sleep is impossible in the early morning because of the deafening clatter of the servants starting their day's work. Lucius Marcus tosses on his woollen mattress, buries his head in his pillow and pulls his blanket up over his ears—for the bed has no sheets, only one blanket on top and one underneath—and finally opens one reluctant eye. If he can't sleep, there is nothing to keep him in his dark, little room, which, beside the bed, contains only a chest, a chair and a silver chamber-pot.

196

Rome. City of crowds and clamour, of bread and circuses.

Dressing does not take long, for Lucius will go to the public baths later in the day, and as for clothes, he is already wearing his linen loincloth and tunic with elbow-length sleeves. He puts on his sandals and wishes he could add one of the light, hooded cloaks which are becoming fashionable, but today he has to go to pay a call on some high official and must wear his formal toga. This consists simply of a piece of woollen cloth about six yards long which is pleated round the waist, thrown over the right shoulder and the loose folds draped over the left arm*. It is heavy, awkward and easily soiled besides being almost impossible to put on without help. At last Lucius is dressed and breakfasts rapidly, since, like most Romans, he takes only a glass of water in the morning. His litter is brought to the door and Lucius reclines in it at full length,

193

197 198

199

resting on one elbow, and draws back the curtain as the bearers move off.

The first thing he sees as he leaves the house is Crassus, the wine merchant* whose shop is next door, already behind his marble counter serving customers. Lucius feels a moment's envy. Of course Crassus does not live as comfortably as he does himself; his house is cramped and he has only one slave, but he has none of this business of beggars and callers coming and going, his life is without cares. Crassus closes his shop on the *Ides* in the middle of the month, the *Kalends*, at the beginning, and the *Nones*, the 5th or 7th, as well as for the *Lupercalia*, the *Vinalia*, all days when there are games, races or processions, the birthdays of Augustus and the Emperor Hadrian and the anniversary of Hadrian's accession—Marcus makes a swift calculation that Crassus' shop is open one day in three and then only for seven hours. Marcus sighs: if only he were a man of the people and could work for a living. True, if he were not rich he would live in an *insula*, five or six storeys high and housing an assorted population, without heating or water, and in the minimum of space, instead of in a large, light and airy *domus*. These insulae caught fire on the slightest provocation and the conflagration would spread through a whole district with terrifying speed, despite the constant vigilance of the fire brigade. Hardly a day passed without an accident. Here was another reason for sleeping lightly. In addition the streets were filthy: where they were paved, the stones fitted badly and where they were not, the road was little more than a sewer and the litter bearers would be splattered with mud to the eyebrows before they reached home. If the streets of Pompeii* appear broad and clean to us, it is because they are the streets of a deserted city.

194

200

195

It seems as if the whole city is jammed into the narrow thoroughfare. A crowd has collected round a snake charmer, and a little further on a man selling sausages has been knocked down by a horse* outside the bakery with its big grinding stones*. Marcus passes the shop of Calpurnius Marco, whose cellars* are stacked with amphorae full of the immortal Falernian wine, and sees Velleius, the olive merchant, standing on his doorstep*. All this activity finds its symbol in the scales*, a legacy from Rome to the whole world.

196 197 198 199 200

Roman weights and measures, Roman justice, set a standard for the world.

# Pompeii, entombed in the ashes of Vesuvius, enjoys the sleep of the centuries.

201

202

203

204

Meanwhile Flaminia is at home bullying her servants. Since Lucius' departure her hairdresser has been fussing round her, curling her hair and piling it up on her head in a towering edifice of curls. But milady is irritable, as the red weals left by her rawhide whip on Galla's shoulders sufficiently show. At last Flaminia is dressed and the slave is free to run the errands that are her next task.

First Galla goes to fetch the piece of fine red cloth which her mistress has ordered from Vecilius Verecundus. Verecundus is a cloth merchant and Galla likes his warehouse because of the cheerful bustle filling his workrooms, to which the sign* 201 hanging outside bears witness. There are men dyeing woollen cloth, weavers finishing bright lengths of stuff and salesmen displaying the wares. Next Galla goes to the cobbler* for a pair 202 of *solea*, simply soles fastened to the feet with leather thongs, which are being repaired. On the workbench there are rows of leather shoes (*calcei*), and tall boots called *caliges*.

The rope-maker who works next door to the cobbler is always ready to flirt with Galla but she has no time to stop. She passes Rabinius, the dyer who stocks the best Tyrian purple in Rome, and the sight of his amphorae*, brimming 203 with colours, reminds her that she must ask if the saffron yellow cloak is ready yet. Now she has only to call on the money-changer* and get new 204 sesterces in exchange for some old ones dating from the time of Augustus. She argues for some time with the old man, who smells of garlic and drives a hard bargain, for she knows her mistress will beat her if she does badly.

One small Campanian town, Pompeii, has been preserved under a layer of ashes just as it was one busy day when Vesuvius erupted suddenly and buried it. From its excavated streets* we can 205 reconstruct the Roman life which spread and served as the pattern for the whole of Europe.



205 →

# The hours pass, marked by the water clock. The Roman dines with

Some time later Lucius has come home and his wife is repairing the damage done to her appearance by an outing in her litter. At the other end of the house the servants are getting dinner ready and polishing the splendid gold and silver dishes that are the household's pride. Lucius looks fondly at his newly acquired water clock. It is just on the hour and any moment little multicoloured stones will leap into the air and fall back into a bronze basin. The Roman day began, like ours, at midnight, but the hours were counted from sunrise to sunset and their length varied with the seasons in order to make a consistent 12-hour day and night. At midwinter the hour was only 44 minutes long while in summer it corresponded to 1 hour 15 minutes. Now it is the tenth hour and the day being the ides of May the time is about four o'clock in the afternoon according to our reckoning. So far Lucius and Flaminia have eaten very little today: only a glass of water in the morning and a little cold meat and some fruit at midday. The main meal, the *cena*, is taken after the day's business is done. When the *nomenclator* announces that dinner is served everyone goes into the *triclinium* while the slaves are mixing the water and wine and filling ewers with scented water to pour over the guests' hands*. The diners 206 recline on couches with their heads towards a table spread with a white cloth. Today's menu has been chosen with especial care: for *hors-d'œuvre* there are pickled sow's udders and oysters from Tarentum, then come roast dormice sprinkled with honey and poppyseed, and the meal is rounded off by fritters and dried fruits. An aromatic wine is served with the *hors-d'œuvre*, and a pleasant and palatable Muscatel from Béziers with the roast. The Romans sat long over dinner and ate heavily; they would not leave the table without giving audible proof of their satisfaction, if indeed they did not tickle the back of their throats with a flamingo feather so that they could start all over again. Rome boasted many gourmets, and the banquets offered in some houses, that of Lucullus is an example, have

206

207

208

sts and after the meal there is dicing by lamp-light. *Tempus fugit.*

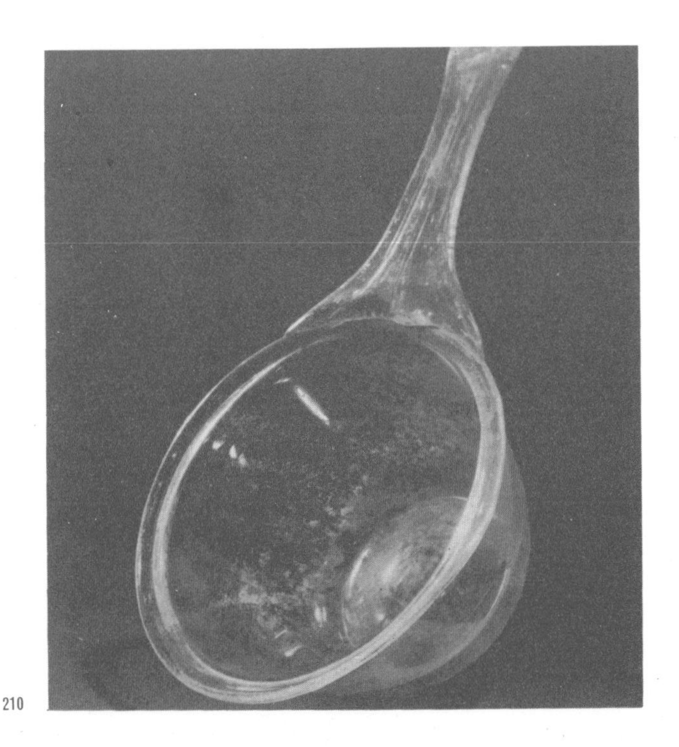

210

212

211

209

become legendary.

We shall leave our party to finish the evening playing dice* by the light of an oil lamp* and go on a tour of the kitchens. There are a surprisingly large and varied number of utensils. This cheese grater and the strainers and skimmers* would not disgrace a twentieth-century kitchen, neither would the glass saucepan* anticipating the invention of Pyrex by some two thousand years. At one end of the kitchen is a huge open fire with spits turning above it; there is a brick oven in the middle and in one corner a sink with running water from cisterns*. There is even a baby's bottle* on the table.

208 207 209 210 211 212

# An emperor's gift to his people—the Baths of Caracalla.

213

214

Lucius Marcus has a bathroom in his own house but this afternoon he went to the baths of Caracalla, one of the finest buildings in the city and as much a centre of public life as the forums, the great squares which house the hub of the administration, with their temples, libraries, columns and the enormous five-storey market built by Trajan. The building housing the actual baths has a central-heating system, called a hypocaust. The first room, the *apodyterium*, is a changing room*; next a sweat bath in the 213 *sudatorium* to clear the system is recommended, then patrons go to the hot room, the *caldarium* to be showered with hot water and scraped down by a slave with a strigil. From there they move into the *tepidarium* which is slightly cooler, before taking a cold plunge in the pool in the *frigidarium*. The bath relaxes body and mind and is very good for the health.

If the bath does not seem to have done you any good, the best thing is to go to the doctor. He will smile sympathetically and feel your pulse* and if 214 it is variable, racing or jumping, he will probably resort to cupping or induced vomiting. The remedies are generally speaking as unpleasant as the illness, and their effects are very far from certain. Doctors in Rome tend to be of foreign birth.

The baths provide many facilities in addition to those strictly connected with cleanliness. In the same buildings, although outside the baths themselves, is a wide promenade surrounded by columns. On the right is a shady walk where some hearty characters are playing at handball in the palaestra, and others, with bandages on their hands, are boxing. For the less energetic there are libraries, exhibitions and rest rooms, to say nothing of shops full of the luxuries and precious goods brought to Rome from the East. The city has no lack of other entertainments: games at the circus, racing, contests of gladiators and wild beasts in the arena, and at the theatre the ever-popular comedies and mimes*. 215

215

## traight roads, swift couriers and good inns facilitate communications.

216 217

Lucius Marcus' son, Decimus, is not travelling away from the city in the imperial courier's heavy wagon* for pleasure. He is rejoining his legion which is on garrison duty at Colonia Agrippina (Cologne). All the way to Cologne Decimus' journey will be through Gaul, which at that time covered Belgium, Switzerland, southern Holland and the part of Germany along the Rhine. The wild, barbaric Germans were causing trouble along the Rhine frontier. The Roman road is straight and well kept up and the vehicle relatively fast and comfortable, but all the same the mile-stones (every fifteen hundred paces) seem to creep by with terrible slowness. As he watches them pass, one after another, Decimus lets his mind dwell on Rome and the inexhaustible pleasures and luxuries of the city from which they are slowly dividing him. But he tells himself proudly that Gaul has certainly taken on a new look since the Roman conquest. Then the driver pulls up, the first stage has been reached already and it is time for lunch. Decimus strolls into the wayside inn, the Nigro Pullo—the Black Hen—whose friendly, smiling hostess is already approaching with a jug of beer and a mug in her hands to welcome the traveller*. The meal lives up to the promise of the welcome, for the food is good in Gaul and there is plenty of it. Decimus is offered trout, then some excellent sausage and ham, for Gallic ham is the best in the world, with asparagus, the whole accompanied by a round loaf—the Gauls are great bread-eaters —and a very good local wine. Some men wearing kilted-up tunics come into the room. They are bargees like those Decimus passed not long before, hauling their heavy vessels up the Saône*. Next a team pulls up before the inn drawing one of those heavy metal-bound barrels* which only the Gauls have the secret of making, and which are a continual source of astonishment to the Romans, who have nothing but earthenware amphorae.

218 219

# The Roman taste for good living spreads through the Province of Gaul.

220 221

After finishing his meal Decimus climbs back into the wagon and, lulled by the movement, allows his thoughts to wander. The question uppermost in his mind is whether he will find Cologne as well provided with amenities as the many Gallic cities he has already passed through, such as Forum Julii (Fréjus), Arelate (Arles) and Lugdunum (Lyon), which were almost indistinguishable from the Roman. In Romanised towns in Gaul stone blocks and manufactured brick and tile had replaced mud and wattle and there were fountains of clear water, often brought for many miles by aqueduct, large theatres and, in particular, vast amphitheatres seating an audience of up to fifteen thousand. There were shops bursting with Gallic specialities; here is a draper*, 220 for instance, about to cut a piece of cloth while his assistant holds it taut—scissors had not yet been invented and people used instead the sharp pincers that were also used for sheep shearing. There was also the cobbler's shop*, the basket 221 maker's, with its attractive stock of baskets and cane chairs, and the maker of soap, a product of Gaul which was made with tallow and cleaned much better than the powders and pomades common in Rome. Then there were the shops selling the highly praised cooked meats and in the busy streets where a salesman was crying: 'Apples. Buy my lovely apples!' one could stop for a moment to watch a showman with his performing monkeys, while a fashionable beauty, holding a circular fan in her hand* was standing framed 222 in a nearby window.

Life was pleasant in Gaul, as this young couple* 223 with the dog curled up at their feet seems to suggest; they may not have had all the refinements that came to Rome from the East, but the great landowning aristocracy and the town bourgeoisie possessed a strong sense of comfort, as the very up-to-date looking divan bed, with its warm covers and soft pillows, bears witness.

222

# Roman organisation is reflected in the majesty of country estates

224

226

Decimus plans to break his journey at Augustodunum (the modern Autun) to stay with Julius Florentius Nertomaros, whose name is half Latin and half Gallic and who is an important personage of senatorial rank to whom the young officer's father, Lucius Marcus, had rendered some service when he visited Rome. Julius owns a large estate, and the buildings of his domain are arranged round a semicircular entrance court bounded by a covered walk, with the flour mill on the left of it. The house itself is built round an inner court*, and the place as a whole gives an impression of style as well as comfort. Small buildings of one or two storeys are linked by colonnades through which servants come and go wearing the Gallic hood, called *cucullus*, which is so useful that it has been adopted all over the empire, pulled over their heads*. (The *cucullus* was the original model for the cowl still worn by certain monastic orders.) Julius and his family give the traveller an enthusiastic welcome. During dinner Julius' elder son, Cintus, who is studying rhetoric at the celebrated Romano-Gallic University of Autun, plies Decimus with all sorts of questions about life in Rome, and afterwards Julius takes his guest on a tour of the house. Decimus is particularly amazed at the fireplaces, which were a Gallic invention and very necessary in a country where winter could be bitterly cold. Outside, grapes are ripening on the trellised vines watched over by a slave sitting in a little willow cabin built in the fork of a tree and playing a flute to scare away the birds*. The afternoon ends with some quiet fishing by the river*.

224 225 226 227

225

227

Before three more centuries had passed the first sounds of disintegration were beginning to be heard on the furthest borders of the empire. The nomads who lived on the edge of civilisation poured in on all sides in raids which carried them thousands of miles from their starting points. Beginning in central Asia with the unknown races who were the forebears of Huns, Avars, Turks and of the Mongols of today the reverberations of their movements swept from east to west.

In the twentieth century the Mongols' life is becoming less primitive, but the appearance of their camps has not altered for over a thousand years. They still wear enveloping sheepskin capes* (228) and fur-lined robes with felt leggings and boots, and at the end of the day put up their huge tents made of felt, called yourtas, which are supported by hundreds of pegs and have a round hole in the roof to let the smoke escape* (229). And they still make *koumys*, a delicacy of fermented mare's milk. The steppe is not only their home; it is their heaven, and in the days when they invaded cultivated lands they would not stop until they had destroyed all vestiges of civilisation and re-created the desert from which they came. This is what happened in the invasions which ravaged the Roman Empire in the fourth and fifth centuries A.D. and in those led by Genghis Khan and Tamerlane which took place in the Middle Ages.

228

229

At first the Asiatic invaders were probably seeking fresh pastures after a prolonged drought and were content to harry the semi-barbaric tribes on the borders of the empire. Under pressure from their rear these begged admittance to the empire and used force when it was refused. The first barbarian infiltrations were easily dealt with, by creating colonies for them which were absorbed into the empire and in turn developed into defensive outposts. The newcomers fitted into the Roman civilisation and even contributed to it with their own forms of art*, the art of the steppes. (230) Later, as the stream of barbarians asking for admittance to the empire became a rushing tide, they were forbidden. But the pressure grew until at last the *limes*, the fortified line running from the mouth of the Danube to the west coast of Britain which defended the empire like a dyke, gave way, and the wave of invaders broke in.

230

## . . . until the invading barbarians thunder over the protecting dykes.

# Mongols, small, ferocious, bring yellow peril to Euro

231 232

We can gain some idea of the effect on the citizens of the empire of these iron men, whose descendants today peacefully tend their flocks* and drive their long caravans of camels across the Gobi desert*, from historians of the time who reflect the terror they inspired: 'The Huns are more fierce and barbarous than can possibly be imagined. They slash their children's cheeks to prevent their beards from growing. They look like monsters with their squat bodies, huge upper limbs and outsize heads and they live like animals, feeding on roots and meat which they have a way of cooking by keeping it beneath their saddles. They never change their clothes but wear them until they rot to pieces on their bodies, and they spend so much of their lives on horseback that they might be glued to their saddles.'

The townspeople built hurried defences against the Huns or fled into the country for refuge—but nowhere was safe; the land was given over to fire, rape and pillage. No sooner were the Huns subdued and the ruins rebuilt than other tribes loomed on the horizon. Goths, Vandals and Lombards drove into Italy itself, Rome fell to the barbarians and on 4th September 476 the empire crumbled.

Several times again the civilised world would be threatened with destruction in the guise of this stocky little Mongol* with his grinning face and fur cap, clambering, lance in hand, onto a small shaggy pony as wild-looking as himself, as though he were once more riding to conquer the world, setting up his tents in a new place each night*. In the fifth century A.D. an ancient tradition was broken, and in western Europe only the fast-dying memory of civilisation remained. It was to be a long time before the tree flowered again.

233 234

d from the North the Viking longships harry a defenceless continent.

235

Yet by the seventh and eighth centuries, especially in the West, the barbarian rulers had begun to re-establish the order they had overthrown. Their warriors shared out the lands with their former owners, though the thunder still growled occasionally. Hungarians penetrated into the heart of Europe, Saracens plundered the Mediterranean coast and the Norsemen came on their sudden, violent forays from Scandinavia.

These last were not total barbarians; they made a livelihood from cultivating rye and barley, as well as from hunting and keeping flocks and herds. The houses in their villages were built of wood and clay and the chiefs who ruled them knew considerable luxury, owning fine furniture, chariots, 235 carved sledges, helmets with great horns*, delicately engraved silver buckles and heavy iron 236 crowns*. These Vikings were primarily warriors and 237 seamen. With their swift, efficient warships* they raided the coasts of Britain and western Europe, and ravaged the fertile farmlands; the inhabitants would flee, taking with them all they managed to carry, and it was not long before their warlike pursuers discovered that inland were huge areas of rich, almost undefended country. For several decades a new terror hung over the West, the terror of seeing the high, beaked prows of the longships on the horizon. The Vikings sailed up the rivers, besieging towns, burning and laying waste; and the monasteries, with their rich store of treasure and sacred vessels, were especially vulnerable. Flying over Denmark today one can still make out the sites of Viking burials with their oval formations of stones marking the places where 238 chieftains are buried beneath their ships*.

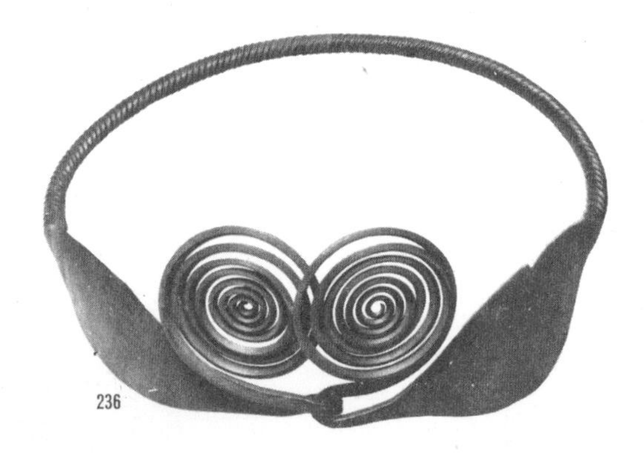
236

237

238

# Peace comes too late to save the Roman Empire. The noble spirit lingers amo

239

240

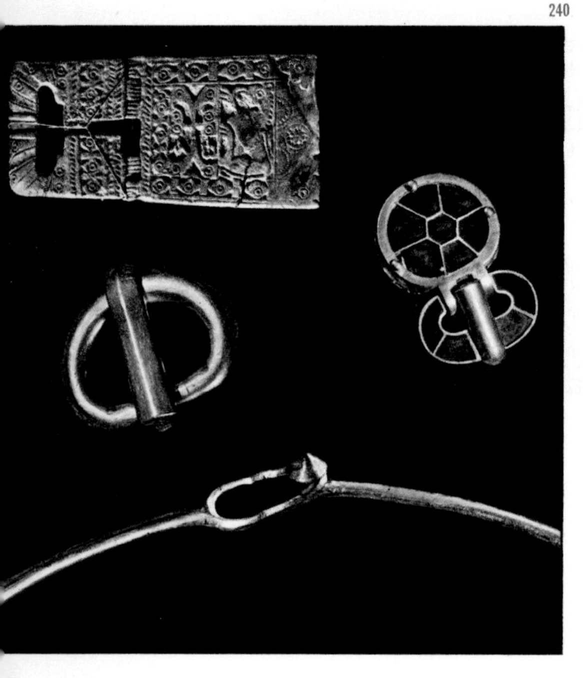

242

243

When at last the thunder of the moving hordes had subsided and the din of battle and the wail of victims grew quiet, it seemed as though a great silence had fallen on western Europe. Excavation of the levels corresponding to the sixth and seventh centuries reveals nothing but a few crudely carved tombstones* (239) and swords with sheaths made of wood and leather, decorated with roughly-fashioned jewels made of cloisonné enamel* (240), to replace the relics of elegant living left by the Romanised peoples.

Of course life went on, but it seemed as though the great edifice of civilisation, built up stone by stone over so many centuries, was ruined for ever. Even Latin had been replaced as the common language by the *lingua romana* in Gaul and Germanic in the German parts of the Frankish Empire. The looks, clothes and customs of the Franks became the chief influence on a vast area, covering ancient Gaul and a large part of Germany, and differed greatly from those of their conquered predecessors. This is how the Roman Gauls saw them: 'Their blond hair is combed forward on their heads making a fringe on the forehead and leaving the nape of the neck bare . . . it is carefully combed and scented. . . . Their faces are clean shaven but for flowing moustaches.' They wore two short tunics, one cotton, the other wool, one on top of the other, clasped at the waist with a leather belt, and breeches bound with criss-cross gaiters and a cape fastened with a pin on the shoulder. The princes of the realm were cruel and brutish and spent their time in hunting* (241),

241

fighting or drinking themselves into a stupor at banquets. With the exception of one or two saintly men the higher clergy plunged as eagerly as the courtiers into the most disgraceful debauches. The monuments of Roman Gaul, converted to fortresses during the invasions, sheltered whole populations from towns that had been burned or sacked, who lived there in conditions of appalling squalor perpetually menaced by robber barons, famine and epidemics of plague, dysentery and smallpox. The many nervous disorders they suffered from were attributed to possession by devils. Everywhere people were turning back to the old pagan religion with its primitive practices, superstitions and portents. Even with the rise of a strong power under Charlemagne the immense commercial prosperity that had existed under the Romans showed no signs of a revival, and the only foreign goods imported into the realm were luxuries destined for the court. The towns, lacking either trade or native craftsmen, remained dead for centuries.

In the country, life went on in the great estates owned by Franks, or Roman Gauls or by the monasteries. The lord, in his Frankish dress*, 242 lived in a *villa*, usually built of wood. Round the villa were many out-buildings with bakeries, ovens and wine presses, for the domain was entirely self-supporting. Nothing was purchased from outside and generally anything left over was stored as a precaution against future lean years. Of the peasants and serfs dependent on the lord, some were carpenters, joiners, masons or smiths who kept the fortifications in good repair*; 243 others worked in the fields and brought in the harvest*. 244 245

The most important part of the house was the great hall, with its whitewashed walls and high, beamed ceiling, furnished with chests containing clothes and valuables. It was in the hall that the lord with his wife and guests assembled at about five or six in the evening for the main meal of the day*. 246 The meal consisted of fat joints of meat, stewed or roasted, hams, geese and occasionally such rare dainties as peaches, which had only recently been cultivated in Europe and were still a novelty, or Roquefort, a cheese that Charlemagne probably knew. The poor lived meanwhile on gruel or a sort of barley soup, which was the forerunner of Scots porridge, and vegetables such as beetroot, cabbage, radishes and onions and mallow leaves which were eaten like spinach. In times of famine bread was made out of bran or even clay or beech leaves.

244

245

246

247

For the Franks, as for the Romans, the world ended at India in the east and in the west there was only the ocean. They would have been surprised, indeed utterly incredulous, to hear of the New World, for they believed that if there were islands in the ocean they could only be inhabited by monsters, and the existence of a whole continent would have been unthinkable to them. They could never have imagined that across the sea in countries now called Mexico, Guatemala and Honduras majestic temples and pyramids* rose **247** towards the sky, and that around them flowered a brilliant and refined, but also strange and disconcerting civilisation: that of the Mayas.

Long before the time of Charlemagne these distinguished and dignified people* had carved **248** out huge areas of forest to grow maize. They had invented an extremely complex method of writing, and, although they knew nothing of the use of metals, had raised the great monuments which we incorrectly refer to as Maya cities. This pipe, representing an old woman* in huge terracotta **249** ear-rings, gives us a very clear idea of these people's appearance; their houses were built with wooden stakes, lianas and panels of bark in the clearings beside their fields. There they grew cotton for spinning and weaving, maize for cakes and soup, and cultivated gardens of sweet potatoes, cocoa, pawpaws and avocadoes. They had only one domestic animal, the turkey. It was not until after the Spanish conquest of Mexico in the sixteenth century that maize, green beans, turkeys and cocoa reached Europe, but it was to be centuries later before another Indian discovery, rubber, revolutionised Western life. The furniture of their huts was simple and rudimentary: stone benches, a flat stone for grinding corn, a few fibre mats and some fine painted pots, like this one in the shape of a human being*. Their **250** most domestic objects show an often startling originality, like this doll* resembling a grandee **251** accompanied by a person pulling a face, perhaps a servant. The main figure wears a necklace of jade beads and on his head, as a sign of rank, a huge

248 249 250

# On the other side of the globe, deep in the jungles of the New Worl

252

crown made of feathers of the quetzal bird, which was held sacred and which has shimmering green plumage. A priceless, feathered cloak hangs from his shoulders to his feet. This lordly person is probably a priest, dressed for a temple ceremony, for religion played a basic part in the lives of the Mayas. People from the surrounding villages crowded into the holy city for religious festivals and poured onto the wide terraces between the towering masses of temples* and pyramids to the spaces reserved for the ball game resembling pelota. This was not a competitive game, but intended to illustrate the progress of the earth and the march of the stars in heaven.

252

The priests, adorned with jade and feathers, entered the sanctuary, which was heavy with the fumes of copal, the native incense, and presented themselves to the god, begging his help for their people. They danced the sacred dances which represented mythological stories*. Some of them had painted their bodies black and drawn weird signs on their faces*. Dressed in their magnificent ceremonial attire, with its brilliant colours, and richly adorned with jewellery, these priests would assume a terrifying, superhuman appearance, as though they were larger than life; in the eyes of all the people they were the incarnation of the gods, the masters of men's destiny.

253 254

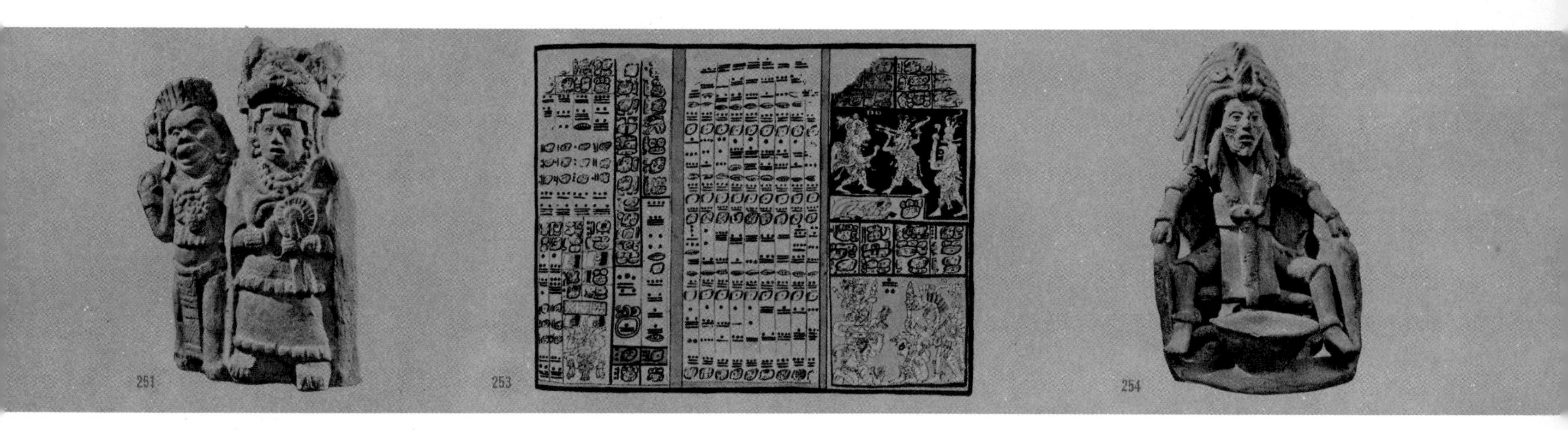

251 253 254

strange, baroque civilisation flowers unknown to the West: the Maya.

256

255

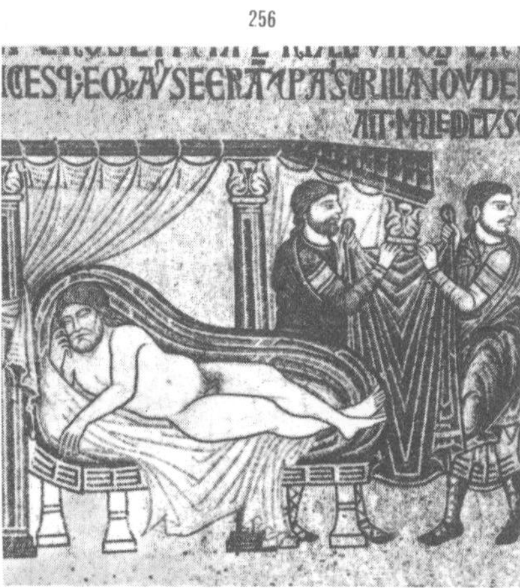

257

Although Romano-Egyptian and dating from the second century A.D., these portraits* are sufficient to suggest a racial likeness to Byzantines of later periods. After the fall of the Roman Empire, Constantinople had inherited the glory of Greece and Rome and shone with unrivalled brilliance. Byzantine power extended over Asia Minor, Greece and part of the Balkans, but its influence spread far further, to the western limits of Europe and to Russia, which had been converted by Byzantine missionaries and where Vladimir, the ruler of the first real state, the principality of Kiev, had married a Byzantine princess. 255 257

Let us take a look at a typical house in the city, home of a fairly prosperous bourgeois family. It is on two floors and the walls are covered with coloured stucco while there are little glass panes set in plaster in the windows. Everything indicates a level of comfort far higher than was usual at the period. The main living-room, the *triclinium*, where meals are served, rises to the whole height of the house. It contains a large rectangular table surrounded by high-backed chairs called *cathedra*. Above the table hangs an elegant bronze lamp, in which burns a wick soaked in oil. The master's room is on the first floor and has a mosaic floor and a ceiling panelled with cedar of Lebanon. In one corner is the bed which stands on four legs and has a slightly raised head. It is surrounded by silken hangings*. Demetrios* is wealthy enough to have accumulated in his apartment innumerable objects whose luxury makes a striking contrast with the poverty found in a Frankish or Russian household. There are incense burners*, ivory chests, icons, gold ear-picks and even what is probably one of the first commodes in history. The long fitted robes of the Byzantines* were made of brightly coloured silk brocade and bore a much closer resemblance to eastern costume than to the simple Roman or Greek wear. Other points of difference were their hair, which they wore long, and their headgear: these high dignitaries in council wear hats whose shape and colour vary according to the wearer's office. 256 257 258 259

## Byzantium the golden : the first Christian civilisation.

258



259 →

261

The traveller disembarking at Constantinople in the tenth century must have been amazed by the great capital with its high walls, 'enclosing the city all round about and her splendid palaces and tall churches . . . and the length and breadth of the city'. The Frankish knights who took it by storm three centuries later could 'not believe that there might be another city as mighty in the world. And there was no man so bold that he did not tremble.' Constantinople was often besieged but it placed its trust in its walls on which an army of workmen was constantly employed, strengthening and repairing them*. Within the walls lived a population that must have exceeded a million, among whom were Armenians, Georgians, Arabs, Norman knights who had come to sell their swords as mercenaries, and Venetian merchants, for Venice was the trade link between Constantinople and the West. It was a polyglot crowd that one would meet in the Mese, the Champs Elysées of Constantinople, with the entrance to its marble arcades surmounted by a statue of Constantine raised on a porphyry column, or in the *agora* where street hawkers moved among the tables of the money-changers, piled high with gold and silver, and the desks of the public scribes. There were astrologers, magicians and guides always ready to serve the stranger dazzled by so much splendour. They would take him to visit churches, gleaming with gold and mosaic, or to the hippodrome where the Emperor patronised the chariot races, events of two- or four-in-hand that raised the crowd to a frenzy of excitement*. The guide would find the stranger a good vantage point to see the many processions* when the Patriarch in his splendid robes, holding the tau, the shepherd's staff shaped like a crutch, might be seen carrying some precious relics of the Passion, the object of many pilgrimages, while the trumpets sounded and the air was heavy with incense. True there was another side to the picture: slums, narrow alleys and streets that were unsafe and filthy, for theft and murder were a commonplace and there was no public refuse service. But to all these disadvantages the traveller would pay no attention at all, for things were as bad at home and he was quite used to them.

260 261 262

260

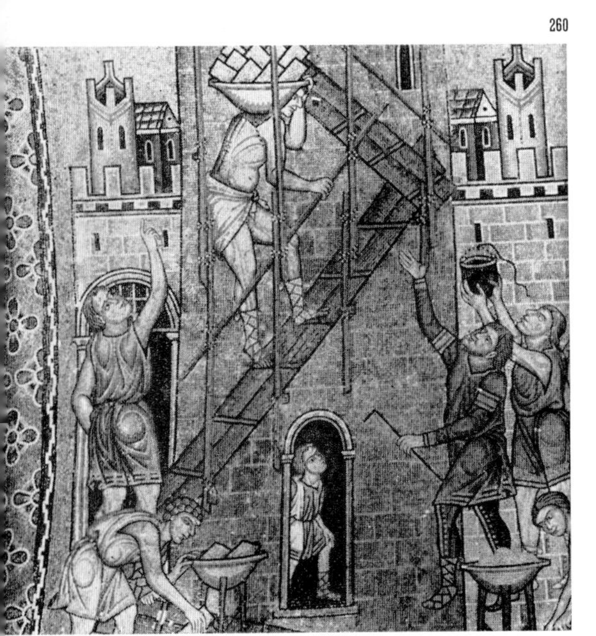

262

The splendours of Constantinople awe the western visitor.

# At home the pillagers settle down and become respectable.

263

263 This bronze key* opens the door to a new era. It is Viking and stands for the part played by the descendants of the plundering Norsemen in building the Europe of the eleventh century. Already important innovations were creeping in quietly to improve conditions of life. The transport of goods had become easier since the advent of horseshoes, stirrups and a rigid collar to replace the throttling band around the horse's neck. The rudder, replacing the steering-oar, improved navigation, while the windmill, borrowed from the Arabs, and the waterwheel harnessed natural forces.

Still, the man of the times was a warrior, a feudal baron responsible for maintaining order in the lands in his fief. His life was consecrated to violence, to baronial wars, hunting and the tournament. The rest of his time was passed in the great hall of his keep, the sole room which was really habitable. The only light came from narrow apertures sealed with oiled cloth, and it was cold despite the huge hearth, big enough to hold stone seats inside it. The trestle table stood in the centre of the room* and a squire carried the dishes to it, covered as a precaution against poison. The meat was served on trenchers of bread which soaked up the gravy and could be eaten afterwards. There were often entertainments during the feast and travelling minstrels were always welcome. They accompanied themselves on the flute or harp* and sang such songs of noble and heroic deeds as the *Chanson de Roland*. The bed with sheets and a down coverlet also stood in the great hall*. Everyone slept naked, and it was accepted practice to ask a guest to stay the night. Also in the hall, behind an arras, was the wooden tub where they took their none-too-frequent baths*.

264 265 266 267

264

265

267

266

# The peasants live in subjection to their lords and in fear of God.

268 269

270

Close under the castle walls, within which he sheltered when danger threatened, lived the peasant, a serf compelled to carry out his lord's work. This left him very little time to tend his own little plot of ground, which he held on a precarious tenure from the lord, who was well within his rights to trample it with his hunt. The villager's day began at dawn with the ringing of Prime from the monastery bell-tower. He crossed himself three times then put on his breeches, shirt and hood and went to mass, and afterwards went home to breakfast off a bowl of cabbage soup and a hunk of black bread before leading his pigs out to the wood for acorns, or making his wine in the common press* which belonged to the lord, or setting off, axe across his shoulder, to chop a clearing in the forest*. Meanwhile his wife would be busy in the outer keep, tending the animals, cooking, and weaving the wool from their sheep into clothes for her household.

268
269

270 The land yielded very little. A good harvest* brought only three times what had been sown and famine raged nearly one year in ten. The peasant lived on his produce—or, more accurately, on what his lord left him—and ate little meat other than pork, which was killed at the beginning of winter and the flesh salted and preserved. In Lent people ate fish, freshwater fish or sea fish salted or smoked, and in particular dried whale meat, for there was a thriving whaling industry* in the Bay 271

271

# All life centres on the Church and nobles flock to the Crusades.

of Gascony in the Middle Ages. Life for the layman centred round the castle of which we have a detailed description through the eyes of a contemporary, Jean de Colmieu, archdeacon of Thérouanne: 'A mound of earth is raised as high as possible which is surrounded by a wide, deep ditch. On the inner slope is a palisade of sharp wooden stakes and this is reinforced by watchtowers built at various points. The house, or rather the keep, is built on top of the mound where look-outs can see in all directions.' Still, people looked essentially to the Church, and to the monasteries in particular. They lived in perpetual terror of heavenly signs and strange portents and always they went in fear of robbers and the ever-present menace of famine and plague.

272

Their only hope lay in the untiring stream of prayer rising from the churches to a God of power. It was above all in convents and cathedrals that the priceless heritage of civilisation was preserved and handed down and began to spread beyond the walls into the lives of the people. All material and spiritual knowledge was enclosed in their manuscripts, copied lovingly by the monks.

274

273

In them we find precious medical prescriptions and instructions for performing such surgical operations as the clerks ventured on, such as removing polypus from the nose* and lancing piles*. And who if not the priest could stand up to the baron*? For few barons were too brutish to be moved when they heard fulminations from the pulpit against the heathen who held Christ's Sepulchre. Here was a noble quest that would ensure absolution for all sins, and eternal salvation was the prize for death in battle. In the year 1096 the first barons and knights set out on the long trail across Europe and the Mediterranean towards the conquest of the Holy Land.

272 273 274

275

276

277

Another civilisation, as unknown to the contempory mediaeval world as the Mayas of Central America, reached its climax in the twelfth and thirteenth centuries in what is today Cambodia. The capital of the Khmers was Yagodharapura, which we call Angkor, and it was surrounded by lakes, filled with all kinds of fish. In the pleasure boats which plied the lakes, ladies in embroidered jackets and with hair twisted into a bun on the nape of the neck would sit holding sunshades. In the centre of the city was a huge building called the Bayon on which, as on western cathedrals, the people had tried to show every facet of the lives of gods and men. These bas-reliefs* are all that allow us a glimpse into the lives of the whole race. 275

Near the lake a fish-seller has set up her stall and is crying her wares*. She is dressed much less elaborately than the ladies in the boats, in a pleated cotton skirt, but she has heavy silver necklaces round her neck and bangles on her ankles. The lobes of her ears have been gradually stretched since childhood by means of progressively heavier weights, until now they hang onto her shoulders. This custom is widely practised among Buddhist peoples, and the long ears of the Buddha are a sign of spiritual elevation. A little further off under the mango trees, in whose branches are apes and peacocks, a group of workmen engaged on building the temple are taking a rest. Cooks belonging to the royal household, dressed in loin-cloths, are preparing a meal for them. Fires crackle under the pots and men are carrying bowls of rice on trays among the workers, some of whom can be seen shaping beams with adze and chisel. More cooks are about to plunge a whole pig into boiling water and others are spitting meat on skewers ready to grill at the fire to make shish-kebab, a dish still popular in the Middle East today*. A family is moving house, and a bullock-cart piled high with their belongings comes in sight, while the people follow behind, parents with children perched on their shoulders*. The king has a fever and lies on his bed in his palace of a thousand columns surrounded by doctors and healers trying to ease his pain*. 276 277 278 279

278

## ...ople of which the West would know nothing for many centuries . . . Khmers.

In another room the lords of the realm are waiting, two of them playing chess* (280), a game the Khmers learned from the Hindus, but whose origins go much further back in time. A showman is amusing the crowd in the public square, and sword-swallowing* (281) held as much fascination for young and old seven centuries ago as it does today.

This ancient, dead capital, isolated in the jungle, shows us a way of life that persisted almost unchanged to its last years. It was a simple life, but one perfectly suited to both the climate and the natural resources of that part of Asia. Rice, sugar cane, bananas, coconuts and groundnuts, of which the last three were later cultivated in

280

Africa, were among their basic properties, as well as chickens, which were first domesticated in south Asia. This was another of the centres of civilisation which were developing independently in various different parts of the world, unknown to each other. Soon it would be time for the West to break out of its isolation and make contact with these new worlds.

281

279

282

In the palace courtyard at Nagaoka, the modern Kyoto, high officials sit cross-legged on checked cushions waiting, hieratic and expressionless, in their ceremonial lacquered bonnets with a single ribbon curving out at the back of the head*. They 282 are waiting outside the entrance to the *Room of Perfect Freshness* in which are the private apartments of the Emperor Toba (1107–1123). Word has gone out that the princess Murasaki, first imperial concubine, is returning from admiring the cherry trees in blossom. Once inside she will withdraw to the forbidden precincts where the Empress and the royal mistresses have their apartments. In the galleries are red-painted pillars with ornamental tablets of black lacquer and gold inscriptions, and roofs of glazed jade-green tiles enclose courtyards full of flowering shrubs in pots. This is the delightful setting for a court life that embodies the exquisitely refined and delicate Nippon civilisation; it originated in China, but rapidly developed here an individuality of its own.

In this elegant and to all appearances entirely frivolous world everything was in fact ordered according to strict etiquette, from the colour of a robe to the length of a sword or the depth of a bow. There was a formal exchange of short, beautifully executed poems, a highly prized art at which the women in particular excelled. But now we must leave the palace and go to meet the princess. On the way we pass the train of a nobleman paying a visit to his estates*. He travels inside a 283 closed *kago*, a sort of palanquin in which the only comfortable position is bent double, while a servant carries his baggage on his shoulders, and is accompanied by an escort of four armed men, each carrying the regulation sabre. Now at last here is the procession*. Servants in short tunics 284 and full breeches and archers of the guard, dressed in trousers so baggy that they give the appearance of divided skirts, press round the coach,

283 284

ɛgant, but subject at all times to an iron etiquette.

286

287

which is drawn by a buffalo. Ladies dressed in their prettiest dresses, worn one on top of the other in a dazzling display of colour, gather on the verandahs before the houses to watch the officers on horseback and the halberdiers and standard bearers of the procession go by. No sooner has the last of it passed than the streets fill with their usual busy crowds.

Many of the passers-by are free men belonging to fraternities and guilds organised by the government, but others are slaves, some public servants employed in cleaning the streets, others private domestic servants. Travelling salesmen* with their wares slung on long poles across their shoulders go from door to door, selling fish, which is often eaten raw, rice, soya, bamboo shoots, peppers, *shyoyu*, a sauce made from fermented barley, and terracotta bottles of *sake*. At a cross-roads there is a juggler* balancing a precious porcelain plate on a long pole on his nose, while his wife beats a little drum to attract a crowd. White-clad pilgrims wearing their bed-mats folded on their heads as hats* make their way to the temple of Buddha Amida to worship*.

285 288

# Age-old Japanese concerns: elegance, beauty, cleanliness.

289

291

Although in the country, where there is little fertile soil, the Japanese peasant lives very frugally, the tradesmen and artisans in the towns find little to complain of in their lot, for they are naturally sober people who can content themselves with very little. They care much more for a thing's beauty than for its cost, so that their houses are plain but always tastefully furnished and their principal luxury is absolute cleanliness. Daily cleaning is detailed and thorough.

Slaves beat the floor mats with canes in front of the house, and the heavy wooden chest used for storing the brilliantly coloured robes of silk or gauze is hauled out onto the pavement. One servant washes the oiled-paper walls*. Japanese houses of the Heian period were very simple, consisting only of a wooden framework, tiled roof and sliding walls made of paper. Even if these did catch fire easily the damage was never as disastrous as in the West. There was usually time to save the few valuables which were kept in a special room with protection against fire, and a new house, almost identical with the old, could be built in a few days. The rooms were raised slightly above ground level and joined to one another by verandahs opening onto a small garden surrounded by a bamboo fence. Here a few stones, some flowering shrubs and one or two exotic plants were lovingly arranged to make a retreat where the Japanese soul could taste at leisure the bliss of being at one with nature*.

289
290

As soon as the fine weather came the inhabitants of Kyoto poured out into the parks and public gardens to admire the wistaria, azaleas and chrysanthemums in flower or to gaze at the full moon. In the shade of a great pine tree sits a little group of women with lacquered hair and men whose heads are close-shaven, but for a little crown of hair drawn into a tiny topknot, eating a light meal in the cool of the evening*. Beside them is a flask of *sake*, an alcoholic drink made of rice and served hot. One of them reads aloud a short poem he has composed which catches something of the intangible quality of the air: 'The flowering wistaria is mirrored in the lake. Among the pebbles at the bottom precious stones appear.' This peaceful existence was to be sadly interrupted by quarrels among the great warlords. The Emperor became a puppet in the hands of rival factions and the land was pillaged by the Samurai.

291

290

# In the teeming cities of the Arab world, five times a day th

293

294

The lands of Islam once formed a belt stretching from Spain and Morocco in the west as far as India in the east. At the heart of the Muslim religion is the city of Mecca in what is today Saudi Arabia, and every year crowds of pilgrims flock to it from all over the world. Not far away in the south of the Arabian peninsula is the city of Zabid, an important international trade centre which in the twelfth century was one of the world's greatest slave markets. The picture on the preceding page shows a scene in the market*. A merchant has just sold an Abyssinian slave, and his assistants are weighing out the purchase price paid by the lady. All three wear the *qaba*, a sheet with a design in silk, over which is flung a light cloak made of goat hair, called an *aba*. On their heads are tarbooshes round which are wound turbans whose ends hang down loosely behind. The lady is veiled and her dress is caught in at the waist by a *shall* of fine brocade. On her feet are the little morocco slippers the material of which, as its name indicates, is of Arab origin. 292

Now let us go with Guido, a merchant of Padua who is travelling to Islam to trade among the pagans, for wars and crusades have not interrupted all contact between Christians and infidels. In the spring of 1172, after many adventures, our merchant at last reaches his destination, the house of Abu-l-Hasan Al Hahshab in old Cairo, the largest city in Egypt under the sultan Saladin. Guido stares about him in amazement. On either

296

295

muezzin calls the faithful to prayer and time stops. Allah is great!

297

298

them other eastern cities seemed little more than villages. First thing in the morning Abu-l-Hasan goes to the *hammam* where, after bathing in the pool*, he is washed, shaved and puts on clean clothes*. Suddenly a weird cry rings out from the top of a minaret, where the muezzin is calling the faithful to prayer*. Abu-l-Hasan makes his way to the mosque, where five times a day the faithful turn towards Mecca and pray to Allah. They bow their heads and then kneel with their foreheads touching the ground and hands stretched out before them. Abu-l-Hasan describes to Guido the interior of the mosque, which no one may enter before taking his shoes off, with the court of ablutions and the sanctuary in which is the *mehrab*, turned towards Mecca. The imam stands on the *minbar** to preach a sermon. But the mosque is not only a place for prayers. Close by are the school buildings where the master teaches his pupils, sitting cross-legged on the floor*, verses of the Koran which they learn by heart and chant in chorus before writing them down. Guido finds that education is much more widespread in Islamic countries, where half the population is able to read and write, than in his own country.

295 296 297 298 299

One of the most important occasions in the Muslim year is Ramadan. This lasts for a whole lunar month, during which period the faithful must not eat, drink or wash themselves between the hours of sunrise and sunset.

side of the street tall houses rise like mountains to as many as ten storeys with little closed balconies protected by wooden lattices, called *mousharabiehs*, overhanging the street from which the women can watch passers-by without being seen themselves*. Whenever they do go out they are carefully veiled and carried in camel litters*.

293 294

Cairo at this time had some two million inhabitants and Baghdad three million, and beside

299

# The women's world: the harem and the beauty parlour amaze the West.

300

Guido is invited to Abu-l-Hasan's house, which is lighted by oil-lamps made of glass on which [300] are painted verses from the Koran*. But there is one room in the house Guido is not allowed to enter, and that is the women's quarter, the harem; and although he may see the face of the servant [301] girl spinning in the courtyard*, the mistress of the house is always closely veiled and reveals only her eyes. Abu-l-Hasan explains that the word harem does not necessarily imply polygamy. He, like many men in Cairo, has only one wife and, although she rarely goes out, this does not seem to trouble her. Her part of the house opens onto a pleasant [302] garden* where fountains splash into mosaic [303] basins*, and her greatest pleasure is receiving visits from her friends. The ladies remove their veils and sit cross-legged on sofas or cushions scattered on carpets among low, brass tables on which incense-burners fill the air with their [304] scent. Maids offer them ewers* of rose-water and many different kinds of sweetmeats, and the ladies chatter happily. The most important event of the week for Abu-l-Hasan's wife is her visit to the hammam. This is a real beauty parlour, and the ladies arrive at dawn and are not ready to leave until the evening.

The treatment begins with a session in the steam-bath, after which comes a massage, a shampoo and a pedicure. There is an interval for a cold lunch, brought from home, which may consist of meat pasties, a salad of aubergines, honey cakes and peaches with an iced honey drink. There may even be coffee, which is beginning to make its appearance in Arab countries as a substitute for wine, forbidden by the Koran. In the afternoon the lady has a complicated facial, followed by a henna rinse to give auburn lights to her hair. As a finishing touch her eyelashes are darkened with indigo, kohl is put round her eyes and her nails are varnished red.

Western visitors, even the Crusaders themselves, were amazed at the subtleties of Eastern life, for nothing similar was known in Europe. They borrowed many things from the Arabs, including the windmill, new methods of dyeing cloth, silkworm culture and the cultivation of saracen corn and apricots. The hennin, an imitation of the pointed head-dress worn by men in the time of Haroun al-Raschid, was soon to become the newest fashion among great ladies in the West.

301 302

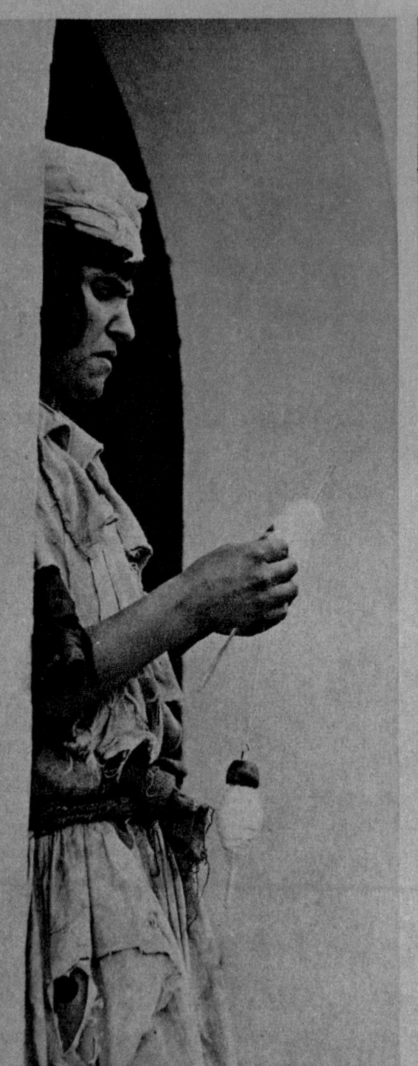

304

303

305

Western towns in the thirteenth century, entrenched behind their high, towered ramparts*, could hardly compare with the great capitals of the East; yet in the course of two centuries a gradual process of development had taken place which produced a class of merchants and craftsmen, some of them extremely wealthy, who formed the new bourgeoisie. Soon these cities would become completely self-governing.

Even before the first glimmer of daylight the bells of countless churches and monasteries would be ringing for Lauds, and soon the first street-cries would begin: a friar ringing a bell and calling, 'Pray for the soul of Eustache Boucel'; or asking for 'bread for the little brothers! Bread for the poor!' The plea was always answered, for the poor and needy lived only on alms and there was always a queue at the convent door for gifts of soup, shoes* or clothes*. A trumpet sounded at dawn for the opening of the town gates, and the night watchmen left the walls and removed the chains stretched across the street to close off quarters of ill-fame. Few people were abroad in the streets after nightfall; in the absence of street-lighting, most people found it advisable to bar themselves safely into their houses after curfew.

Master Guillaume, the goldsmith, is woken at dawn by the bells and wastes little time on his toilet, for modesty demands that he washes himself fully clothed. Already there is a show to draw people out of doors. A huge wheel has been stuck up on a pole in the market place on which a malefactor, his arms and legs broken, has been exposed to the view of all who wish to come and gaze at his agony*.

306

307

308

Western cities are on the rise, and with them beggars, crime and merchants.

# Work, eat, sleep: the pattern is established.

309

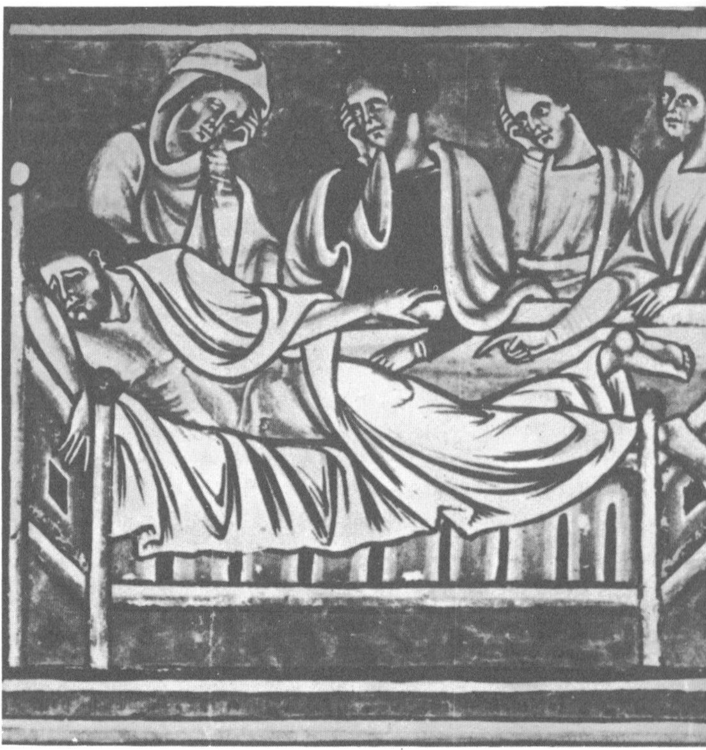

310

Master Guillaume's shop is closed today for the feast of Saint Elias, the patron saint of goldsmiths, so he takes the opportunity to do some tidying up, with the help of his apprentices. While he is occupied with his accounts downstairs his wife, Dame Pernelle, is on the first floor, which juts out over the street, supervising preparations for dinner. She and her children will eat by themselves today, for her husband is going to a banquet for the master craftsmen of his guild. For the occasion he wears a full, sleeveless gown of blue cloth lined with squirrel fur over his woollen tunic, and a blue hat, also fur-lined, on his head. Here he is at table* (309). On the cloth in front of the diners are covered pewter dishes, chalice-shaped drinking cups and many different kinds of food, including bread rolls, a carp and a boar's head. We still have the bill of fare from this feast: first, goose with chitterlings and jugged hare flavoured with herbs, followed by dressed carp, boar's head and sucking pig with a sauce of garlic, verjuice and breadcrumbs. The meal finished with tarts, wafers and other sweets and a plentiful supply of claret. But after the feast Master Guillaume does not feel very well and has to go to bed* (310). Soon the doctor, dressed in a long purple gown and red gloves, arrives on his mule. He examines the patient, advises that the barber be sent for to bleed him and prescribes, in addition, a medicine made out of powdered stag's horn.

While Guillaume is resting Dame Pernelle looks after the children. Etienne, the baby, is asleep, tightly swaddled up to his neck in bandages which leave only his head in its little bonnet uncovered* (311). He is no trouble, for a wet nurse has been employed to look after him. Of the remaining seven—four more are already dead—the eldest girl is destined for the convent, where she is already learning to read and write. Two of the boys are at school learning Latin, but Martin, Pierre, Nicole and Jeanne are still clinging round their mother's skirts. The girls are playing quietly enough with the earthenware dishes, making dinner for their painted wooden doll, but the boys are in the shop playing at tournaments like the one they saw only a week ago, and Dame Pernelle is afraid they will wake their father, for the house at the sign of the Unicorn is not very large. Downstairs is the shop, with the kitchen behind it with its huge pot hanging from a hook over the fire; the main room, where the whole family sleeps in one bed, occupies the first floor, while above it is the loft and the attics where the servants and apprentices live.

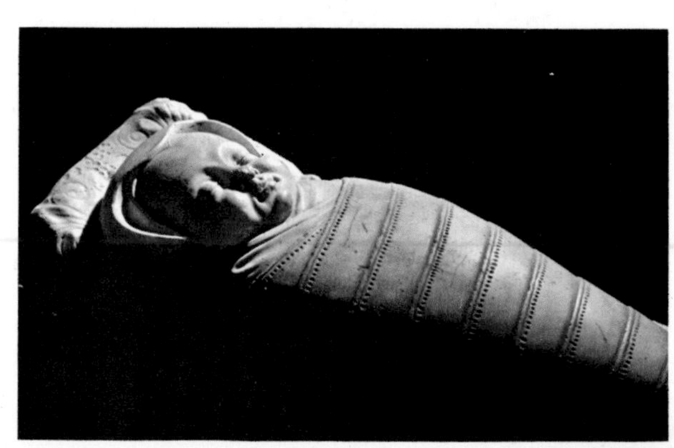

311

# The impecunious English scholar looks mainly to the Church for his career.

England in the fourteenth century was already a powerful and prosperous country made rich by trading in wool with foreign lands; but to find out how a student, or as he would have been called then, a scholar, lived let us look at the life of John Wyndham. His father, Geoffrey Wyndham, is a plain yeoman farmer, that is a farmer who owns his own land, who has scrimped and saved to send his son to Oxford. John has already learnt French, which is still the language spoken by the upper classes, and Latin at school. In 1345 at the age of sixteen he is enrolled in the faculty of arts and begins his initiation into the seven liberal arts: grammar, rhetoric, logic, arithmetic, geometry, music and astronony. It sounds a full programme, but there are plenty of things to occupy his free time. The students have picturesque battles on stilts* (312), on which John rapidly becomes an expert, and every day there is archery* (313) practice with his friends, for this was a very popular sport in the England of the time. The library* (314) is one of the finest in Europe, but John Wyndham uses it very little, for the precious manuscripts are reserved for the use of dons and he must either borrow the books he needs page by page from the bookseller, or take notes, sitting on the ground, from the master giving his lectures. These lectures are often delivered out of doors* (315). Every morning John goes to mass in his college chapel, where he plays the organ while a younger student works the bellows* (316). He has little money left over after paying his college dues, and he lives with several friends in a cheap lodging house, sharing a room and a bed with them. He forms one of a rowdy and undisciplined band of students who are a terror and scandal in the town. On leaving the university, with his degree, John will become a clerk, perhaps even a priest, and hope to find a church benefice for his livelihood.

312

315

314

313

316

317

# Through the green English countryside to Canterbur

318

In the Easter vacation of the year 1346, John Wyndham decides to go on a pilgrimage to Canterbury. He journeys to London and joins up with other pilgrims at the Tabard Inn in Southwark. Among them was Geoffrey Chaucer, and he gives us a lifelike picture of the scholar:

> As leene was his hors as is a rake,
> And he nas nat right fat, I undertake
> But loked holwe, and therto sobrely.
> Ful thredbare was his overeste courtepy;
> For he had getten hym yet no benefice,
> Ne was so worldly for to have office.

This is a sharp contrast with other much more worldly and successful churchmen Chaucer describes, such as the monk:

> . . . a fair for the maistrie,
> An outridere that loved venerie,
> A manly man, to been an abbot able.
> Ful many a deyntee hors had he in stable.

or the Prioress, Madame Eglentyne:

> Ful semely hir wympul pinched was,
> Hir nose tretys, hir eyen grey as glas,
> Hir mouth ful smal, and therto soft and reed . . .
> Ful fetys was hir cloke as I was war
> Of smal coral about hir arm she bar
> A peir of bedes . . .* (317)

Leaving the town through a gate in the walls, above which can be glimpsed the spires of churches and chapels*—some still standing today*—the pilgrims trot on horseback through the green English countryside, stopping at midday at an inn. We can see them all* sitting round a well-laden table. If we try, we are able to make out the Knight, in his long fustian robe and round hat, with his son, the Squire, the Prioress with another nun, her Chaplain, the Franklin, a rich red-faced farmer, the stout monks, the Merchant with his forked beard and the Wife of Bath, 'a worthy woman all her life':

318 319 320

> Of cloth making had she swich an haunt
> She passed hem of Ypres and of Gaunt . . .
> Hosbondes at chirche dore she hadde fyve
> Withouten other compaignye in youth.

Next is the Doctor of Physic, learned in astrology, dressed in a red and blue gown lined with taffeta and sendal (a very soft silk), the Sergeant of Lawe and many others representing all levels of English society in the fourteenth century. The Prioress is an example to them all, for:

> At mete wel y-taught was she withalle
> She leet no morsel from hir lippes falle
> Ne wette hir fyngres in hir sauce depe . . .
> Ful semely after hir mete she raughte.

After the meal they sit talking, and the Wife of Bath's mind runs on foreign travel, which was becoming almost a commonplace to English ladies. Disembarking in France, while porters

320

haucer's pilgrims make their way, passing time by telling tales of daily life.

319

321 carried her heavy travelling trunks*, she had found herself among elegant Frenchmen dressed according to the latest fashion in tight-fitting hose and padded doublets and shoes, made of pony-skin, with points so long that they had to be supported by slender chains fastened below the knee. The Merchant listens but wants only to be back home, snug and warm in his big bed with its silk curtains, wearing his gown and nightcap, with his wife preparing a posset of herbs in a cauldron over the fire, her book of recipes open on her knee*. As for the Doctor of Physic, he can talk 322 of nothing but the cure of beryl he gave a young woman which not only healed her of an eye disease but actually helped her to make an excellent marriage*. 323

321

322

323

# In Italy the merchants come into their own. The clothworkers of Prat

324

325

326

327

Two years after this Canterbury pilgrimage the whole of Europe was ravaged by a terrible epidemic, the worst ever known, called the Black Death. One of the countries to suffer most was Italy, yet barely two years later prosperity had returned.

Compared with the nearby city of Florence, Prato, in 1392, was only a little town with about twelve thousand inhabitants, but it was busy and made a very prosperous living from the cloth 324 industry. Within its protecting walls*, guarded by two castles, were fine public buildings like the palace of Pretorio, meeting-place of the council of Priors, who administered the town, and streets crowded with citizens and peasants who had come in from the surrounding countryside either 325 to sell their produce* or to bring corn to the owners of the farms, who lived in the town. The

## ule the town council—in their hands are money, power and prestige.

dress worn in Sardinia to this day is almost 326 identical with that of the peasants of the time*.

Within the city limits, beside the sumptuous public buildings and new white churches, was a mass of mean streets, as often as not running sewers, and hovels built of wood or brick. Shops opened directly onto the squares: the barber shaved his customers in full view of everyone, and the baker took his loaves out of the oven among a crowd of maids waiting to collect their bread. The butcher chopped up his meat as his wife sold it, and the assistant knelt beside the stall slaughtering a 327 sheep*. Houses belonging to the most prominent citizens were still very simple in appearance, with outside staircases, but it was becoming the fashion to add a decorative loggia with ornamental frescoes and sculptured cornices. The most

328

important people in the town were the consuls of the guilds, to which nearly all adult citizens belonged. There were fifteen guilds at Prato: those of the goldsmiths and money-changers, the doctors and apothecaries, the notaries, the cooks, the smiths, the cobblers, the butchers, the grocers, the wine merchants, the tailors, the bakers, the millers, the barbers, the carpenters, and the most powerful of all, the clothworkers guild, called *l'Arte della Lana*. It was their vote which carried 328 most weight at all municipal elections*, and their influence was especially widespread because the local administration sanctioned loans to citizens temporarily in need of money. Perhaps one of these 329 three dignitaries* dressed in their full gowns (called *gonelle*) and large hats may be Francesco di Marco, a shrewd businessman who at the age of fifteen was orphaned by the Great Plague and set off for Avignon, then the seat of the Pope, and made his fortune. On his return to Prato, he became its foremost citizen and built himself a splendid house, which is still standing although it was completed in 1392. His account books and correspondence allow us a glimpse into his home life.

From time to time he would talk to his family about the splendours of the papal court at Avignon and the magnificent banquets which took place in the houses of great lords there, to which he was sometimes invited*. 330 Even the ladies in their high, horned head-dresses and the barons in their surcoats and furred gowns were amazed when a girl, preceded by the carver, carried in the roast peacock in all its gorgeous plumage while cup-bearers refilled the guests' goblets with wine.

329

320.512M Nevada's legal whore's safe.
VOTE LIBERTARIAN.

331

332

Messer Francesco di Marco often spends long periods away in Florence on business. While he is gone, his wife, Donna Margherita, supervises the servants, who include slaves from Africa and Tartary. Like all good housewives she does her own share of the work, allowing no one but herself to decant the precious malvoisie wine from Cyprus. Indoors, Margherita wears a purple velvet gown, lined with green cloth, with her hair plaited round her head*, but when she goes out she puts on a *mantella* and covers her head with a hood to match her dress. On top of this she wears a beaver hat in winter and a straw one in summer. Margherita is very proud of her house, which is the most comfortable and best appointed in Prato, and of her salting tubs full of meat, her faience dishes—faience ware was something new; its name is the French for the Italian town of Faenza—and her silver, which includes a dozen forks, something still so rare that even the Pope himself possesses only a few. She also has hangings and curtains made of painted cloth, triptychs set in gold and a store of linen, which includes openwork napkins, embroidered table-cloths, bath-towels and the plain towels decorated with a little red embroidery which her maids, Domenica and Nana, bring her to wash herself*. But all this does not keep Margherita busy at home all the time, and she often takes the faithful Domenica and goes as far as Messer Lapo's shop to see if he has any fashionable novelties in stock, such as belts with big silver-gilt buckles, painted ivory combs, embroidered silk handkerchiefs or coral rosaries, or perhaps has herself measured for a new surcoat*. On Lapo's table, next to the ell, are the new scissors which have not long replaced the old tongs. Another of the lady's great pleasures is visiting the apothecary in whose shop many strange things can be found from far-away countries. There are all the spices of the East; ginger from Alexandria, cinnamon from China, cloves from the East Indies, pepper, nutmegs and perfumes, ready-made sauces, electuaries to be taken as cordials or for clysters, parchment for writing, candles—a fourteenth-century apothecary's shop had much in common with the American drugstore of the twentieth. Behind the shop the apothecary and his assistants distil mysterious liquors in glass alembics, the stove bubbles and an alligator—stuffed—hanging from the ceiling, is lit up with strange terrifying lights. Margherita has good reason to believe she is peeping into hell with all its devils.

(Margin references: 331, 332, 333)

333

## Fine linen in the home, and in the shops, silk and spices from the East.

# China awes the West with a civilisation that is already old.

334

Trade with the East had long been in silk and spices. Ever since Marco Polo's travels to Pekin, Italy had led the world in exploiting the commercial possibilities. Her merchants were the adventurers and intrepid explorers who played the main part in opening up the new trade routes. Other travellers returned from China with such fabulous tales of the unimaginable wonders they had beheld there that in the end people ceased to believe them, although we know now that they spoke the truth. Since those times the Chinese have changed very little, and this ancient sculpture, with its expression curiously similar to that of the smiling angel in Rheims, tells us more than the conventional nineteenth-century portraits about the timeless Chinese character*. The landscape has changed as little as the people. In the south, paddy fields lie between low hills, and peasants in wide straw hats plant the rice shoots by hand*. But China in the thirteenth and fourteenth centuries was a country much richer and more advanced than Europe. In her arts and sciences as well as in her daily life she was ahead of her time. 334 335

Things were already common in China that were not in use in the West until several centuries later, such as paper, printing, bank-notes, compasses and powder. Hang-Tcheou, the old capital, was then the most modern city in the world. Let us make the acquaintance of one of its citizens, Fong-Tch'ang, a mandarin of the sixth degree and a high official in the ministry of rites whom we can see here in his official dress*. 336

335

336

# China has Time. The mandarin writes verse; his wife creates her elabor

Fong Tch'ang's life, like that of every official, is ordered round the routine of his duties. He goes to his office very early in the morning while the monastery bells are ringing and monks are going round the streets calling out the hour. On his way Fong-Tch'ang happens to pass four dainty ladies, their hair dressed high on their heads with large combs, climbing into a carriage*. These are cabaret singers just going home from work. At five o'clock, drums call the people to work—and no one is late, for the penalty for unpunctuality is the bastinado. But to compensate for this strictness there are many advantages: one day's holiday in every ten as well as fifty-four days' regular holiday, and not to mention long periods of official leave. Moreover, custom decreed three years' leave on the death of either father or mother. Fong-Tch'ang has plenty of time to devote to his favourite pastimes of poetry and painting.

His wife, Tao-t'ien, leads a peaceful, leisurely existence, hardly ever going out. At a time when children were frequently abandoned—either drowned at birth or left in the streets—Tao-t'ien pays close attention to the education of hers. Perhaps the fact that the children of the concubine Wou-Kang, whom her husband brought back from his official residence in Ou-tcheou, also live in the house has something to do with it. Up to the age of seven, when they start school, children are allowed almost unlimited freedom to chase butterflies* and play with the magnificent golden carp in the lily pool.

It is bath time and the big tub of hot water is ready*. Any moment their nurse will arrive to rub them with liquid soap and shave their heads so that only a few small tufts of hair are

338

337

339

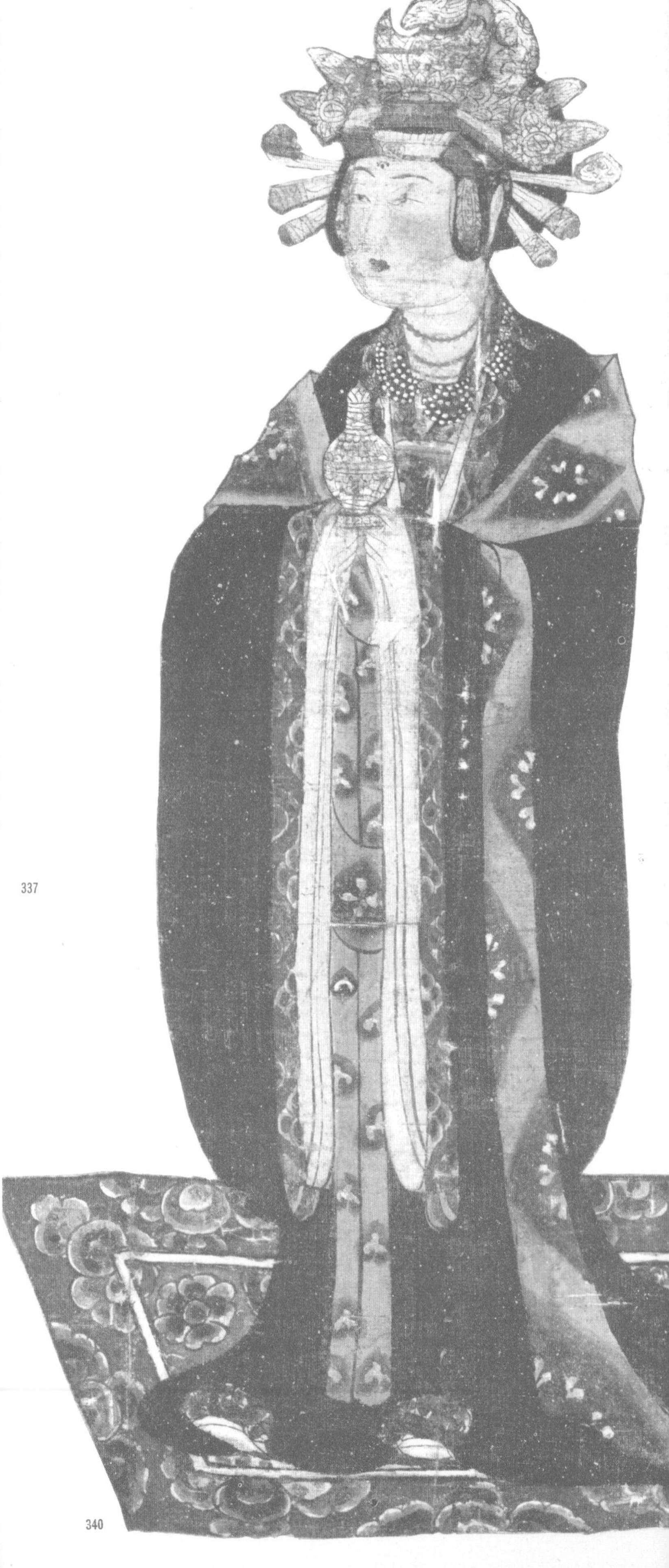

340

*iffure*; and endless patience becomes a Chinese virtue.

344

343

345

allowed to grow. The children's mother has also washed herself thoroughly, for the Chinese are accustomed to wash themselves every day—a custom their Western visitors might have done well to imitate—and never sit down to a meal without first having bathed. Tao-t'ien then plucks her eyebrows and draws a pencil line over them, and makes up her face with a white foundation covered by a coat of powder and rouge on her cheeks. Next she puts on her robe of dark-red brocade worked with fine gold thread which has a train and huge sleeves hanging almost to the ground, and folds a light painted silk stole carefully round her shoulders. But most of the time spent dressing is devoted to her hair. This is plaited and wound in a chignon on the nape of the neck, and in it are stuck anything up to thirty large gold and silver pins, carved like dragons and lotus flowers, to form a crown*. Dressed in these formal clothes she places an offering of incense on the altar of the ancestors, each of whom is represented by a lacquered wooden plaque inscribed with his name. After this she receives the humble salutations which are the privilege of a lady of her position*.

340

341 342

Fong-Tch'ang's house is fairly modest in appearance*, but it is set in the centre of a beautiful garden containing a broad lake, covered with lotus flowers and spanned by a marble bridge*. There is also a bamboo plantation and a rock garden, for which the stones were brought at great cost from the distant mountains, planted with dwarf trees and rare flowers. Beside a spring at the end of the garden is a pretty wistaria-covered pavilion*, where Fong-Tch'ang and his scholarly friends meet to raise their brimming cups of wine to the full moon and read each other the verses they have composed.

343 344 345

341

342

# Buildings grow upwards to save space—and to grace ornamental gardens.

346

The town lay between the River Tche-Kiang and the western lake and had little room for expansion. Western visitors mention that the cramped situation made it necessary to build houses several storeys high in order to accommodate the population*. 346 Some of these houses had as many as five floors or even more. But on the hill of the Ten Thousand Pines, the residential district where high officials lived, there were spreading parks and gardens scattered with small kiosks and intricate pagodas*. 347 In the town centre were ten principal markets, open regularly on three days a week, with an abundance of meat, game, poultry, fruit and vegetables, spices, aromatic wine made from rice, and flowers, as well as pearls, jewels and books. Not far from the imperial highway lay the quarter of the cabarets and tea-houses. Their walls were decorated with the work of famous painters and calligraphers; and vases of flowers and miniature trees in pots completed the décor. Rich merchants and officials came here to be served with *pâté*, made from silkworm cocoons, on lacquered plates, minute cups of jasmine tea and fruit liqueurs. Some of them took lessons in the *khin**, 348 a musical instrument closely related to the Japanese *koto*. But these sensitive pastimes were too delicate to encourage more athletic sports, and even polo*, 349 which came originally from Iran and had been very popular in China several centuries earlier, had few adepts.

348

347

349

# In Europe, Flanders basks in a new prosperity derived from trade and industry.

Returning to fifteenth-century Europe, it seems as though a great change has taken place. The period brought a startling increase in wealth and comfort, and one has only to look at almost any Flemish town to realise this. The high, gabled houses are very attractive with their wooden beams, carved with gargoyles, flowers and animals, and their mullioned windows in which small glass panes replaced the earlier oiled parchment. Everything is neat, clean and pleasant*. (350) Domestic architecture during this period reached a perfection that in Bruges, and many other Belgian towns, remains unchanged to this day*. (351)

The time is 1452 and the place Flanders, one of the group of states that go to make up the Duchy of Burgundy, which runs like a broad stripe across the map of western Europe from Franche-Comté to the Dutch coast, taking in, besides a large slice of northern France, the whole of Belgium, Luxembourg and most of Holland. These countries, with their wide variety of races and languages, were all united under one ruler who was sometimes at war with his cousin the King of France and sometimes his ally. The good Duke Philip lived in the castle of Hesdin in what is now the Pas-de-Calais, with his son, the future Charles the Bold, and he had gathered round him a court whose strict etiquette and fabulous splendour made it the wonder of all Europe. There were many excuses for general holidays: festivals such as feast days of saints or days of ceremonial royal processions, when fountains ran with beer and wine, and pretty girls dressed up as nymphs. The Duke's natural dignity was enhanced on these occasions by the scarlet mantle of his newly created Order of the Golden Fleece.

This ostentation was no more than a reflection of a prosperity which was general throughout the country and was mainly due to the increasing spread of industry and to the great ports of Bruges and Antwerp. Bruges was the great centre of commerce; cloth was manufactured at Ghent and linen at Ypres. All these towns had from sixty to eighty thousand inhabitants and boasted impressive public buildings, town halls crowned with tall belfries* (352) from which the bells pealed out several times a day and opulent churches containing many pictures painted with oils, a new technique which was to revolutionise the art of painting.

350

352

351

It is a fine morning and a group of merchants are busy gossiping in the town square surrounded by its gabled houses—in one of which a woman can be seen taking clean sheets out of a deep coffer*. Older men in Flanders still cling to the long furred gown and hood, but the young gallants follow the new fashions for long hose and a close-fitting, padded doublet, and over it a jacket with the upper part of the sleeves padded out into a sort of balloon of cloth which is slashed to reveal the doublet beneath. The subject of their conversation is most probably business, more precisely the business of the guilds to which they belong: Saint Joseph for the carpenters, Saint Crispin for the shoemakers, Saint Anne for the glovemakers. Each guild has its own special feast day, and there is great rivalry between them for the most ingenious display to delight the crowds. One of the duties of the master craftsmen is to administer the common

353

disperse to their shops and workshops. They have to force their way through streets packed with carts, women carrying home buckets of water and artisans who have set up their stalls outside their doors. Here is the carpenter with his lathe*, 354 the sculptor, busy carving a wooden figure of Christ, the tailor cutting out a doublet*, and the 355 butcher slaughtering a pig*. 356

There is someone to say good morning to every few paces, for everyone knows everyone else, and mendicant friars and whining beggars exposing their sores to be avoided. Perhaps these are some of the notorious *coquillards* who terrorise the citizens at night. The people stand aside as a leper approaches shaking his rattle and pause for a moment to watch a tumbler, while a file of prisoners goes by gagged and chained, with heavy iron balls dragging from their ankles.

Our group of friends has reached the merchant

353

356

354

355

fund into which are put the contributions of the members of the guild and which forms a kind of welfare chest.

The decision before the guild at this moment involves a large sum of money. They are debating whether to build a chapel, and whether to send meat and wine to the poor at the hospital and to prisoners in the ducal dungeons every week, or to put on a mystery play similar to the one of Saints Crispin and Crispian which the shoemakers of Paris acted so successfully a year ago. But the belfry tolls the hour, and it is time for them to

arcade, where all the luxury trades are to be found, and each goes to his counter. Gilles Perrotin takes the three pieces of silver which a customer extracts from his purse* to pay for a pair of shoes with 357 long, pointed toes. The length of a man's shoes indicated his social position; a common man's could be only half as long as a burgher's, while a nobleman's might be twice as long again. A strict and unfailingly observed order also prevailed in the choice of cloth, colours, furs and head-dresses; clothes were always an index of rank. Equally rigid distinctions applied to hangings, counter-

The shops are full and the guilds grow rich. Painters, with th

358 357 359

panes and bed curtains: only queens and princesses had the right to a green bedroom. Moreover, each colour had its own special meaning to show joy or sadness, friendship, love or indifference, and it was thought improper to wear a colour at odds with one's state of mind.

The next shop belongs to Christophe van Eycker. His wife is standing next to him and has just handed him some buttons, from a cupboard, and a mirror, backed with quicksilver, whose ivory cover is engraved with an old-fashioned tournament*. Denis Pastel displays ewers, chalices and goblets on his counter, and the pride of his stock is a silver knife with the music of the 'benedicite' engraved on the blade*. Our three friends have agreed, without telling their wives, to pay a visit to the stews that evening, where a licentious atmosphere still prevails in spite of all the rigour of the law*; but there is always the possibility that their plans may be forestalled by a fire in the neighbourhood, in which case they, like everyone else, will spend part of the night helping to form a chain to pass the buckets*.

360

361

ew medium, oils, mirror a life that is easy and comfortable.

# Rings are exchanged, the dowry paid; the bride wears red.

362

363

Today is a holiday in Ghent, for the very high and mighty lord Charles de la Tour is marrying his son, Hugues, to the daughter of Count Vernon. The marriage has been arranged for a long time, and a few weeks ago the betrothal took place. Hugues took a ring from his own finger and put it on that of his betrothed, saying, 'With this gold ring I bind you to love me and be true to me for ever.' Then Berthe gave him her ring in return. After this they went to the church and the pair plighted their troth before the priest, who then said to them: 'I betroth you in the name of the Father and of the Son and of the Holy Ghost, Amen.' The day before the wedding the father-in-law handed over the dowry in front of witnesses*, and on the wedding morning the bishop comes to pronounce his blessing over the young couple in the great hall of the de la Tour house*, where the floor has been strewn with flowers for the occasion. Hugues wears a surcoat of poppy-coloured velvet, lined with marten fur, and a crown of roses; and Berthe a long gown of red brocade—since fashion decrees red for weddings—edged with a broad band of ermine and a cloak to match. The hair on her forehead has been shaved to make it look higher under the tall red hennin covered with muslin, from the point of which floats a filmy veil. After the ceremony Hugues takes off his cumbersome surcoat, and he and Berthe open the ball by dancing a Burgundian *branle* to a fanfare of trumpets*. After the feast which follows, the young couple are escorted to the bridal bed, which has been blessed by the priest.

A few weeks later the noble lady Berthe is sitting with her back to the fire in a richly decorated chair reading her illuminated book of hours*. Every now and then she lays the book down on her lap and her gaze wanders round the room from the carved sideboard, with its gold ewer and basin, to the window, open to let in the spring breeze.

364

365 →

366

Hugues is bitten by one of the hounds in his pack. At once Berthe writes down the magic charm on a crust of bread: *Bestera + bestia + brigonay + dictera + sagragan + es + domina + fiat + fiat + fiat*. Hugues laughs at her, but he is in a high fever. He sits by the fire, a goblet and a flask of hypocras (white wine sweetened with cinnamon and spices) at his elbow*. Gravely the doctor* 367 368

367 368

inspects the sick man's urine, brought to him by a valet, and, without troubling to examine the patient himself, declares it fetid and purulent. Meanwhile Messire de la Tour is growing worse; he becomes so weak that, feeling his last hour upon him, he makes his will, leaving large sums to the neighbouring monastery for masses to be sung for his soul. Then he summons all his family together, relations, friends and servants, and asks their pardon for any wrong he may have done them. A candle is put into his hand and he receives the Last Sacraments and piously recites the Creed*. 369

Courtly love might be a fine thing in principle, but it rarely survives marriage. It is no more than a fairy story. When Berthe married Hugues she had no means of knowing his violent temper. He has only to lose at chess and he throws the board at 366 his partner's head*, and from there it is a short step to daggers drawn. He neglects her shamefully. Either he is out hunting all day or, if the weather is not fit, he shuts himself up in the room he has furnished for himself in the tower and sits there, well wrapped up in his warm, furred gown, with his lectern before him reading the exploits of the great conquerors of antiquity translated by Latin authors. Slowly Berthe forgets her young girl's dreams; the knight with the green banner, for whose coming she waited so many years, never existed outside the story-books. Now she spends her time supervising bakers and cup-bearers, carvers, water-carriers and cellarers. The years pass and she bears eight children, three of whom die, and the others must be brought up. One day while he is out hunting

369

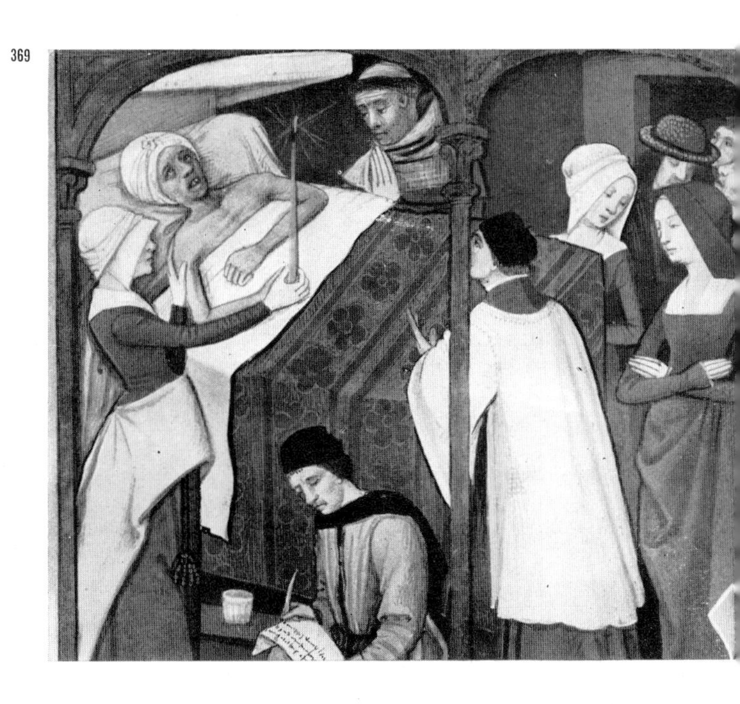

## But all too soon the honeymoon is ended. Neglect sets in.

# In the south a new zest for living quickens and glows in the sun.

370

371

Bruges, Ghent or Ypres in 1452 still had something of a mediaeval atmosphere, luxurious and even slightly morbid and very different from the rough simplicity and burning faith of feudal times, but still mediaeval. It was the last flourish of a dying way of life and thought. But only one generation later, in Florence in 1497, a new feeling could be sensed in the air. Twenty-seven years have passed and the people are no longer stiff and formal but full of natural grace. It is partly to do with the sun, but there is also a real change of spirit. Man's attitude to the world has altered. Life is no longer a vale of tears to be withstood only as a preparation for eternal bliss; it is to be lived to the full here and now.

Even in a plain country farmhouse, the tiled floor is scrubbed clean, the animals are relegated to the stables, there are chairs just as there are in town houses, and the sheets on the big bed where all the family sleeps, head to feet, are freshly laundered and scented with lavender*. The peasant women wear thick dresses made of cloth woven from goat's hair, called camelot, which was known in England as shoddy. Here in Tuscany there is no such gulf between the city burgess and the country peasant as there is between lord and villein north of the Alps.

370

In towns the beds are softer and tucked away in curtained alcoves; there are hangings and oriental rugs and huge linen chests, called *cassoni*, decorated with mythological scenes painted by artists*. But everywhere life has the same frugality, and this rich townsman, dressed in his full black *lucco* lined with fine mauve silk, sitting down to table and saying his grace*, will dine simply enough off a round loaf, a pigeon, a few vegetables, sweets and fruit. Meal-times are about nine o'clock in the morning and in the evening, and butcher's meat is usually only served on special occasions. But there are plenty of delicate faience dishes and pieces of fragile glassware on the table, and plates and goblets are no longer shared, unless with one's wife. It would be considered bad manners to dip one's fingers in the sauce, and every well-equipped household possesses forks, many of which have exquisitely wrought handles. These forks were not used as we use them today but planted upright in the meat to be cut up; as a rule they had only two prongs, those with three or more being still very rare*.

371 372 373

372

373

This was now a period of unprecedented splendour, the finest in the whole history of Florence, under Lorenzo de' Medici, whose rule continued until 1492. It was a time of good living, and although there were still epidemics and the threat of war the people were able to write proudly beneath Ghirlandaio's fresco in the church of Santa Maria Novella: 'Florence, renowned for her beauty, her victories, her arts and crafts and her buildings, now rests in health, peace and plenty.' The buildings of Lorenzo's Florence can still be seen, almost intact, in our own time, and it increases our delight in her pictures to be able to see the life of the city going on in surroundings which we can immediately recognise. This procession of gay young people is passing the Baptistry. They walk under a richly coloured canopy escorted by a fanfare of trumpets. The girls wear dresses and cloaks of crimson, scarlet and green brocade, sewn with embroidered trellis patterns of gold thread and silver buttons. Their tall head-dresses are still mediaeval in style, but one girl is wearing a huge, smart hat made of peacock feathers, and pearl necklaces; scented gloves and gold trinkets add the finishing touch to their immaculate elegance. The materials used for the young men's clothes are every bit as rich and bright; their capes and tabards are pink and blue, edged with velvet and lined with silk. They wear parti-coloured hose, and hats of purple and mauve cloth cover their long, bleached curls. Everything indicates a dandyism never since attained by masculine dress. The wedding they are celebrating is that of Boccaccio Andinari*. 374

In a moment the bride will stop in front of the garland of flowers placed at her feet by the young people of the city. The prettiest of them will make her a little speech of good wishes. Weddings like this became so extravagant and ostentatious that they soon provoked protests from the more conservative citizens, and the anxious authorities passed law after law forbidding the wearing of expensive clothes and limiting the number of guests and the number of courses that might be served at wedding breakfasts. The cook had to present the menu for the banquet to the municipal authorities, and this was limited to three courses and twenty-five places. But it was almost impossible to enforce these restrictions, and the rich continued to spend thousands of ducats on a single banquet. Prophets thundered against extravagance and blamed the women particularly: 'O women! You provoke the wrath of God by your extravagance, by the exorbitant length of your trains, by the immodest display of your bosoms and the paint with which you cover your faces. A fine thing it is to see young girls dressing themselves up in frills and furbelows, fabricating themselves outlandish head-dresses and flaunting sleeves that bear more resemblance to dangling sacks. Not one of them can take up a cup at table without trailing her

374

Florence, city of youth, fashion and extravagant gaiety, hears

sleeves in the food and soiling them or the cloth.' Prominent among those who fulminated against all luxury was the Friar Girolamo Savonarola, a young Dominican from the monastery of San Marco, whose recriminations were especially vehement and eloquent, and who was responsible for burning many precious treasures before he himself finished at the stake. Florence certainly had no lack of occasion for displaying the pomp and show that expressed the joy of living. There were balls, jousting in the Piazza Santa Croce* (375) and pageants, including among their attractions floats representing mythological subjects designed and painted by some of the greatest artists the world has ever known. As they passed, the crowd took up the nostalgic carnival song: 'How lovely is youth, and how quickly it flies. Rejoice he who may, for tomorrow he dies.'

375

376

Venice had known wealth for longer than Florence, and from contact with the East had acquired the taste for the rarest and most exotic pleasures. The Grand Canal was lined with palaces with delicately fretted balconies, and even comparatively small houses were decorated with carved lintels and had roof gardens which carpets and hangings transformed into outdoor salons* (376). There were countless processions where, behind the priests, came a throng of members of the Signoria and the Council in their long robes, while lovely Venetian ladies watched the ceremony from their windows, which were hung with fine silks for the occasion* (377).

377

Savonarola fulminating against pomp and luxury, and burns him.

# Enjoyment and wealth may have their advantages: escape from the plague.

378

In the summer the Florentines and Venetians were in the habit of making excursions into the country round the cities. Any citizen of means owned a farm, and from this developed the fashion for villas surrounded by gardens attractively laid out with cypresses and shrubberies. Often the men rode out into the country with their spears and a pack of hounds to hunt any game they met on the way*. Once at the villa there was plenty of company and diversion, for some of the guests were excellent and lively storytellers and many played the lyre, the lute or the flute well enough to improvise a concert in the open air*. Card games were also popular, and the packs were often painted by extremely skilful miniaturists.

But there was another side to this picture of a free and liberal society. There were often cases of sacrilege, sacred vessels stolen from churches or a chamber pot emptied over a statue of the Virgin, and for these crimes punishment was swift and merciless. The offender, if he were caught, would be hanged at once from the nearest bell-tower. Superficially the Italians of the times might have been sceptical and materialistic, but underneath they were still extremely superstitious; the most unlikely portents and miracles were accepted without question, and there were numerous astrologers and magicians who exploited this very profitably. Natural hazards were still a continual threat. Bad harvests meant famine. The price of bread rose to astronomical heights and free distributions soon became free fights in which many citizens were trampled by the crowds. Earthquakes, frosts and freak hailstorms brought more catastrophe, but the Florentines' greatest fear was the *moria*, the grim plague which stalked the land and ravaged the towns mercilessly before precautions could be taken. The Florentines would leave the plague-stricken town and flee to the country taking the infection with them, and in the city all shops were closed, so that it became almost impossible to obtain food. Those citizens who stayed at home roamed through the streets holding flowers, medicinal herbs and sponges soaked in medicines to their noses. All law was in abeyance; thieves broke into the deserted houses and murder was rife.

Modern Venice still has its pink palaces, its canals of greenish water and black gondolas, and even the strange picturesque chimneys can still be found in some parts of the city; but to see it in all its glory we have to conjure up a picture of gondoliers in parti-coloured hose and plumed bonnets, noble lords in severe yet sumptuous robes, lovely ladies clad in silks and pearls and a procession of white-robed priests moving slowly across the centre of a covered bridge, part of which can be raised to allow tall ships to pass*.

379

Yet in spite of all this, Italian travellers in Germany in the late fifteenth and early sixteenth centuries were loud in their praise, and the comparisons they made were rarely to their own advantage: 'In no country are the towns more delightful than in Germany. They have a pleasant, smiling appearance and an air of having been newly built, and there is a freedom there which is to be found nowhere else.' At Nuremberg 'the burghers' homes are princely'.

The town was the scene of frenzied activity. Its industries included wood- and copper-engraving, map-making and the manufacture of compasses; the population rode on the crest of an unprecedented wave of luxury. Merchants grew rich through foreign trade, the mining industry was expanding rapidly and the bankers had established a monetary fund which advanced loans to the Emperor himself, for which they were granted valuable indemnities. Yet still the narrow, winding alleys were heaped with refuse; farm animals were stalled in the town centre and it was unwise to walk about the streets without heavy, wooden-soled clogs.

382

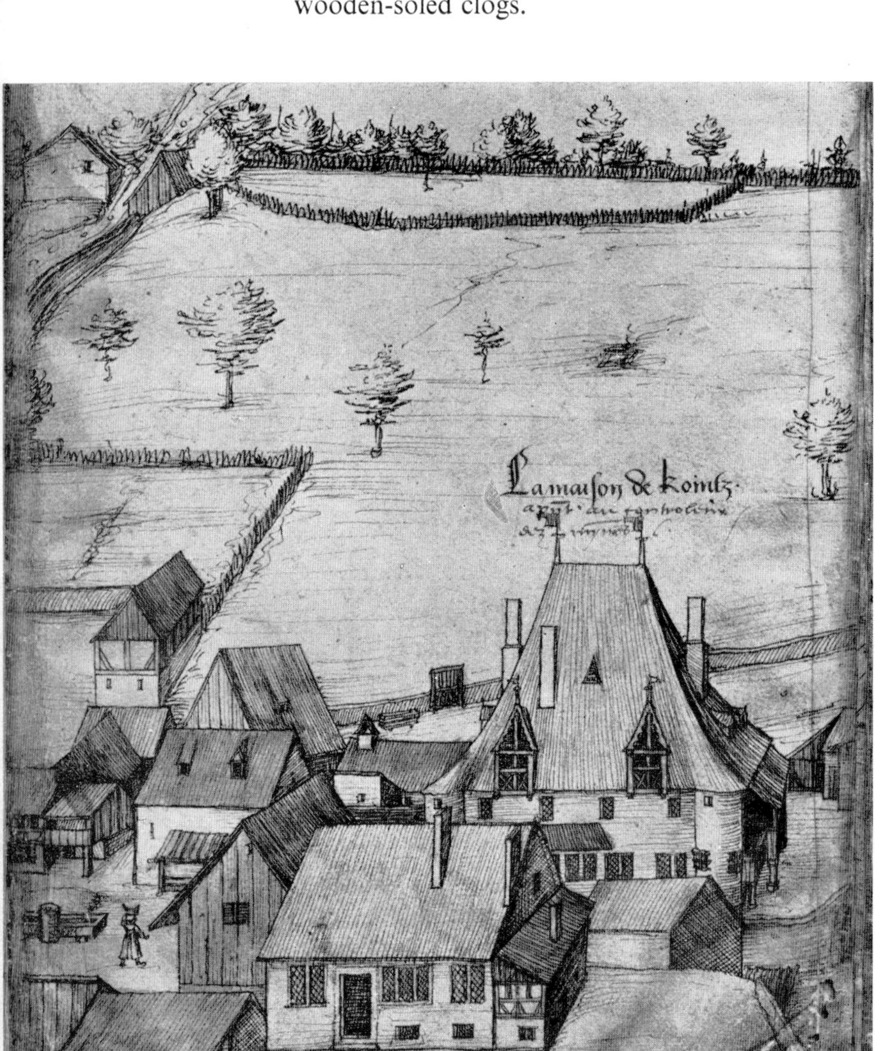
381

Nuremberg, 1502. The house we are looking at belongs to Julius Kaintz, master clockmaker and member of the town council. It is on the outskirts of the town and is surrounded by out-houses and farm buildings. The house itself has a high, mansard roof topped by weather vanes* similar to (381) those which are still found in great numbers in German provincial towns today*. The rooms are (382) well lighted by large windows with small leaded glass panes, and in one corner of the living-room, which has a shallow, vaulted ceiling and tiled floor, is a solid table, replacing the trestles common in the Middle Ages, and carved oak chairs. These chairs look very hard, but in other rooms in the

383

In Germany, the wealthy merchants live like princes.

# By 1500 printing is widespread, and the commonest book in the house is a Bible.

384

house there are leather-covered armchairs padded with horse-hair. The art of upholstery was first introduced at this period—a sign that people were becoming more preoccupied with physical comfort. The heavy, lidded beer mugs and pewter plates* were arranged on a flat sideboard—shelves 383 were the privilege of nobles, two for knights and as many as five for ruling princes—with comfit dishes of gold and silver plate containing separate compartments for fruit and different kinds of sweetmeats, and spice boxes for pepper, nutmegs and ginger.

In her room upstairs Frau Kaintz is sitting in a three-cornered chair with a rush bottom, spinning wool and talking to a visitor still in his riding apparel*. Her forehead is carefully shaved, and 384 she wears a head-dress of folded material surrounded by a kind of starched veil known as a *huve*. The room contains a massive dresser on which Frau Kaintz has placed some of her best dishes and the printed Old and New Testaments, bound in parchment. Their owner takes a great pride in these, for printing is a recent invention which brings the pleasures of reading within the reach of ordinary people like herself. Until now books had been almost entirely the prerogative of the clergy and of princes lucky enough to obtain manuscripts.

Soon the weary traveller will retire to refresh himself with a hot bath*, and Frau Kaintz will 385 seize the opportunity to pay a visit to her neighbour who has just had a baby, and of course take her a present. These are simple people, and there are no curtains round the bed or tapestries on the walls, only a few plain wooden benches in the room, but the new mother has white sheets on her bed and is covered by warm woollen blankets and her husband is busy writing the baby's name and birthday in the family Bible*. 386

385

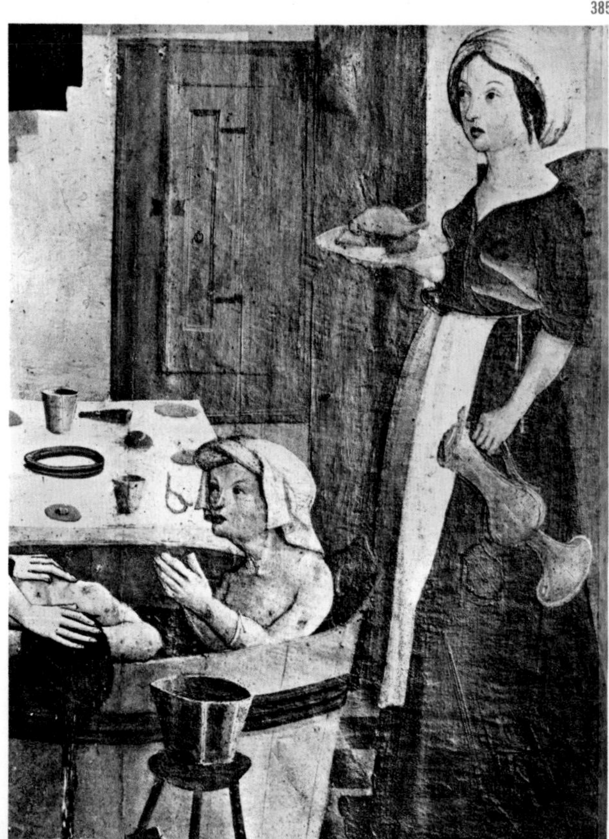

386

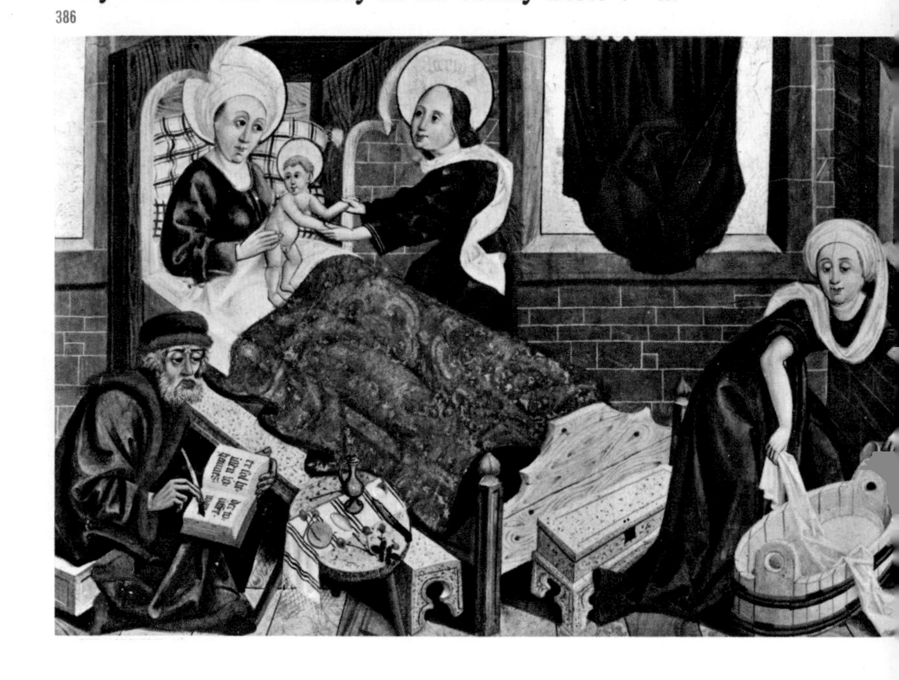

387

Nuremberg in 1502, like similar cities such as Lübeck, Strasbourg and Augsburg, was only a small town when judged by the number of inhabitants, but it was a free, self-governing city within the Holy Roman Empire and owning allegiance only to the Emperor himself. During the last few decades its appearance had settled into a mould which time would do little to change; the houses had tall, crenellated roofs, and there were broad squares with fountains, like this one at Augsburg*, with symbolical or satirical statues. But today's peaceful charm is deceptive, for in 1502 the square would have been cluttered with shops and stalls*; the houses were crooked and even the very few streets that could boast paving were heaped with mud and rubbish.

387 388

Herr Kaintz has told his wife before leaving home that he has business in the town which will prevent him coming home for dinner, so he eats

388

ıd their wives to toast one another's health and wealth in taverns.

389

390

his midday meal in a *Bierkeller*. At this period this was still an innovation, for although beer itself was almost as old as civilisation, the real, German beer, made with hops, had only just started being brewed by a brewer instead of at home.

The host has redecorated his premises to attract customers from all levels of society, and has made small private rooms in the cellar where the town burghers can meet and talk business among the barrels fitted into the walls*. But today the weather is cold, and Herr Kaintz prefers the public room where he can sit close to the big stove with its glazed tiles. The stove gives out plenty of heat, so his fur-edged mantle is open in front to reveal the top of his doublet. His beaver hat is tilted over one ear, and he appears to have done full justice to the roast sucking-pig and beer*. Now he is raising his goblet to toast the rather odd-looking business friends who seem to be wearing bonnets and skirts. Perhaps Herr Kaintz did not tell his wife the truth. Still it looks like a good party and everyone seems to be enjoying themselves. For, like many Germans of his time who have lived through wars, famine and pestilence, Herr Kaintz is making the most of the new-found peace, which brings great freedom of manners and morals in its wake. The Emperor's subjects relish good cheer and hearty fun.

Early in the afternoon Kaintz goes home, takes off his fine clothes, and gets down to work in his shop with his apprentices*, putting the finishing touches to his latest manufacture. It is not only a particularly beautiful clock but it embodies a new kind of mechanism: it works by means of a spring instead of the pendulum and weights which have been in use up till now. The hours and half hours are marked by a little hammer striking a bell perched on top of the

391

clock. Progress is being made in all directions. The craze for spectacles—probably first invented in Italy in the late thirteenth century—has swept through Europe, and everyone in the streets can be seen wearing them. The foreign market is flooded with all kinds of little wooden novelties manufactured in Nuremberg: caskets and boxes attractively painted, delicate ivories, children's toys, musical instruments. In addition, the town is full of the latest fashions in clothes. Even the men are in the habit of going to the barber to have their heads smeared with a weird mixture of sulphur, resin and white of egg which will give them the fluffed up hairstyles which have become so fashionable.

## Gay squires joust in the market place where witches are burnt.

392 393

The country too has a holiday air. The washer-women still heat their cauldrons on the river bank and scrub and hang out their linen, as they have always done*, but on Sundays they go to mass wearing fichus, scarves and aprons made of silk brocade over their heavy cloth dresses. At some village festivals in Bavaria the young girls still wear today fantastic head-dresses of flowers made with metal and pieces of coloured glass*. There is a cheerful crowd of people amusing themselves in the meadow, skirts are flying in the dance and other couples are sitting at tables eating and drinking. The prospect of customers soon attracts the pedlar*, who has his tray full of pretty things for the ladies: mirrors, silver chains, scented gloves and playing cards, and terracotta horsemen and charming wooden dolls dressed in the latest fashions for the children*. True, this free and pleasant existence has its meaner side. Even in Nuremberg the Jews are segregated and compelled to live in a ghetto, called the *judenviertel*, the Jewish quarter, which is chained off at night. It was at this time that Yiddish developed as a language among the Jews, a mixture of archaic German and Hebrew. The Jews' main occupation was usury, and this helped to increase a resentment that has never been quite forgotten. It was also a time for witch hunts, and as a result many miserable women died each year at the stake. It was a time of superstition, the chronicles are full of so-called miracles, and the shameful sale of indulgences was at last beginning to arouse opposition.

On holidays the village put on its best face, and rich and poor went to the tournament* in the lists which had been erected in the main square. The knights no longer wore complete body armour, for the only targets were the head and shoulders, since the tourney survived as a sport and was no longer a serious preparation for war, which in these days was a matter for foot-soldiers supported by artillery.

It was an occasion for displaying the gay silk caparisons in the colours of the different knights together with their splendid shields and plumed helms bearing their arms. The joust was a game, and fools in parti-coloured clothes joked and tumbled round each knight, helping him to mount and pretending to act as his squires.

394 395

396 →

397

398

In the year 1519 a young man of nineteen, who had been king of Spain for five years already, succeeded to the Holy Roman Empire. His name was Charles V and he ruled over people of many different nationalities, languages and customs. Yet even Spain was a world in herself, and there was little in common between the austere Castilian and the sensuous Andalusian. The Spaniards were a people split by fundamental differences of origin, religion and way of life. At the top of the social tree was the Grandee of Spain. Only twenty families in the whole country could claim this title, and they were filled with pride of rank. The Grandee dressed in the French or Flemish fashion, wearing a broad lace ruff even over armour*; his (397) wife carried herself with a rigid, immovable dignity that owed much to the stiff clothes she wore*. (398)

The noble lady's life was as rigid as her clothes. She rose very late and took only a glass of iced water before putting on her mantilla and going to church, accompanied by her duenna. Returning home she took a cup of chocolate before receiving her confessor, and after a light lunch retired for a siesta until two in winter or four in summer.

399

## Spain: tender and violent, austere and sensual. The grande

400

401

402

403

Then, after a cold collation, it was the time for paying calls and perhaps taking a walk by torchlight, and she only returned home in time to take a light supper in bed before going to sleep. The lives, even of the great, were models of sobriety. Their kitchens might be well equipped with brick ovens, pestle and mortar and a range of cooking pots* (399), but the meals they produced were very plain, consisting basically of a bean or lentil stew. This was the life emulated by the hidalgos, the lesser nobility; but however poor they might be, none of them would ever forget their dignity. They preferred to retire to their estates and dream, like Don Quixote, of an outmoded chivalry* (400) that would be an example to the rest of Europe.

The hidalgos were also an example to the rest of Spain, for the Spaniards as a race liked to think that idleness was man's natural state. The number of domestic servants employed reached fantastic proportions, yet it seems the number was not enough, for unemployment led to begging and vagrancy. The streets of all the large towns were thronged with cripples, whom the religious orders made some attempt to help* (401).

The fifteenth century was also the time of the Inquisition in Spain, with its crusade against heresy. The Inquisition was set up in 1482 and was assisted by a secret police organisation called the Hermandad. The *reconquista* had only been finally achieved in 1492 with the conquest of Granada, but the Moors and Jews had not been driven out. They were tolerated at first, but gradually the demand for their conversion or expulsion grew. People distrusted the sincerity of those newly converted, and the Moriscos (converted Moors) and Marranos (converted Jews) were automatically suspect. Denunciation, however flimsy the evidence, meant secret trial and torture, and after a solemn ceremony in which priests conjured them to abjure their faults, those persisting in their errors were handed over to the secular arm and led to the stake, dressed in conical hats and mock chasubles on which all the torments of hell were painted* (402). At the same time priests and monks, following in the wake of the conquistadors, were undertaking the conversion of the American Indians. With fantastic courage the explorers crossed the seas in caravels* (403) to win an American empire for Spain.

re mannered, proud, devout. The Inquisition rages.

404

When in 1519 Cortés and his men sighted the Aztec capital, Mexico-Tenochtitlan, they were overcome by the city's size and splendour. It incorporated three separate towns, covered nearly nine square miles and was criss-crossed by canals bordered with little floating gardens. The city possessed more than five hundred thousand inhabitants.

The Emperor Motacuhzoma II, an impressive figure in his sea-green cloak and triangular gold crown set with turquoises, was backed by fearsome warriors and priests. He ruled over a much more ancient people who were kept in subjection by the handful of warlike men which had conquered their civilisation. Though the Aztec empire crumbled before the conquistadors the old customs have survived to our own day, far from the modern cities, among the Indians whose dress has altered as little over the intervening centuries as their faces*. 404

We shall leave the imperial show of the capital, with its gold, jade and turquoise, exquisitely cut and mounted by expert craftsmen, which aroused the greed of the conquistadors, and follow the humble peasant of the sixteenth century in her cotton skirt and *huipilli*, a sort of loose over-blouse, her baby fastened to her back by a band of cloth*, as she walks through her village far 405 away from Mexico. She is carrying her burden back to her house, with its tall, thatched roof and walls of mud-covered bamboo*—houses in the 406 town are built of unbaked brick, for stone is only used for religious monuments. The whole family lives in one upstairs room over a lower one used as a foodstore. Women kneel before the stone *metate*, pounding maize with a pestle to make the cakes*, called *teaxcalli*, which are their 407 staple diet and were the original of the modern Mexican tortillas. Such food as venison, turkey, and cocoa mixed with honey and flavoured with vanilla is only found in wealthy homes, but the poor have the vegetables they grow themselves: beans, peppers and tomatoes. Their furniture is crude and consists mostly of mats and wicker-baskets, and for warmth they have only a wood fire or braziers. Light comes from pine torches. Next to the house is a small semicircular building which is the *temazcalli*, in which they make them-

405

406

eeds a race of warriors dreaming of immortality through death in battle.

407

408

409

selves steam-baths by heating the walls and sprinkling water on them.

The future of the child being carried on his mother's back was decided on the day he was born, when his umbilical cord was buried, together with a shield and some small arrows. He is dedicated to being a warrior*. At six years old he, like all children—for the Aztecs had a system of compulsory education—will go to the *telpochcalli*, where he will receive a purely military education. When he has fought in some battles and taken his first prisoner he will earn the right to the title of *iyac* and allow one lock of hair to grow long over his right ear. If he is lucky, he will rise in rank according to the number of dead and prisoners he can claim in battle, until he reaches the highest grade of all, that of the *jaguars* or the *eagles*. This means that even in civil life he will be able to wear certain special tokens such as leather bracelets, plumes and gold jewels in addition to the normal *maxtlatl* (loincloth) and the *tilmatli*, a cloak knotted in front or on the right shoulder, for the Aztecs had no buttons or pins, and woven in bright colours with gorgeous patterns which varied according to the rank of the wearer*.

The finest possible end for an Aztec warrior was death in battle. By dying like this he was sure of immortality, and would become one of the eagle company escorting the sun on his triumphant course, and then be reincarnated in the form of a humming bird. Warriors were buried with great ceremony on open biers* for they, like the drowned, were held sacred, and not cremated like the general run of people.

410

# Human sacrifice protects the Aztec. The Inca lives by peace and wisdom.

412

413

The innumerable warlike expeditions punctuating the life of the Aztecs had one principal objective: to take prisoners for sacrifice to the gods. Only the suffering of the entire people could counteract the agonising instability of the world, and only bloody sacrifices were capable of renewing the strength and life of the sun which continually threatened to fall to the ground and extinguish itself. There was no anger in this dreadful condition of Aztec life, only absolute cosmic necessity. Their huge pyramids* still stand in mute witness 411 to the holocausts. When a warrior was taken prisoner he not only accepted his fate but would refuse the clemency of his conquerors, even if it were offered. By his death he became a heavenly messenger to the gods and himself clothed in almost divine glory.

The victim destined for sacrifice led a life of splendid idleness, an object of veneration to the entire people; and then on the appointed day he climbed the steps of the pyramid among the priests, some arrayed in the gorgeous plumage of the quetzal, some with their bodies painted black, blowing into hollow shells*. When they reached 412 the top the priests seized the victim and threw him down on a stone slab, then, while four men held his arms and legs, the chief priest brandished an obsidian knife and plunged it into his breast*, 413 and thrusting his hand into the wound drew forth the heart and offered it to the sun. When the sacrifice was dedicated to Xipe Totec, the flayed lord, the priests flayed the corpse and dressed themselves in the skin.

This weird, secretive face*, condemned to silence 414 by the golden disc representing the sun, which seals its mouth, is the work of another civilisation. It, too, is Indian, but its home is in South America: it belongs to the world of the Incas.

411

414 →

# Europe comes, intent on Inca gold, but takes away far more precio

Today, after nearly five hundred years, roads built by the Incas in the fifteenth and sixteenth centuries still run straight and firm across the high 415 plateaus of the Andes*, from one end of their empire to the other. They were paved with a mixture of mud, maize leaves and pebbles which has withstood all weathers, and it was thanks to these lines of communication, kept in perfect repair, that Pizarro and his Spanish soldiers were able to conquer a land so rich in gold that they called it Eldorado. The empire covered an area roughly two thousand miles north to south and six hundred from east to west. Its people varied widely in origin, and some of them, even before the coming of the Incas, had had their own highly developed civilisation, as this fine mochica vase*, 416 probably dating from the time of Charlemagne, indicates. Functioning from the capital, Cuzco, an efficient and energetic administration governed the whole Inca empire and the lives of all its members, according to a carefully regulated pattern.

At the bottom of the social ladder were the peasant families who formed communal groups, known as *ayllous*, and within these it was the responsibility of the chiefs to divide up the land according to the needs of each family. No man was permitted to leave his land, he must die in the place where he was born, and he himself owned nothing save his clothes and a few personal possessions. All land was owned by the state, which divided the wealth of the country among the population. The course of a man's life followed well-defined rules which depended on his age. Until he was a year old he counted as a baby in arms, and, after that, from one to nine, he merely played, though as idleness was not encouraged he was expected to make himself useful. From nine to twelve his job was scaring birds from the maize fields, and between the ages of twelve and eighteen the young Indian tended the llamas and learned to make all the objects that were needed

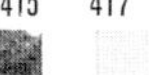
415 417

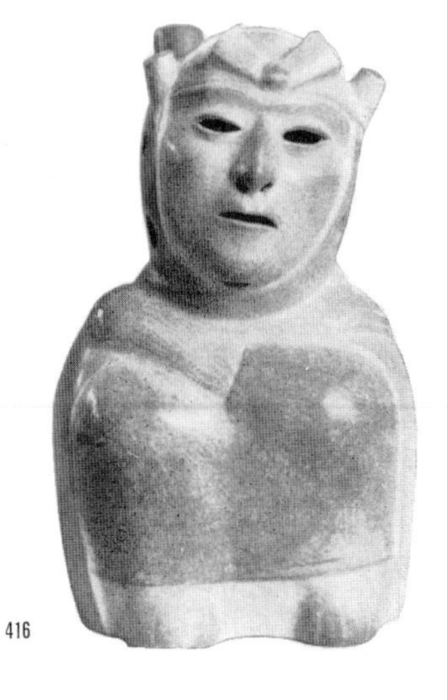
416

reasures: the potato, the bean, the tomato, quinine and cocaine.

418

420

419

in the home. When he was eighteen he was able to help his parents in their work, until he married at the age of twenty-five and settled down to make his own home. From then he paid taxes until he was sixty, after which age nothing more, save good advice to the young, was expected of him.

The thatched houses built of unbaked brick which compose the Indian villages are the same today as they have always been*. The peasants eat in front of the hut*, and their staple foods are vegetables and fruit, most of which were unfamiliar when discovered by the Spaniards. The invaders, and the whole of Europe after them, found in such things as potatoes, sweet potatoes, peppers, beans, tomatoes, guavas and avocadoes a much more lasting treasure than the gold they came to seek. Other useful plants which originated in Peru were the spiny cactuses which could be used as needles, plants whose fibrous leaves could be used to make cloth, and a variety of cane, called the *baloa*, from whose stems were made boats like those still to be found on the surface of Lake Titicaca today. The Indians discovered a useful ally in the animal world in the llama*, a creature as surefooted and reliable as a camel; it could be used to carry burdens, and its soft coat furnished excellent wool.

The peasant had not many utensils, but they were enough for his needs, consisting mostly of different-shaped pots, often representing people* or scenes from everyday life. He also possessed a wide range of drugs such as quinine, balsam and coca, which last was especially valuable when its leaves were dried, rolled into a ball, mixed with a few ashes, and then chewed. It is a remarkable stimulant, and even today the Indians use it to give them their extraordinary resistance to fatigue. It was not until the nineteenth century that Europeans learned to extract quinine and cocaine, which have proved invaluable to medicine all over the world. These Andean Indians, in their poncho blankets and berets knitted from llama wool*, are hardly different from ancestors who created the empire and survived the carnage which followed its collapse. Inca contribution to world progress has been incorporated, almost unnoticed, into the lives of all of us.

421

# The Virgin Queen rules land and sea; England enters a golden age.

In the year 1597, towards the end of the reign of Queen Elizabeth I, small English seaport towns like Plymouth and Exeter in Devon were at the peak of a period of unprecedented wealth and activity. The sailors who strolled their streets and frequented their taverns* [422] were to influence every aspect of English life. They included men like Sir Walter Raleigh, who claimed Virginia for the crown and named it in honour of the virgin queen; Sir Francis Drake, first Englishman to sail around the world; Hawkins, Frobisher and many others who set themselves to oust the Spaniards from the New World and paved the way for the great trading companies of the future. Almost overnight England became the world's most formidable and energetic sea-power, and foreign visitors were amazed at the variety of her imports from all over the world. The country was flooded with new discoveries, such as tobacco, which was first introduced into England in about 1580 by mariners returning from the New World. Initially tobacco encountered a good deal of opposition, as it was believed to cause suffocation and fill the lungs of those who smoked it with ashes. One London bishop was even rumoured to have died from smoking too much. Later, however, there was a complete reversal of opinion; tobacco was credited with all kinds of improbable virtues and the habit of smoking or snuff-taking became widespread.

423

Potatoes and bananas were also to be found in London, though these as yet were a delicacy available only to the rich. But the life of even the poorest people was changing. It was long since the town walls, relics of the wars of feudal times, had been allowed to fall into disrepair, and though the streets were still filled with filth and garbage and rarely paved, watchmen with halberds and lanterns patrolled them regularly all night to keep order. New houses were springing up in town and country. There were substantial manor houses of lath and plaster with heavy black oak beams in intricate patterns* [423], with tiled roofs and large windows whose small leaded panes—for there was still no technique for making big panes of glass—were a great improvement on the transparent pieces of horn formerly used. The great hall was often the scene of merry gatherings, when the sideboards groaned under the load of gold and silver plate and minstrels tuned their theorbos and lutes for the waiting couples to dance the pavan. It was a time of extravagant fashions in masculine dress, and men wore doublets and hose so outrageously padded and laced that they could hardly move. They wore huge pleated ruffs and ear-rings, and whole fortunes were spent on clothes. In the kitchens, scullions laboured* [424] preparing roast beef, boiled mutton, meat pasties and haunches of venison, and on the table were vast quantities of creams, pastries, marchpane and comfits, as well as exotic fruits like oranges, lemons, pineapples and pomegranates. At the end of the meal it was considered good manners to take out one of the new tooth-picks kept in a special case, and clean one's teeth. Feasts on this scale were by no means exceptional, and the English had a reputation for extravagance and ostentation. Even on ordinary days, all but the really poor ate well and plentifully, though

422

424

they had only two meals a day, at about eleven in the morning and five or six at night, and fast days were in general very strictly observed.

The Elizabethans were great devotees of outdoor games of all kinds, and small boys in the Grammar Schools spent their recreations playing football and chasing after hoops. In class they stumbled through their Latin recitations as best they could to satisfy the schoolmaster, who sat enthroned in cap and gown with the dreaded birch in his hand*. One of these scholars has left us his exercise-book, and besides his homework he has filled it with pictures of what will be his favourite sport when he grows up, like that of most other men in the kingdom: archery. Another popular diversion was play-going and the reign of Elizabeth was the golden age of English theatre. Posters fixed to the walls of buildings gave the title of the play, though not the names of the actors, and at one o'clock in the afternoon in summer people would flock to the Globe theatre, a hexagonal wooden building with galleries running round the inside and open to the sky in the centre*. The groundlings, the poorer members of the audience, stood in what is now the stalls while the well-to-do sat on wooden benches in the galleries, and those especially privileged had private boxes or sat on the stage itself. The men smoked their pipes, or played cards while they waited for the performance to begin, and nuts, apples, beer and wine, and even the latest books, were on sale in the theatre. There was no curtain to go up, but when actors dressed as soldiers came onto the stage, the audience grew quiet and the play, a new piece by Shakespeare, began.

425

426

People flock to the Globe where Shakespeare plays to standing room only.

427

The heavy iron-studded door of Richard Hathaway's house in Stratford-on-Avon opened directly onto the single living-room* with its stone-flagged floor strewn with rushes, which were not changed more than once a year, and its broad hearth which heated, though not very adequately the whole ground floor of the house. This was an innovation, and old people were sure that the younger generation caught cold more quickly because of it. The room was hung with tapestries suspended from wooden slats, some distance away from the wall because of the damp. A few straight-backed chairs, some stools, an oak table covered with a thick cloth, and a dresser completed the furnishings. Light came from candles, marked off in sections so that they also told the time as they burned. From a corner of the room a staircase led to the first floor, consisting of three intercommunicating chambers. These had no doors, for the Elizabethans cared very little for privacy. In one of them, the master bedroom, was a carved four-poster bed with an embroidered tester and curtains. Underneath the big four-poster was a little truckle bed, only taken out at night, where the page slept. Maids did the housework*, somewhat inefficiently by our standards, for an Elizabethan house was so dirty and smelled so badly that we should hardly be able to bear it. The rushes on the floor soon degenerated into a sort of refuse heap; the rooms were never aired and occasionally one grew so bad that even the Elizabethans considered it unusable, and burned juniper berries in it to clear the air. Yet great progress had been made since the days when people slept on straw pallets and used logs of wood as pillows. By 1597 some fastidious persons even went to the length of wearing nightshirts, and, though they rarely washed, their garments were very rich and costly. Women wore huge farthingales and rigid stomachers, stiff with diamonds and pearls, and their dresses were very low cut in the front with ruffs of stiffened white batiste edged with exquisite lace. They and their cavaliers diverted themselves playing a game of table bowls*, the forerunner of our modern billiards. Children in this period had a rich variety of games, and the elder Brueghel has painted a kind of encyclopedia of them*. His Flemish schoolboys in their tight stockings and long coats, overflowing with boisterous energy, are playing games that are still popular today: bowling hoops, stilts, a tug-o'-war, leap-frog, blind man's buff, follow-my-leader, marbles, dice, five-stones, skittles, hide-and-seek, hopscotch and many others long since forgotten.

428

429

430 →

431

The Dutch countryside in 1618 looked very little different from what we can see today, with its canals, black and white cows and windmills. Its present appearance dates from the early seventeenth century, when the United Provinces, recently liberated from Spanish domination, began their rise into a great seafaring and colonial power. This sudden world-wide expansion had its repercussions even in the lives of the simplest country folk, as we can see if we pause for a moment by an ordinary country inn. It is Sunday and the peasants are sitting in the shade of trellised arbours drinking small beer or, in a few cases, the new ratafia imported from France, or Hollands gin. Some are playing bowls* or smoking tobacco (431) in long clay pipes. This was a more complicated process then than it is today, as the tobacco had first to be chopped into small pieces before the pipe could be filled. In a back room the barber is operating on a corn with a sharp, red-hot needle*. (432) There are still some poorer homes in this part of the country where people sleep in cupboard beds, like those common in Brittany, some of them so small that the occupier has to sleep sitting up; but close by are wealthy farmhouses with spacious buildings and ample stableyards where the beasts are stalled and groomed, surrounded by deep ditches spanned by swing bridges. These houses are meticulously clean and not without a certain rustic comfort that has considerable charm. One corner of the room is cosily furnished and lined with embroidered hangings*, and the Calvinist (433) Bible is placed on the table ready for evening prayers. Like the vast majority of Dutch peasants, who differ in this way from the rest of seventeenth-century Europe, everyone in the household can

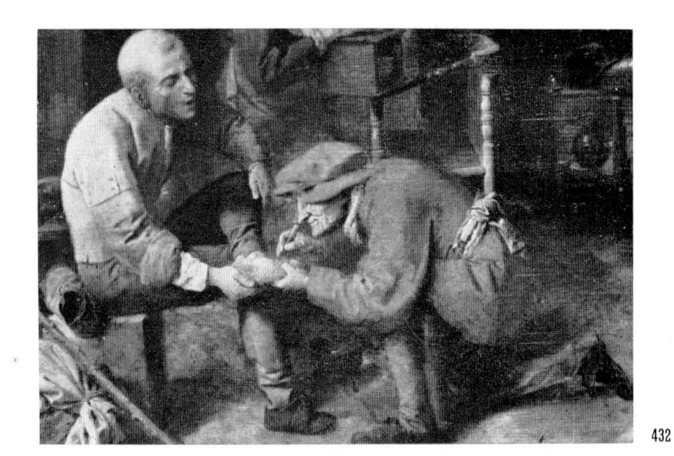

432

# In the country the Dutch peasant eats, drinks and is merry

# In the city the perfect housewife pinches pennies and dreams of a house of her own.

433

read. Dinner is ready, and the farmer's wife is waiting for the men to come home from the fields. Not far away is the village with its provision store*, selling the condiments which, with butter, cheese and vegetables, make up the staple diet of the Dutch peasant. Wealthy people also grow potatoes and tomatoes from the Americas in their gardens, but these are for decoration rather than for the table. In the towns people eat four meals a day. Very early, at about five or six in the morning, there is a breakfast of bread and butter and cheese and a drink of milk or beer; the midday meal consists of a soup made from vegetables and milk, some fish, and a meat course—usually a *hutsepot* of vegetables, chopped meat and lemon juice cooked in fat—and some fruit, as well as the occasional pancakes or waffles. At about eight or nine in the evening the remains of the midday meal are eaten up with some butter and cheese, and when work allows, there is also a light tea of bread and cheese, with some almonds or grapes, and beer at about three in the afternoon.

434

The food was nourishing and there was plenty of it, but the Dutch did not indulge in the subtle recipes and hours of preparation that are the glory of French cooking. Rich households were generally only distinguished by the services of fine porcelain which wealthy merchants were beginning to import from China, and which they often had made to their own designs. When people wanted a meal that was something out of the ordinary they went to a tavern, and some of these had reputations for especially fine cookery.

434

435

Professional men in seventeenth-century Holland dressed on the whole very soberly in dark colours: black, brown, grey or purple. Over their doublet and breeches they wore a coat, usually buttoning in front, with white bands and often a cloak on top, and a soft, wide-brimmed felt hat. These sober citizens are gathered outside the Stock Exchange in Amsterdam, the centre of the country's foreign business*, where the great fortunes were originally made which financed the building of the fine houses with their ornamental gables, some of which are still standing today.

435

# Everything is washed, bright, clean and shining—except the people.

436

The majority of houses were smaller and made of brick, crowded into streets with a canal running down the middle which at this period served as a general sewer*. The canal was bordered by narrow lanes which even as early as this were beginning to prove too narrow for the new traffic of sprung coaches, an invention stemming from France. There were one-way streets in Amsterdam as early as 1615. Dutch women were already very house-proud and their houses were given a thorough cleaning once a week, usually on Saturday, and sometimes even more. All the furniture was taken outside, the curtains were changed and the rooms thoroughly scrubbed; even the fronts of the houses were given a cleaning with a syringe to reach the top-most gables. The cleaning was a national institution as sacred as the *kermesse*. But the result was worth the trouble, for the tiles glistened and the heavy oak tables, waxed cupboards and stamped leather armchairs all shone with polish*.

The main front room opened directly off the street, and it was here that the family spent most of their time. Vrouw Hendrik Tulp of Leyden

437

438

has just called her little daughter Maria away from the wooden cart she was playing with to have her bowl of gruel*. Vrouw Tulp's feet are tucked carefully into her beloved foot-muff, and from her waist hangs a chatelaine with scissors, needle-case and a bunch of keys fitting the precious cupboards inlaid with mother-of-pearl which are stuffed with linen and provisions of all kinds. But for all their cleanliness the Dutch were not over-scrupulous about washing their own bodies.

439

The place is Paris and the date May 1636 at five o'clock in the morning. Two men are duelling in the rue de la Grande Truanderie between the houses, whose doors and windows are still closely shuttered against the early morning sun. The only watchers are their lackeys, standing impassively holding the horses*. 439

A short distance away, the Hôtel Faverolles is beginning to wake up. The *valet de chambre* is shaving his master carefully, leaving only a little pointed beard, trimmed *à la royale*, and a curling moustache*. The business of washing was itself a simple enough process, since it only 440

440

441

442

involved rubbing a small flannel dipped in a pewter basin of water over the most obvious places. True, water was scarce and had to be used economically, but the entire household only needed fifteen buckets a day. To overcome the inevitable smells people resorted instead to a formidable array of powders, scented oils and flower perfumes. Madame de Faverolles has risen earlier than her husband. Her bed is already made and the curtains drawn round it, and her maid has just finished doing her hair. This has two rows of little crimped curls, called *bouffons*, and a *garcette*, a little fringe combed carefully to fall over her forehead. Madame is wearing her flowered taffeta underskirt with a full black gown with wide sleeves and lace cuffs over it. The cumbersome ruff has long since been discarded, and now women wear only a plain fichu, such as Madame is at present trying on*. There is a knock on the door and in comes the shoemaker, bringing a pair of the fantastically fretted slippers with lace rosettes which are the newest craze and which only he knows the secret of making*. He condescends to fit them himself, while his assistant stands by flirting with Fanchon, the lady's maid. 441 442

In Paris blood runs freely ; bath water less so.

443 444

Fanchon is looking forward to the day when she can leave her job and get married, but it is only three years since she left her father's farm to go into service, and she calculates that she will have to put up with her mistress's scolding for another three before she has saved up enough money to do that. The real power in the household is Ferry Rondeau, the *maître d'hôtel*, who rules everyone from the kitchen boy to the head valet and even, the whisper goes, Monsieur himself, with a rod of iron. But if Rondeau is strict, it is because he has to be in such a busy household, with its four horses in the stables and even one of the new carriages, still a great rarity, upholstered in crimson damask. The only person he cannot control is Toinette, the baby's nurse, who is a law unto herself. She swaddles the infant so tightly that he can't move a muscle*. [443] The other maids crowd round the crackling fire exchanging gossip and infallible cures for all ills. The little one has a toothache, so his gums should be rubbed with a mixture of honey, adder's brains and the milk from a bitch with a new litter. Louis, the third child, wets his bed, and the remedy for this is porcupine's meat. In the gallery next to this room, which is furnished with rich tapestries and seats upholstered in red serge with silk fringes, the four other children are playing. François is still dressed in skirts, but is differentiated from his sisters by his big plumed hat, like his father's. Anne, the youngest but one, is learning to walk, and she stands inside a hollow wooden stool which scrapes on the ground every time she takes a step, happily banging a little hammer against the frame*. [444] The noise they are making wakes their baby brother who starts shrieking at the top of his lungs.

In the evening the table is laid in the master's room, which is the largest in the house, and while the company amuse themselves by making apple fritters* [445] round the fire, the maids put a clean white cloth and damask napkins on the table, for hitherto people had only wiped their hands before and after the meal on the towel which hung from the wall. Like all reasonably wealthy people the Faverolles possess a large quantity of valuable silver plate, and there are gleaming dishes and dish-covers on the table. Precious glasses of coloured crystal from Bohemia stand on a side-table with flasks and bottles of wine, and when any of the guests is thirsty he makes a sign to the wine butler, who then removes the bottle and glass when he has finished, for the drink is never left on the table. The meal includes few vegetables, although peas, eaten in their shells, and asparagus have recently become great favourites with gourmets, but there are plenty of tender young chickens and turkeys, pigeons, all kinds of game and meat pies and tarts*. [446]

Madame de Faverolles has pretensions to fashion, for ever since the Marquise de Rambouillet opened her famous *chambre bleue* in the

445

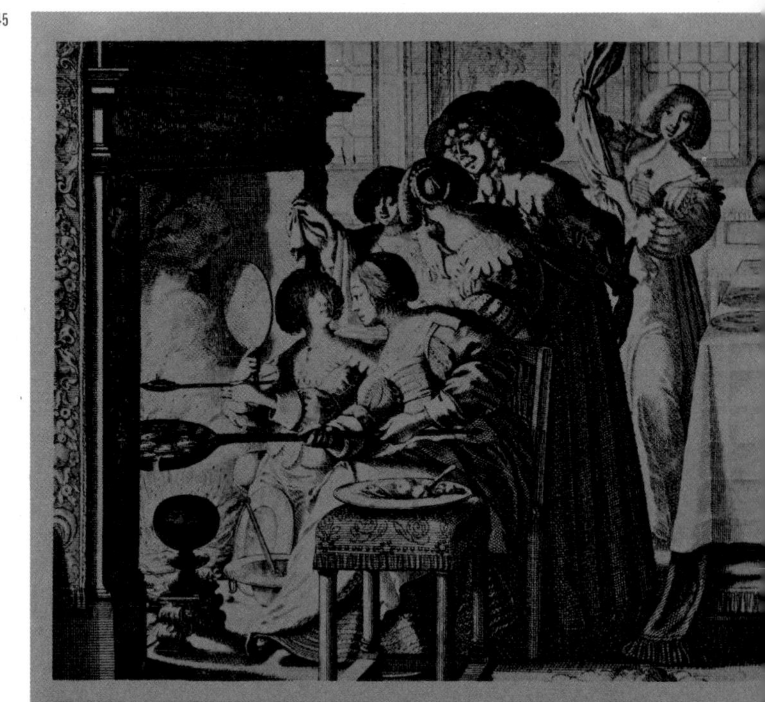

446

## …, music and letters, make rules of good manners and compare their beaux.

rue Saint-Thomas-du-Louvre in 1606 and began inviting wits and ladies of fashion to it, more than one lady has been fired by the ambition to have her *ruelle*, to assemble a select little group of kindred spirits round her bed. It was in great part a protest against the ignorance and bad manners of the nobility and the stubborn materialism of the middle classes, and these ladies prided themselves on their delicacy of feeling and expression. Madame de Faverolles sits, fully dressed, enthroned in her great bed, with its plumes of ostrich feathers*, and leads the conversation. They have laid down very strict rules concerning what is or is not good manners: one must not yawn too loudly, for example, or spray the person to whom one is talking with saliva; and spitting may only be countenanced if it is done discreetly, not too far and not in the face of one's companion. In accordance with this code of manners Madame Petitot, or Thisné as she is known to the ladies, who all have pseudonyms taken from the novels which are the latest rage, is politely turning aside to blow her nose. A few evenings ago Athénaïs went to the Marais Theatre to see M. Pierre Corneille's plays *Le Cid* and *L'Illusion comique*. The performance* began very late: it was nearly half-past three before it started, and it did not finish until after seven. The townspeople, students and lackeys in the pit made a great commotion, eating sweets and oranges during the interval; and when one clique tried to boo during the acts, the play's supporters almost came to blows with the attackers. Like all the *précieuses*, these ladies are devoted to intellectual pursuits; the musical ones play the lute and the spinet and all fancy themselves as poets, delighting themselves and each other with their verses and epigrams. They all dream of love, too, though their love affairs are strictly platonic, and even Madame de Faverolles herself is not averse to the charming d'Houquetin, who accompanies her when she walks abroad*. His long curling hair, wide lace collar and close-fitting breeches ending in a lace frill tucked into wide-topped boots, and above all his beautiful manners make him the perfect gallant.

447

448

449

# The apothecary has the cure for all maladies: bleeding and purging.

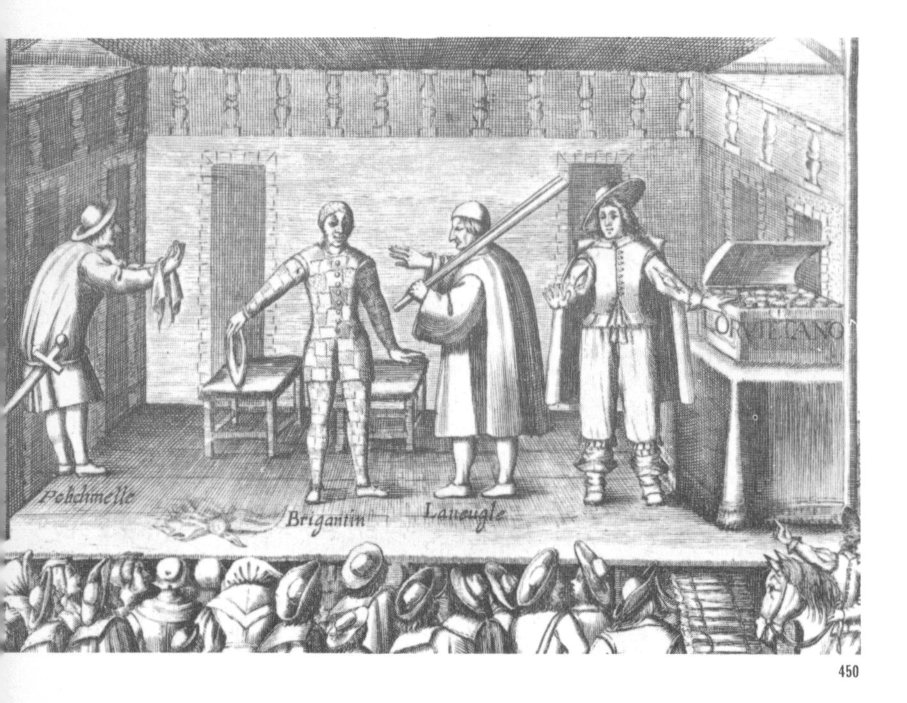


450

452

If Fanchon, the maid, had her own way, she would leave her mistress and her cavalier alone together and run to the Pont Neuf to mingle with the crowd of ordinary people watching Tabarin, the charlatan, whose quackeries are 'sovereign against all evils, bites and sickness, against the devouring worm and the small-pox and other ills'. On the stage, Brigantin, the blind man and Polichinelle with his wooden sword are up to their tricks*. 450 But there is trouble at home, for Madame de Faverolle's sister, the Canoness, is ill. The invalid is lying in bed, looking very pale under her lace cap*, 451 and M. Fragoux, the apothecary, has arrived punctually, as always, for her douche. Behind him comes a chambermaid carrying the commode. The illness is causing a great deal of inconvenience in the household, but there can be no question of sending the lady to the hospital, where the nursing sisters take in all comers without distinction of race or creed, and the sick lie two by two on straw pallet beds*. 452 On the evening of 17th June, 1636, M. Rendant, the doctor, prescribes bleeding again to remove the bad blood and enable the good to increase, but it is too much for the patient's strength and she passes away. Two days later she is buried. The coffin is carried by six Franciscan friars and preceded by the priests of the parish of Saint-Eustache carrying a cross, while all the men of the family, wearing long black cloaks and crêpe bands round their hats*, 453 follow the cortège. At the end of the procession come two hundred poor; they are carrying torches, and have been dressed in black by the Faverolles for the occasion.

451

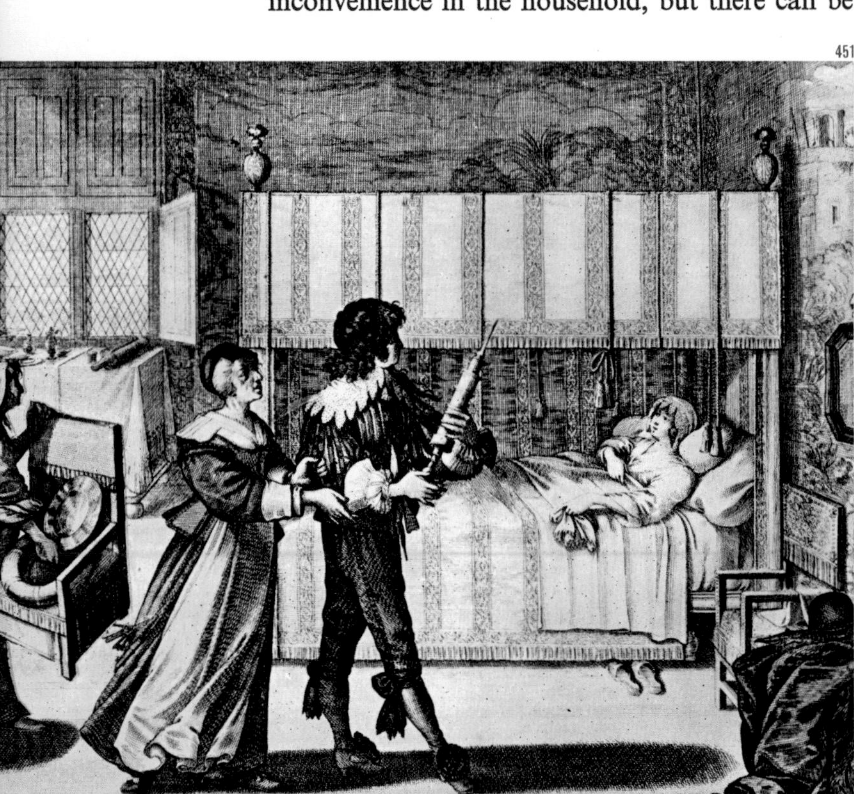

453

# Shaggy moujiks and Western merchants distrust each other, but trade begins.

In the time of Louis XIII the Grand Duchy of Muscovy was no more than a name to the French, but English, Dutch and, most of all, German merchants had all visited it, although the Russians had so great a distrust of Europeans, whose beliefs were incompatible with the orthodox religion, that they were only allowed to stay in one particular part of Moscow, known as the German quarter. There was plenty to trouble and amaze the foreigner in the vast, flat expanse of country, with its immense birch and pine forests, its cruel climate and wild-looking people, with hairy, unshaven faces under their shaggy hats, and long 454 shirts and thonged boots*. The peasant girls wore thick, all-enveloping coats and big fur hats, with 455 one long fair plait hanging down their backs.* Winter was long, and in the village, with its windowless wooden houses, the people fought the cold outside with a huge stove built of masonry, and the whole family were employed indoors while the fields were covered with snow. They 456 made sandals*, called *lapti*, from the bark of the

456 454

455

lime tree dressed and cut into strips, and carved wooden knives and spoons and dolls to sell in towns. After drinking their steaming cabbage soup or a sort of gruel laced with kwass (a drink made from fermented barley), and praying before the holy icon with its lighted lamp, there was nothing to do but go to bed. The moujik, the head of the household, had the place of honour on top of the stove, and the women and children slept on a heap of rags on the ground. Yet, however primitive he was, the Russian peasant loved to wash himself. On the eve of holidays the whole village went to the bath-house*, and in the steam-filled 457 hot-room they beat themselves with bundles of birch and massaged and trounced each other so heartily that they needed vast quantities of drink to replace the moisture they had sweated out.

457

458

The year of 1613 saw a completely new city of Moscow beginning to rise from the ruins of the old, which had been almost wholly destroyed by civil war. Its crooked streets were lined with innumerable single-storeyed wooden houses, all heavily bolted and barred with iron doors and shutters and each standing in its own high-walled garden. Some of the more important houses were built of stone blocks, and there were countless large churches with gilded or brightly painted domes. Dominating the whole city was the Kremlin, surrounded by an earthwork and guarded by wooden towers set at intervals along the ramparts. Red Square, which was so named as early as the seventeenth century, was already the centre of the city and the place where the great religious processions took place. The most impressive of these was the Palm Sunday procession, in which the file of priests with their swinging censers was followed by the high nobility, called the Boyars, carrying

459

# The Kremlin and Red Square are already built,

willow branches. The heavy sable garments they had worn all winter were changed for full cloth caftans surmounted by tall fur hats*. 458

In the churches the iconostasis, a screen separating the nave from the choir, was always a mass of serene, heavily gilded icons*. The many churches were never empty although the services were very long, and there were frequent holy days which all the people kept piously. After baptism—which involved total immersion in a tub*—all members of the Russian Orthodox Church faithfully observed the strict rules of their religion. 459 460

At the end of the century there was a sudden and very noticeable change in the style of the *loubki*, the traditional wood engravings* of the country. The Russian way of life, hardly altered for centuries, was suddenly shattered to its core by one man: Peter the Great. One day while talking to some Boyars, this Tsar suddenly seized a pair of scissors and 'to their great astonishment and chagrin' chopped off their magnificent spade beards. Thenceforth it became an offence to wear beards and long robes, and all who refused to conform were punished*. The new edict ruled that in winter caftans of the Hungarian style should be worn, and in summer German fashions in dress. The Church protested that 'such measures meant depriving man of the shape he was given by God', but the old fashions were gone for good. The lords started to dress in Western clothes and began speaking French. Women too emerged from the *terems* in which they had been shut up. Yet their new wigs and tricorne hats did not stop the men adhering to the good old customs, such as that of dragging their wives about by the hair and beating them with the knout* for any misdemeanour. 461 462 463

But paving-stones and clearing the streets of the beggars, for whom the Tsar built a special hospital, could not change the appearance of Moscow, and

461

Peter decided to build himself a new capital city, accessible from the sea and facilitating traffic with the West. He built Saint Petersburg, which remained the Russian capital until the Revolution.

463

460

462

# ›ut Peter the Great founds a Western capital: Saint Petersburg.

464

Lunch, in milady's room, with its walls covered in 463 tapestries and pictures, is just over*. Dessert of dried fruits, sugared fennel and sugared almonds is being served, and the mistress of the house has allowed her little girls to come down and be fed on tit-bits. After the meal the ladies go down 464 to the market square in their carriages*, where, without the necessity of putting a foot to the ground, they can watch a play being acted on a scaffolding stage by a company of travelling players. The fashion for carriages originated in France and spread quickly through Holland and Flanders until all the ladies of the nobility and the rich bourgeoisie were clamouring for them. No lady was content unless she could parade in her carriage and compare its luxury and splendour 465 with others*. The new carriages possessed the advantage over the old coaches that they had springs and glazed windows, but those who could not afford the luxury of a carriage of their own had to possess a *vinaigrette*, a two-wheeled sedan pulled by a lackey and pushed from behind by a woman or child, or at the very least a sedan chair. There were even public vehicles on hire in Paris, and had been for some time.

465

They were in fact a strict necessity, since it was hardly possible to walk about the streets without soiling one's dress. This was not altogether a matter for surprise, since most houses had neither drains nor cess-pits and all waste was emptied into the gutter. In summer 'the streets are too foul smelling to be endured. The great quantities of fish and meat decay and rot in the heat, and this, added to the number of people relieving themselves in the street, causes such a stench that it is impossible to remain there.' All those who were able retired to their country estates, except during Lent, when the sermons of Bossuet and Father Bourdaloue drew enormous crowds. Ladies knelt on hassocks and spread out their wide, flounced skirts, lavishly decked with tassels and fringes. On their heads they wore a tall creation, known as a coiffure *à la Fontanges*, built up of goffered lace on a wire framework. After the extravagant fashions of the early years of Louis XIV's reign, masculine costume had become much more sober and was to alter only in superficial

Wheels of sumptuous carriages roll through the filthy mud of the streets.

466

467

468

details until the French Revolution. Its main outlines were a full-skirted coat, fitted to the waist, a waistcoat as long as the coat and under it tight knee-breeches fastened by an elaborate garter at the knee. A periwig, called *in-folio*, rose to two points over the forehead and hung in long curls to 466 the shoulders*. When not following the service in his book the gallant would take out his orna- 467 mental grater*, rub some leaves of tobacco on it and take snuff very loudly, a habit which soon called forth recriminations from the pulpit. Yet though the basic lines of men's costume might be simple there were plenty of exquisites who soon adorned it with all manner of expensive trifles. These could be bought at Perdrigeon's shop at the Sign of the Four Winds in the rue de la Lanterne, and they varied from sashes to be knotted low on the hips, lace cuffs, knots of ribbon for the shoulders and gold and silver fringes to huge fur capes for the winter*. 468

Spain, where, since the reign of Philip II, dress had been noted for its conservatism and severity*, 469 was one of the last countries to submit to the leadership of French fashions. But, in return for the clothes she finally introduced there, France adopted from Spain that sensational drink of Mexican origin, chocolate*. Chocolate made its 470 appearance in Paris at the same time as tea, which was brought from China and Japan, and a little earlier than Turkish coffee. For a long time tea and coffee were great luxuries and only chocolate was a reasonable price. All three beverages were looked on as having medicinal virtues, and their merits and demerits were gravely discussed.

469

470

## 'he beau attends to his wardrobe. Hot chocolate becomes all the rage.

# The unemployed turn to innkeepers for help. The pedlar relies on his feet.

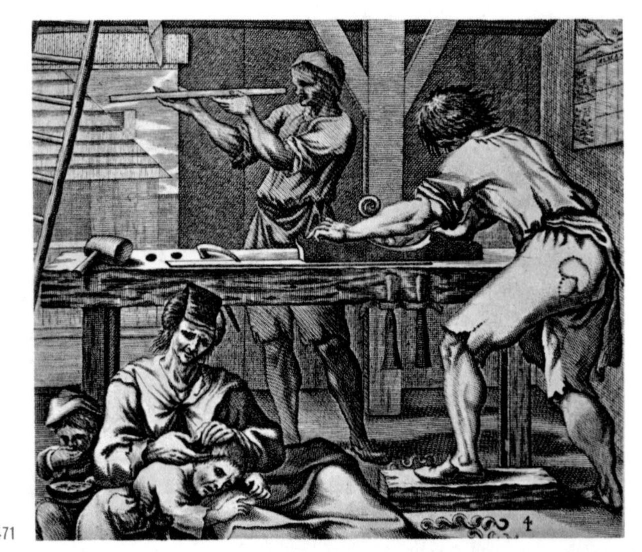

471

473

474

472

There were also travelling salesmen, like this pedlar with his stock of scissors, needles and thread, as well as things like spectacles, combs, almanacs and religious images*, who were free but desperately poor and wore out their shoes in search of trade; and others who hired out their muscles as porters, carrying coal*, wood and water. None of these poor people could read or write, and when this was necessary they resorted to the public scribe who set himself up in front of the inn with a barrel for a table*.

Last of all there were the unemployed of all kinds: deserters, servants who had been dismissed and the crowds of beggars who haunted the Cour des Miracles. It is hardly to be wondered at if the streets were not safe at night however vigilantly the watch patrolled. Over these poor people, as over the country-peasants, hung the constant threat of starvation. Every four or five years brought bad harvests and famine in their wake, and these led in many places to riots and uprisings which were ruthlessly put down by the militia.

On the edge of this fashionable world lived the great mass of the working classes whose life altered hardly at all with the passing of centuries, and the progressive increase in the ease and comfort of daily life among the rich made their lot harder to bear. The carpenter worked with his apprentices in the only room he had, and in which he and his wife and two children all lived*. The state-run guild only worked in favour of the bosses. The workers were compelled to organise themselves and founded secret associations with mysterious private rituals. They met in a bar, and while the front room of *The Throne of Bacchus** was filled with a motley assortment of servants, musketeers, poets and students enjoying sausages and pickled pork sprinkled with claret, the innkeeper, known to the workers as *mother*, secretly took in the unemployed and sheltered them until work could be found for them in a *boîte* (workshop).

475

# Byzantium has become Istanbul. The sultan idles on the Golden Horn.

476

478

After the Turks, who came originally from Central Asia, had become converts to Islam and overrun the Middle East, something had changed in the lives of the peoples over whom they ruled. In 1705, although already being thrust back by the might of Austria, their empire extended from the Balkan states in Europe to Morocco in North Africa, and wherever the *padishah* (the sultan) ruled, the supreme law, regulating all aspects of public and private life, was the Koran*. Constantinople, now called Istanbul, had a population at this period numbering some six hundred thousand, and here the sultan* lived in his vast palace, the seraglio, on the Golden Horn, clad always in the most sumptuous clothes and served by pages and black eunuchs. He was a man softened by a life of absolute pleasure, yet capable of great cruelty, and he passed his time in amusements and visiting his harem, which contained as many as six hundred *odalisques*, brought from all parts of his wide dominions. No one was permitted to enter his presence unless summoned, upon pain of death. Sometimes the sultan, surrounded by his splendid escort, would visit the hippodrome, where the people of the city put on magnificent shows in his honour, which included richly mounted masques*, musical performances and processions of floats, covered in flowers.

477

The officials who served the sultan lived in constant terror for their lives and lands, but although their hour was usually short they used it to spread a reign of terror and profited by it to enrich themselves. The pashas, known by the title of One-, Two- or Three-Tail, on account of the number of horse's tails which were carried in front of them on lances as a sign of their rank, had no scruples in resorting to all degrees of punishment and torture at their disposal in order to extract from their wretched victims the tithes due on all harvests and the tax which was levied on all males not Muslims.

# Turkey: a military empire. Persia: land of A Thousand And One Nights.

479

481

The Turkish Empire was based on military power. Its permanent army was a force called the Janissaries who were young Christian boys recruited and carried away for ever from their homes and families, made to become Muslims and vowed to the service of their lord. They also acted as a police force and can be seen here arresting a pair of lovers in a public garden*. (479) In addition to the Janissaries, the army contained the *spahis*, small feudal lords who each contributed their own troops of cavalry. Turkish life was so efficiently organised as a machine for exploiting subject peoples that it allowed little possibility of progress in everyday life, and the old habits still persisted, almost unchanged. The day was spent in dividing the time between the mosque and the *hammam**. (480) The *hammam* was in fact several centuries old by the time of the Ottoman conquest, but it was first known in Europe by the name of a Turkish Bath. Women were still closely veiled and confined to their own part of the house, called the *haremlik*, and could only be visited by their husbands and near relations such as fathers or brothers. The higher placed officials added to the numbers in their harems by importing slaves from Europe and Africa, and especially popular were Circassians, talented musicians who played the theorbo, a forerunner of the guitar, on all special occasions*. (481)

Although the majority of the sultan's subjects were Christian, no attempt was made to convert them to Islam, since it was they who supported the major burden of taxation and were especially oppressed by Muslim governors. Escaping the rigours of Islamic religious law, their cases were tried by their own bishops. They benefited from the Greek schools, where education was immeasurably superior to that in the Turkish, and some even managed to rise to very high positions in the Ottoman administration.

Not far from Turkey lay Persia, still a fairytale country. There are pictures of great lords sitting on marble terraces spread with rich carpets*, (482) waited on by houris in billowing trousers and floating, diaphanous veils sewn with gold and pearls.

480

485

483

484

Over the whole of Isfahan, a town of some six hundred thousand inhabitants, loom the blue and gold domes of its mosques and minarets. In the Shah's palace, composed of a host of delicate pavilions scattered over a park several miles in circumference, water flows in jasper bowls, the walls gleam with mirrors and in the windows are panes of crystal and many-coloured glass. The second floor of one of the largest of these pavilions has a room opening onto a broad balcony, surrounded by slender columns and overlooking the Maidan, the great square. Here is to be found the Shahinshah, the wonder of the world*. 483

The Shah is sitting on costly cushions, a rose in his hand, listening to the report of his Grand Vizier, who bows humbly before him, while in the background there is a continual coming and going of servants in pleated white skirts. In niches, lined with pink stucco, stand flasks of agate and cornelian containing priceless wines brought from Georgia, Shiraz and Kerman. In one of the many flower-filled courts of the palace, cooks in short trousers with their robes tucked up into their waistbands are busy all day long concocting delicacies of game and pastries and sorbets of roses, each more exotic than the last, for the Shah and his large

n the streets of the town are mullahs, veiled women and merchants.

486

484 harem*. On one occasion the Shah deigns to appear before his people, gathered on the Maidan to see him. This is the *ashoua*, the tenth and last day of the feast celebrated in honour of the Imam Hussein, one of the principal personages of Shiism, the variant of the Muslim religion current in Persia. Then actors portray the martyrdom of Mahomet's grandson, while the crowd lament and tear their hair. The Shiites have their own priests, called *mullahs*, who wear black robes and huge white turbans, and there is even a theological seminary at Isfahan, called the *Madraseh*, with libraries and lecture rooms whose walls, of brick enamelled with intertwining patterns in blue and green, are mirrored in the waters of a wide, still 485 pool*. Students can live here, and they are paid a certain amount of money for their food and light.

In the streets of Isfahan are the solemn, turbaned townsmen, their beards dyed blue, yellow, green or purple, and their black-veiled womenfolk. There are heavily burdened donkeys and camels belonging to caravans. Here the camel is a basic part of life, for it is he who turns the miller's enor- 486 mous wheel*. In the bazaar are the silks, silverware and carpets which merchants from Europe travel 487 half across the world to purchase*.

487

488

The place is Madrid and the date 30th August, 1744. On the plaza de le Cebada the *feria* is in full swing. The square is filled with booths and hawkers, and visitors are sitting drinking in the open air amid the milling crowd of gipsy fortune-tellers. Priests and countesses in panniered dresses rub shoulders with lackeys and orange sellers. When the Duchess of Medina-Sidonia passes in her crested carriage everyone greets her politely, 488 but not obsequiously*.

489 In Vienna, on the same day*, housewives with their baskets over their arms are going to the butcher; a procession is taking place; and a wine merchant is delivering a hogshead on a sledge drawn by horses. This is a town of modern buildings—some are seven or eight floors high and already foreshadow blocks that will not be common in Europe for another century—and it is full of life and gaiety. The Viennese believe in good living—Viennese pastry is world-famed—and they love the countryside and music. They make the most of fine days to stroll in the woods near the

489

490

Madrid rejoices at the feria. In Vienna not only the Danube is blue.

town and dance in the open-air cafés. Work stops at five in the evening, and there is a typically Viennese arrangement, called a *Blue Monday*, an extra holiday by which they can prolong the joys of Sunday. Vienna is a cosmopolitan city where all races are at home, and in its streets one might hear any language from German and Hungarian to Serbo-Croat. Yet it is still to Paris that the eyes of all Europe are turned and to which the foreign visitors flock in greatest numbers. In Paris, too, the streets are an ever-changing show where people dance and drink and talk*. There is the knife-grinder sharpening knives, the vinegar seller in his red bonnet, wheeling his little barrel on a barrow*, the water carrier with his weird, croaking cry and the porter with parcels and packages on his back*, all shouldering their way through the busy crowds, while the air resounds with the coachmen's oaths. On this same 30th August, 1744, the nine days' fair of Saint Ovid has just begun and offers all kinds of delightful things to do. On a scaffolding stage the characters of the *Commedia dell'Arte* are up to their tricks, and next to them the ballad singer has unrolled a huge canvas with the subjects of all his songs painted on it and is pointing them out with a long pole. Two sous buys you admission to a Chinese pavilion, to be entertained with the wonders of the magic lantern*. When Saint Ovid's fair is over there will be another one somewhere else, for the calendar is full of feasts. But there are more intellectual pastimes in Paris as well. At the Opera there are Italian *prima donnas* and violinists who possess the finest instruments in the world, made at Cremona and in the Tyrol*; and there are plays at the Théâtre Français which strolling companies of players, making a picturesque troupe as they travel from town to town*, have carried to every corner of the provinces. French companies are even performing as far afield as Stockholm, Saint Petersburg, Vienna, Naples, Cadiz and Warsaw.

490 491 492 493 494 495

494

491 492

493

495

After Sunday comes another holiday: Blue Monday. Paris, too, makes merry.

# In France the coffee-pot has a place of honour among the family plate.

At about the same period a new appreciation of physical comforts swept over France. Let us go back now, in 1744, and pay another visit to the Hôtel de Faverolles, whose occupants we met a century earlier (p. 149). The Faverolles have preserved the family mansion but they have added another wing to it, more in tune with modern tastes. The ceilings are higher; tall windows make the rooms lighter and the marble fireplaces are much smaller but heat the rooms more efficiently. The new bedrooms are all separate and each has its own dressing-room communicating with it.

At eight o'clock the whole family gather in their morning-gowns in Madame de Faverolles' room for breakfast, and it is she herself who feeds her baby daughter, Sophie, while M. de Faverolles pours the coffee, which is now a common drink*. 496 Everyone has café-au-lait at breakfast time and drinks several cups of black coffee in the course of the day, so the coffee-pot* occupies a place of 497 honour among the household possessions.

Yet, if M. de Faverolles' great-grandfather could come back and see his house, the thing that would surprise him more than anything would be the elegant new furniture made of precious inlaid woods, its delicate curves and its endless variety of shapes. The huge coffers and massive cupboards have given way to neat, practical pieces; tea-tables, chiffoniers, escritoires and many others.

In the pantry a maid is polishing the family plate. She rubs it first with whiting, dips it in bran-water and then polishes the dishes, covers and silver candlesticks until they shine*. In the evening, 498 when she has finished her work, she will take a few moments to go to the public letter-writer. He will write a beautiful letter to her fiancé with his goose quill, sand it carefully to dry the ink and charge her five sous*. 499

The maid must be suffering from love-sickness, for here she is the next day at the apothecary's*. 500 While she is being examined the doctor writes out a prescription for a little balsam, containing some toads that have been boiled in oil. Whatever the cause of the fever, this should cure it promptly.

499

501 502

It is 1753 and Kouen-Tch'oang, a scholar who has recently received an appointment in the imperial service, has been made lieutenant of Tchou-Tong. Today he is on his way to his new post with a full official escort. He has left his palanquin, in which he was getting cramp, and mounted a white horse, and now, with a following of servants and preceded by a pair of heralds carrying banners proclaiming his titles and dignities, he is able to travel on in comfort*. (501) His clothes also announce to anyone who meets him that this is an important personage; on the top of his hat he has a red ball surrounded by oak leaves, and no one approaches him without great bowings and scrapings.

Tchou-Tong, the young mandarin's new home, is a quiet little town where the inhabitants mostly make their living from tea plantations. Three strangers from a far distant country across the sea are being entertained in the house of Kin Wou-li, the most important tea-grower in the town. They are English merchants who have come to trade with him*. (502) While they are drinking jasmine tea and watching the servants blending the dried tea leaves with their bare feet we can take a closer look at the house. Kin's home is made up of three blocks of single-storey buildings, set one behind the other and separated by two paved inner courtyards. In the main room the tablets representing the ancestors are enthroned on a sort of altar on which are laid regular offerings. In the master's room stands a solid brick stove, similar to those used in northern countries, which is called the *kang*, and on this Kin sleeps. The women of the household are relegated to the further rooms, out of the way. Life in the town has little variety. The peasants in their plaited bamboo hats and waterproof straw capes* (503) come to bring their produce and buy supplies, but the town only really wakes up for the festivities marking the new year, which in China is the first moon in February. The celebrations last for a fortnight during which everybody is on holiday and a wooden scaffolding is erected in the centre of the town, covered with pine branches and decorated with multi-coloured lanterns*. (504) This is called 'the mountain of the tortoise carrying the mountain'. It is a time of religious ceremonies, of worshipping the ancestors and burning incense before the family shrine, and of family parties. The days pass in games and feasting, and at night fireworks explode all over the town.

The end of these festivities marks the beginning of the school year, which is only broken by short holidays for the harvest, the autumn gathering and the new year. In the class-room* (505) the pupils

503

ice paper, the schoolboy learns to write. The father smokes opium.

505

506

507

504

learn to read and write in Chinese fashion with a paint brush, reproducing the thousands of different characters in the Chinese language. Each child brings his own materials, and these include a rod of Indian ink, a phial of water, a bowl for mixing the ink, a paint brush and some rice paper. Like all Chinese, these schoolboys have their heads shaven except for a single plait which legends say was imposed on them by the Manchu emperors as a sign of servitude.

Another occasion for festivities is a wedding, which in respectable families cannot take place without a great deal of previous negotiation by go-betweens and formal exchanges of presents. On a day fixed by the astrologers the ceremony of the cups can then be gone through*. The betrothed couple meet each other for the first time. Both wear elaborately embroidered silk robes, and the man wears either a conical straw hat or a silk skull-cap, and the girl a flowered head-dress. On their feet are satin slippers with felt soles. The two young people exchange little cups of an alcoholic drink, four for the man and two for the girl, who as a sign of submission must offer one to her mother-in-law into whose despotic power she passes when she marries. If his prospective bride pleases him, the young man adds two more to the number of pins in her hair. After this the arrangements are considered final and the servants begin fattening the ducks and geese in the yard for the wedding feast. Evening comes and the men gather quietly to smoke a pipe of opium together*.

506

507

# London throbs with life, but the gentry can escape from th

508

There had been great changes in London since the time of Queen Elizabeth. Her port had now become the largest in the world and many tall ships from America and the Indies rode at anchor 508 there*, unloading spices, tobacco, silks and exotic plumes for ladies to wear, and, most important of all, tea; this was fast becoming the national drink.

English ports were also busy with passenger traffic, for all the English who could afford it travelled widely. In 1765 it was estimated that over thirty thousand British subjects were living on the Continent either temporarily or as permanent residents. There were also large numbers of emigrants, often younger sons for whom there was no place at home, leaving England to people the colonies, especially New England.

In the streets of London, with their busy shops and ever-increasing number of new buildings, there was always a throng of coaches, hackney carriages, carts and street porters crowding the thoroughfare* through which the town crier* 509 510 could be seen making his way and crying, 'Oyez! Oyez!' in his stentorian voice. The social life of London had never a dull moment. People met in coffee-houses or in their homes, and wherever they were they talked continuously, exchanging news and ranging over every subject from politics to the latest scientific discoveries and the nature of man. The stern-faced Mr Justice Mumford was not the only man with new ideas*. Ever since England 511 had abolished official torture to extract secrets from prisoners—the first nation in the world to do so—Mumford had been troubled by the severe punishments the law compelled him to inflict in the course of his duties, and in this he was by no means alone. There were still more than two hundred crimes carrying the death penalty; one man had recently been hanged merely for attempting unsuccessfully to cut a purse, and another for having falsely impersonated a royal pensioner. An old man who had stolen a few potatoes was whipped at the cart's tail, and many people sat in the stocks* for much less. Moreover, the public 512 frankly enjoyed the spectacle. It is true that at this time many charitable institutions were being established for the assistance of such poor wretches. The Foundling Hospital had recently been opened and there were hospitals and maternity homes as well as foundations such as Sunday schools for the benefit of those who had hitherto had no possibility of acquiring an education.

The judge can relax in his fine, new Georgian house with its sash windows* and enjoy the com- 513 pany of his guests and his greyhounds, his two best friends, as he is fond of calling them. His house is full of fine things and he has pictures, engravings, ornaments and rich, calf-bound books

509

cial whirl by travelling abroad or retiring to the country.

510 511

513

514 brought from all over the world*. Soon it will be time to sit down to dinner, and one eats well in Mr Justice Mumford's house. Tonight's menu includes roast pigeon garnished with asparagus tips, sweetbreads with mushrooms, lobster thermidor, apricot tarts and gooseberry puddings, all elegantly served on the dishes of Wedgwood china which have replaced silver on the table. For the men the meal ends over decanters of port and madeira, while the ladies retire to the drawing-room.

Tomorrow evening, when business is over, Mumford will climb into his carriage and go down to his house in the country. Like many English people of his time, he has formed the habit of going away to breathe a little country air during the weekend. Since the Scotsman, McAdam, invented his new method of surfacing roads, it has been possible to travel like the wind in England. In the country, Mumford can stroll in his newly completed park; he has had it entirely replanted; all the old box hedges and clipped trees and statues which cluttered the garden in the Dutch fashion have been removed to make way for a landscaped wilderness in which every vista is carefully planned; it includes numerous tasteful ruins, pavilions, imitation Arab mosques, Turkish kiosks and Japanese pagodas.

514

512

In the country he will find peace, which is impossible in town where the fashionable world, now swollen by the addition of the *nouveaux riches*, the nabobs who have made their fortunes from speculation, from the spoils of the Indies and the slave trade, live in a never-ending round of pleasure. Everyone dresses above their station, petty shopkeepers ape the middle class, and the middle class ape the gentry. People cover themselves in costly jewels, and snuff-taking is all the rage, even with the ladies. Balls, routs, dinners, masquerades, the play, the opera, the carnivals at Vauxhall or Ranelagh all follow one another in an unbroken whirl of gaiety. After dancing all night long there are picnic lunches out of doors beside grottoes and Gothic ruins, where concealed musicians play harps and horns.

515

appear. This was boxing*, the noble art of self-defence, as it was sometimes called. At first, matches were fought with bare fists, but the sport found its first law-giver in the person of Jack Broughton, the inventor of boxing gloves which were initially scorned by the champions but soon became an accepted part of the game. Broughton's academy was patronised by many of the aristocracy for swordsmanship, fencing and singlestick. Rowing, too, was an English sport, and the first championships were rowed on English rivers. 518

The English no longer travelled about their own country only from necessity; nature lovers made long pilgrimages to the Lake District and the Scottish Highlands, whose wild and romantic scenery had roused only genteel horror in the civilised people of a century earlier. Some went on their doctors' recommendations to take the sea

Mr Justice Mumford's hospitality is as lavish in the country as it is in town. In the drawing-room 515 a game of whist is in progress*, but the host really prefers those guests who share his interest in the country and to whom he can show off his model farm. Thanks to the new methods of scientific stock-breeding, his cattle and sheep are fattening splendidly and do him credit. It is only in recent years that the quality of English meat has become sufficiently good for fresh meat all the year round to replace the heavy autumn slaughtering for salt meat in the winter. The pride of the

517

516

air at Brighton, Scarborough or Margate, and a few daring spirits even used the bathing-machines which were drawn out to sea by horses until the water was deep enough for the intrepid bather, modestly covered by a cloak, to climb down a ladder and plunge into the waves.

In the villages, new houses, built of brick with small, bottle-glass panes in their windows, sprang up among the old cottages with their exposed beams and thatched roofs which clustered round the church in its green, turf-covered graveyard.

farm are the horses, descended from Arab stallions and trained for the racing which was 516 rapidly gaining popularity in the British Isles*.

There were many other diversions in the country. In the autumn the whole county turned out in hunting pink for the fox hunting, but this was a sport reserved for the gentry. With the popular village game, cricket, things were different, and here the squire and his tenants often played side by side. Enthusiasm for the fierce sport of cock 517 fighting* was just as general, and sometimes whole fortunes were laid in bets. Towards the end of the century a completely new sport began to

518

Fox hunting and racing are sports for the squire; he joins his villagers f

519

520

Not far from the church stood the inn. Here on Sundays the farmers of the neighbourhood, in smocks or overcoats, came to drink their pint of beer and listen to somebody reading the news sheet, which had been a feature of English life since the early years of the century*. The vicar of the parish joined his flock there after doing his rounds on his old black mare. But the inn's day of glory came with election time. Coaches bulging with travellers clattered in and out of the inn yard*. The innkeeper and his staff went almost out of their minds wondering who to serve next, for there were rooms to be got ready, tea to be made, a leg of lamb to be boiled, a sirloin of beef to be roasted and plum puddings made for supper. The next day the voters would go to the polls and cast their free vote for their Member of Parliament—but cartoonists of the period made great play with the exact degree of freedom to be found in most elections*.

Behind this easy, boisterous façade, a very different England was beginning to emerge. Almost without realising it the country was going through the first stages of an industrial revolution, and the machine age, the age of coal and iron, was being born. In 1767 the invention of a spinning machine threatened to take away the livelihood from the cottage industries; henceforth spinning would be done in factories in the rapidly growing towns. In 1769 Arkwright took out a patent for his hydraulic loom, and James Watt for his steam engine. The new mechanical power had a profound influence on the textile industry, and as a result on the lives of thousands of English people.

A few years later the first iron bridge in the world was built, across the River Severn. The union of iron and coal opened up unlimited prospects for industrialisation. Out of the nine million people who made up the population of England and Wales at the end of the eighteenth century only three million still worked on the land.

521

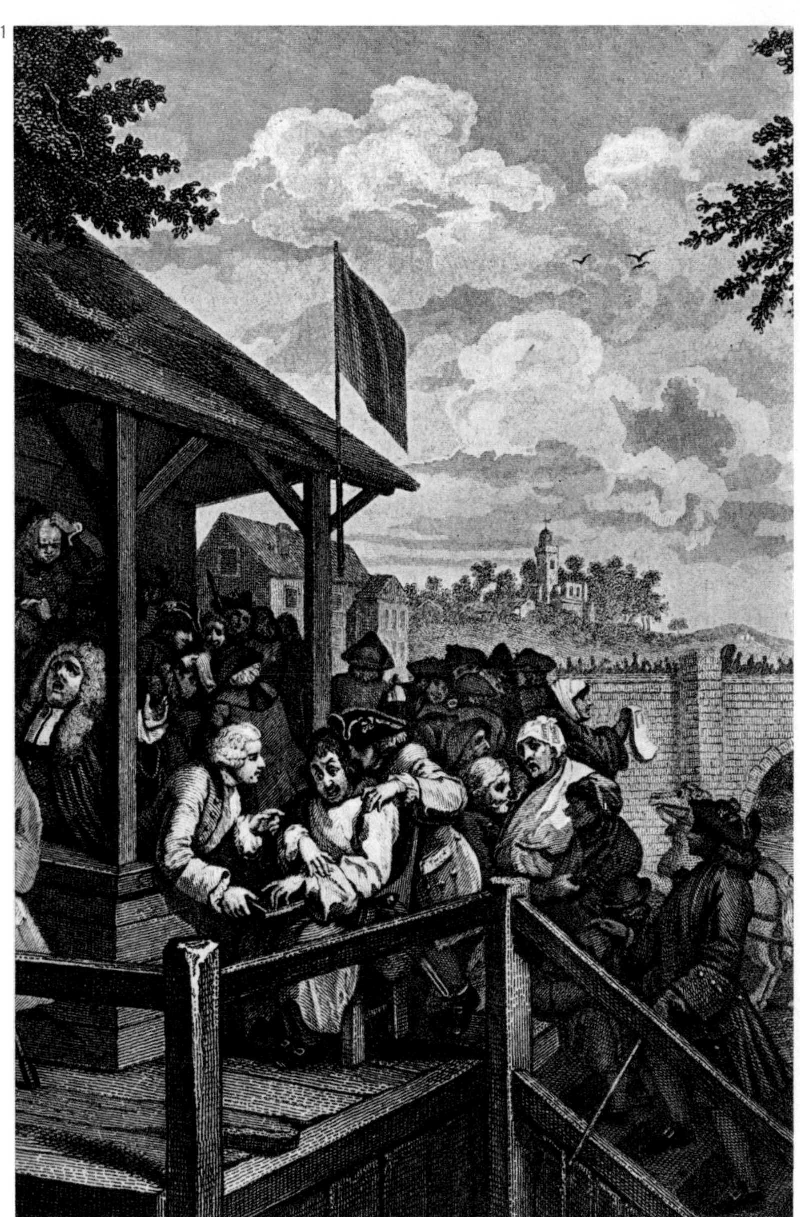

cket and boxing. Meanwhile the industrial revolution is beginning.

522 523 524

In the far north, where the descendants of the Vikings still lived, the people had been converted to Christianity much later than the rest of Europe and had become Protestants during the Reformation in the sixteenth century. All they retained of their sea-roving past was a great aptitude for deep-sea fishing, and in their fishing ports life was very similar to that of any French or English port of the same period. This butcher boy from Copenhagen* (522) might equally well have come from Paris or London, and the herring exporter's warehouse* (523) would look little different if it were in Holland or on the Baltic coast of Germany. Fisherwomen's dress varied little from place to place, and the local costumes of Holland or Denmark* (524) were very like those still to be seen in the west of France.

After the beginning of the seventeenth century, as the wood trade developed, peasant life became more prosperous, but in the high Norwegian valleys, cut off from all contact with the outside world, traditions still went directly back to the Middle Ages. The old houses, made of enormous logs, had no windows; all daylight and fresh air came in through a hole in the roof which was also the chimney, and a cooking-pot hung by a chain over the open fire* (525). The Norwegian peasant lived the whole of the long winter in a house perpetually filled with smoke. There was a huge larder for storing food and deep cupboards in the walls, and the main pieces of furniture were a solid

525

526

## No longer pirates, the Vikings are not very different from fishermen

wooden bed in one corner, a massive chair carved out of a single piece of wood and decorated with simple flower patterns, and a bench. The table was simply a wooden board set up on trestles and stacked away against the wall when not in use. In the more accessible parts of the country there was a certain amount of comfort: designs painted on the walls, attractive carved chests to hold clothes, brightly coloured rugs with primitive patterns on the floor, and a row of wooden beer mugs carved into animal shapes on the dresser. Such was the home of Olaf Mankeliv, painted here by a local artist with his wife and nineteen children, all dressed in their Sunday best*, just as they were about to set off for the service in the old wooden church, with its six-tiered roof and gables carved with fiery dragons. In the very far north, within the Arctic Circle, life was even more primitive. Here fur trappers, dressed in long protective clothes made of skins, scoured the immense, icy wastes on skis, with their ski-pole in one hand and a gun or a cross-bow in the other*, returning at night to the big wooden house where the bales of furs were stored. An Arctic hare was roasting on an improvised spit over the fire, and a barrel was turned into a miniature Turkish-bath*. In the course of their long trips the hunters met the Lapps, the permanent inhabitants of these frozen lands. They were stocky people dressed in sealskins, with their hair piled into a curious top-knot on their heads, and from them the Norwegians could obtain supplies of oil, seal-meat and, most important of all, the milk of the reindeers which the Lapps bred. Sometimes, too, they would even play a game of ball together*.

526 527 528 529

527

528

529

ɜr the world. But in the frozen North time is at a standstill.

530

The English way of life was rapidly gaining ground on the Continent. It was perhaps less impressive than the old, but it was infinitely more comfortable and practical, and progress was especially notable in transport. People travelled more and faster and more comfortably in the new post-chaises, Berlins and stage-coaches*. They were better sprung than coaches had ever been, and they seemed to eat up the miles. In 1722 it took twelve days to travel from Paris to Strasbourg, but by 1784 this had been reduced to five and a half. It was cramped in the narrow, box-like vehicles carrying eleven people—eight inside and three on top with the coachman, paying only half fare—and the roads were very bumpy, but what did people care if Rome lay at the end of the journey? The city was already attracting tourists to see its ancient monuments and, best of all, its carnival. The show lasted eleven days and was worth the trouble of the journey. As soon as the bells on the Capitol gave the signal for the festivities to begin, the windows on the Corso, all decorated with flowers and branches and hung with rich carpets, began to fill with the privileged few who had booked their places long in advance. The horse guards stood by ready to keep order, and the procession of masqueraders appeared*. There were Cossacks, Turks, beggars and thousands of Harlequins, Pantaloons and Polichinelles all wearing black *morettas* (little masks) and throwing confetti and paper streamers. In the evening the carnival continued with magnificent balls in the great palaces, where foreigners marvelled at the marble staircases* and picture galleries but found hard things to say about the discomfort, the almost complete absence of furniture and heating arrangements. The city offered other, gentler pleasures too, and one of the most fashionable was the promenade. These two lovers sharing a sunshade* in a park where art imitates the wildness of nature are enjoying one of the novels that are all the rage, and no doubt weeping copiously over it. He is wearing a blue coat with a yellow waistcoat and a flowing muslin cravat, and she has a mob cap perched on top of her high-piled curls.

In northern countries the great tiled stoves which heated the whole house had become works of art in themselves, decorated with religious subjects or mythological and allegorical scenes*.

531

532

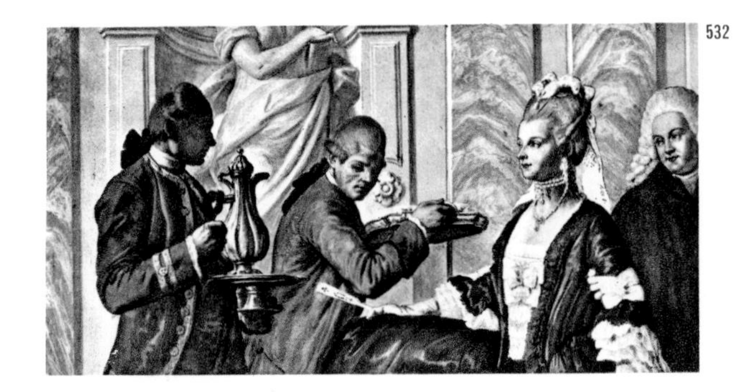

533

# Travel is easier and faster, and all tourist roads lead to Rome.

LE CHARME XIX
XLIX
L'OISEAU XXII
XLII
XLVI

535

536

Back in Paris again, we find that the Hôtel Faverolles has changed its name since we saw it last, forty years ago. The writing over the door, which is kept by a uniformed guard, now reads Hôtel de Marchainville. The Faverolles family still live here, but they have forsaken the legal profession followed by their ancestors and become part of the nobility. The Vicomte de Marchainville is colonel of a regiment and lives at court, as he is entitled to by the coat of arms that cost him a good deal of money. The Vicomte's levée is a small ceremony*. (535) His chief valet is busy curling his wig, which must then be powdered with starch. Meanwhile Madame de Marchainville pays a visit to her daughter*. (536) She wears on top of her massed curls a deep cap supposed to be an infallible guarantee of conquest, decked with ostrich plumes, called *volages*, and her silk gown in the fashionable puce colour has a fine lawn fichu. If too little heat escapes from the fire in the hearth, at least every effort has been made to conserve warmth in this cushioned apartment. There are soft carpets, screens and thick curtains; figured wallpaper has replaced the silk brocades, as these in their turn had superseded the ancient tapestries of the previous century.

The mistress of the house follows all the latest fashions except one: she refuses to breast-feed her children herself. Her new baby has been put out to nurse in the country at Auteuil, and the wet-

537

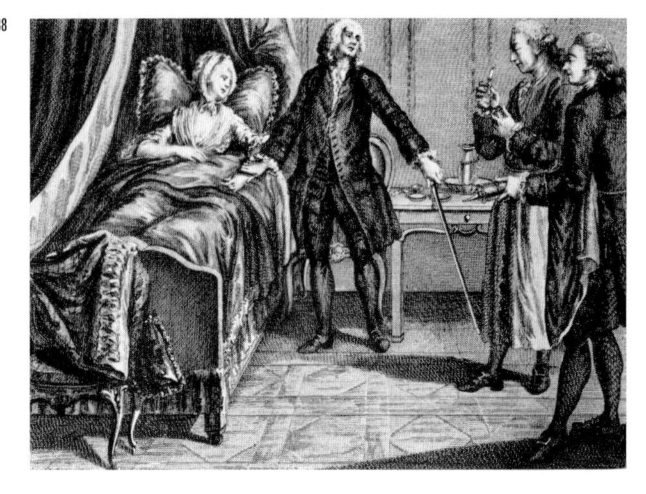

538

## Medicine becomes a science, but warm homes mean less call for the doctor.

539

541

540

542

537 nurse* is a young farmer's wife, recommended by the 'bureau for placing nurses', whose milk has first been tasted by the bureau's own doctor. There at least the child is brought up in the fresh air away from all artificial luxuries. Cleanliness is in fashion, and in the great Marchainville house there is even a 'hydraulic privy' brought at great expense from England. No sooner has someone fallen ill than the doctor and surgeon come running, ready to bleed him, and the apothecary 538 with his inevitable syringe*. Doctors have discarded their mysterious potions with their magic robes and now they are almost men of science. Rumour has it that a cure has even been discovered for the smallpox, which still claims one out of every twelve people in Europe, by inoculating the victim with the germ of a similar disease occurring in cows, which is called a vaccine. Out in the street the seller of brushes* and other petty 539 salesmen are hawking their wares, and up on the fifth floor, in the attic where they sleep—there are three big curtained beds for nine people—the seamstresses are waking up and starting to get dressed*. Shoppers are doing their marketing*, 540 541 buying cabbages and carrots from the vegetable stall, to make a stew, before going off to their day's work behind the counters in the big new shops with their tall glass windows.

Most of the people are cheerful and carefree, resigned to their lot and respecting the crown*, 543 but still in the cafés and factories, and the workshops* of the Faubourg Saint-Antoine, there is an 542 under-current of ill-feeling about the survival of medieval despotism, the extravagance of the court and the arrogance of the nobles. People are beginning to whisper that all men were created equal.

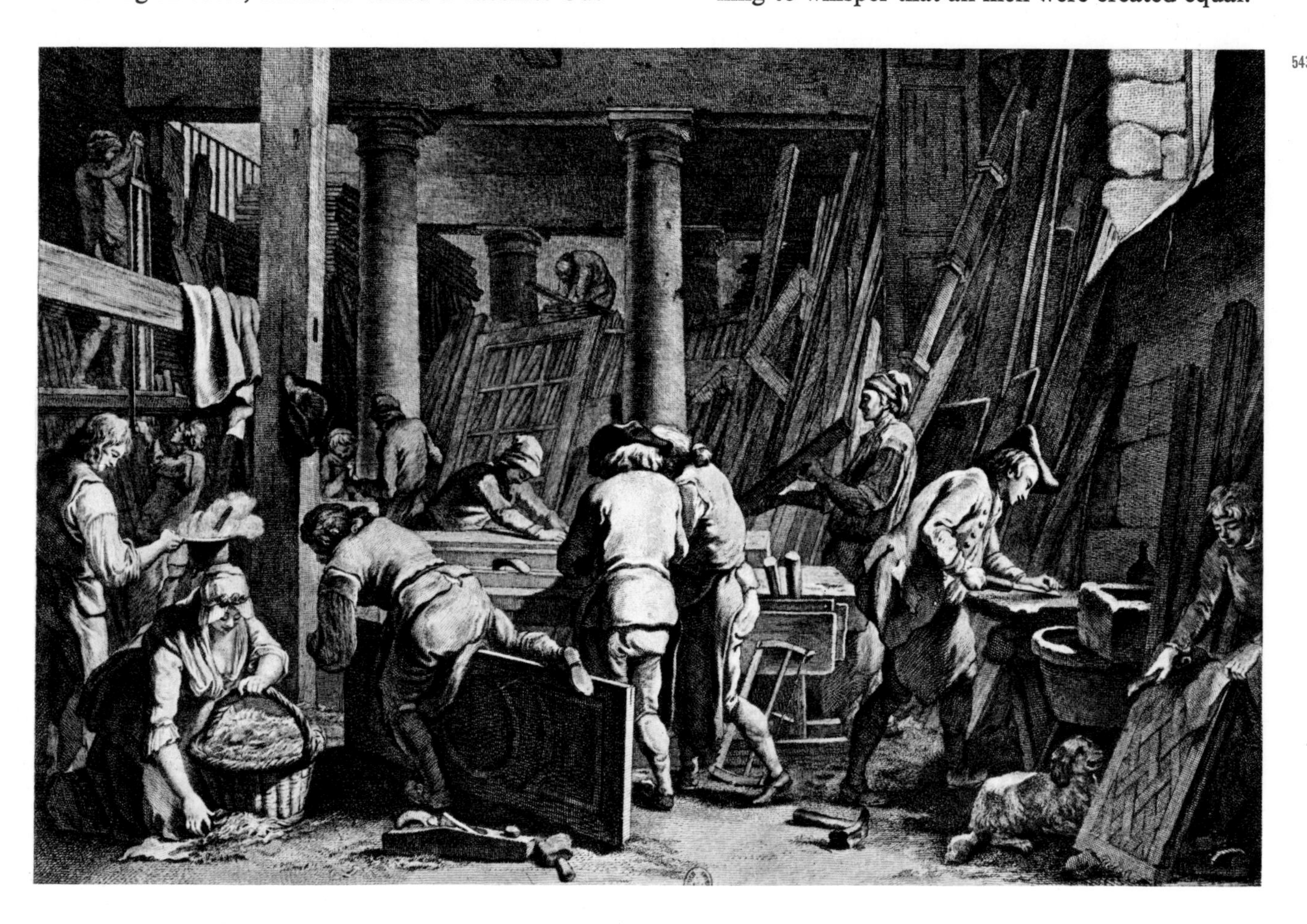

543

In the cafés and workshops revolution is already afoot.

# Half a million Red Indians in the whole of North America, bu

544

The immense spaces of North America stretching between Mexico and Alaska and from the Atlantic to the Pacific Ocean belonged to the Indians. Since the sixteenth century the white men had been encroaching more and more on this territory, and their conquests were made easier by the comparatively small number of Indians—there were probably no more than half a million in the eighteenth century—and the lack of unity among their scattered tribes, for the Indian way of life was quite different from one area to the next.

In Louisiana, in the South, the Natchee lived in villages composed of tunnel-shaped huts roofed with bark and surrounded by maize-fields and well-tended gardens*. (544) They worshipped the sun and fire; each village had its sacred fires which were never allowed to go out, and their lives revolved around the tribal dances and warlike expeditions. The Natchee were divided into two quite distinct castes: the chiefs, who were supposed to be descended from the sun himself, and the common people. The tribes on the north Pacific coast were salmon fishers, and, further north still, the Canadian forests were peopled by primitive hunters. The central prairies were the home of tribes who had learned the use of horses from the white men and spent their time in hunting bison*. (545) The Sioux and Dakota lived partly in fortified villages composed of round, thatched huts called wigwams surrounded by wooden palisades* (546) and partly, when they were on the move on the trail of bison, in portable tents made of skins stretched over a wooden framework. Inside the tent was a platform covered with a bed of skins or leaves, and when they were hunting or at war the men would sit outside smoking their long pipes, which were built into the haft of their tomahawks, between forays*. (547) The men went half-naked and their bodies were painted with symbols. Their hair was shaved back from the forehead, and on the back of their heads they wore feathers and jewels to indicate rank and prowess, and they carried their provisions, which consisted mostly of the precious pemmican—a nourishing and highly condensed food which was basically the flesh of deer or bison, dried in the sun and cut into strips —and wild berries, in leather satchels slung over their shoulders. The Indian's wife carried her baby strapped to a board which could be fastened to her back when she was working or travelling. It was her task to gather the wild rice, grasses, roots and berries which, with what game they could catch, constituted the Indians' staple diet.

When a hunting party returned to the village it was an occasion for great rejoicing, and the men painted their faces and decked themselves in their splendid head-dresses of feathers and beads*. (548)

545

## heir fight against the white man will become a legend.

546

547

548

549 This Pawnee chief* is wearing a long, fringed tunic made of buckskin with bands of bright colour on the neck and sleeves. His tight buckskin trousers have fringes too, and on his feet are soft leather moccasins. The large blankets which they flung round their shoulders were used as currency among some tribes. After the braves had danced their scalp dance round the fire, they sat and recounted their exploits in battle or on the hunting field while the pipe passed from hand to hand. The simple lives of the Indians, their sobriety and extraordinary indifference to pain and death made them worthy adversaries, and their deeds became legendary among the white men who fought them.

549

550

551

On 19th April, 1783, General Washington declared the war against England at an end. The new States, which had proclaimed their independence seven years before, were at last at peace, but their origin went back considerably further, to the day, 11th November, 1620, when the English Pilgrims, who had left their homes because of religious persecution, arrived in the *Mayflower* at Cape Cod. A year later, though decimated by fever, the Pilgrim Fathers could still give thanks to God for their first harvest, but it was with drums and muskets that they made their way* to their little wooden church. Their Indian friends, invited to the celebration, brought with them wild turkeys, maize and pumpkins, and these are still the

550

552

# The Pilgrim Fathers arrive in search of peace and religious freedom.

553

principal ingredients oi the traditional Thanksgiving dinner held on the fourth Thursday of November every year in the United States.

The daily life of these early colonists was hard and tough. They lived in plain, log cabins*, and their austere religion, stark to the point of fanaticism, made it even harder. Yet still the new immigrants came, each bringing their different customs. At New Amsterdam (now New York) the Dutch recreated their own surroundings with gabled brick houses and huge tiled stoves. Philadelphia was the centre of the Quakers who had signed an agreement of peace and friendship with the Indians*, and it was soon the largest city in the Union.

At the end of the eighteenth century there was still a striking difference between the lives of North and South. In the North were mainly agricultural people living in simple farmhouses* in settings reminiscent of northern Europe; the Southern plantations, with their great houses with pillared porticoes and white-painted wooden verandahs, created a new, and still living tradition. Inside, the carved over-mantels and elegant furniture brought from England stood side by side with the simple products of a young, local industry*. Outside, the mansion was surrounded by a crowd of offices, warehouses and wretched hovels for the negro slaves who worked in their hundreds in the cotton fields*.

554

555

## Gratitude and turkey become a national institution: Thanksgiving.

556

557

Japan, far away on the other side of the Pacific Ocean, continued to live in stubborn isolation from the rest of the world. In the sixteenth century European missionaries and traders had established themselves there, but in 1640 the Japanese expelled all Europeans.

In 1750 Europe knew almost nothing about everyday life in Japan, and all that had reached the West were a few precious ornaments, bringing a faint echo of their original home and a taste for oriental things. This is Yedo, the new capital which has since been renamed Tokyo, where beside the ancient military ruling caste of the Samurai, a flourishing commercial middle class is beginning to emerge. The house we are looking at* 556 belongs to a fan-and-screen merchant called Hanabusa-san. It is a light wooden construction, built for protection in earthquakes, with a wattle wall on one side only. On the ground floor a verandah, shaded by flimsy blinds, encircles the house; onto this open sliding walls made of wooden frames filled with transparent paper*. Inside, the 557 house is very plain. Its several bare rooms are divided by *fusuma*, movable partitions covered with decorated paper, and there are *tatami*, mats which are always the same size, on the floor*. 558 Everyone takes off their shoes before entering the house, leaving their high peg-soled wooden clogs, called *geta*, which are used in wet weather, on the threshold.

In the main room, Hanabusa-san is about to take tea, and this in itself is a complete and quite silent ceremony. Behind him is the *tokonoma*, a sort of raised alcove containing a few precious objects: a *kakemono*, a long, narrow painting on silk, and a delicate vase holding a single flower*. 559 But at the other end of the house, peace is shattered by the clatter of servants busy cleaning and

-thquake, and develops an architectural solution: paper houses.

559 560 561 562

560 polishing*. The house must always be kept spotlessly clean, and all the mats, and even the paper on the walls, are changed regularly.

The Japanese are even more scrupulous about bodily cleanliness, and every house contains a simple bathroom with a large wooden tub placed over a hearth. Everyone washes thoroughly before entering the tub, so that the bath water stays clean for the whole family to use it in turn. Hanabusa-san's wife, O-Sune-san, after she has bathed, sits in front of a little dressing-table with a cir-
561 cular mirror* to make up her face with a base of white and paint her eyebrows, and then has a servant do her hair. This is a long and complicated business, and it requires consummate artistry to place the lacquered combs and gold and silver pins
562 in exactly the right places*. For every day O-Sune-san wears a striped cotton kimono over which she ties an *obi*: a long, broad silk sash which goes round her waist and is fastened behind with a bow whose size is regulated very precisely by age and social position. From the sash hangs a *netsuke*, a painted porcelain trinket depicting a woman lacing her
563 sandal*. Under the kimono she wears an *asetori*, a sort of shift which is usually white, but red for young girls, and her feet are covered by *tabi*, cotton socks which are made with a division between the big toe and the rest of the foot to allow the strap of her sandal to pass between her toes.

In another room the children are playing. Takamura has his hair done in three pigtails, which is the fashion for little boys. He is riding his
564 hobby horse*, but his elder brother, Saito, is already learning to write, using a bamboo brush to copy the example his teacher has set him. Kiku, in her pretty flowered kimono, is playing quietly with her dolls, which are dressed in the ceremonial robes of the ancient court.

558

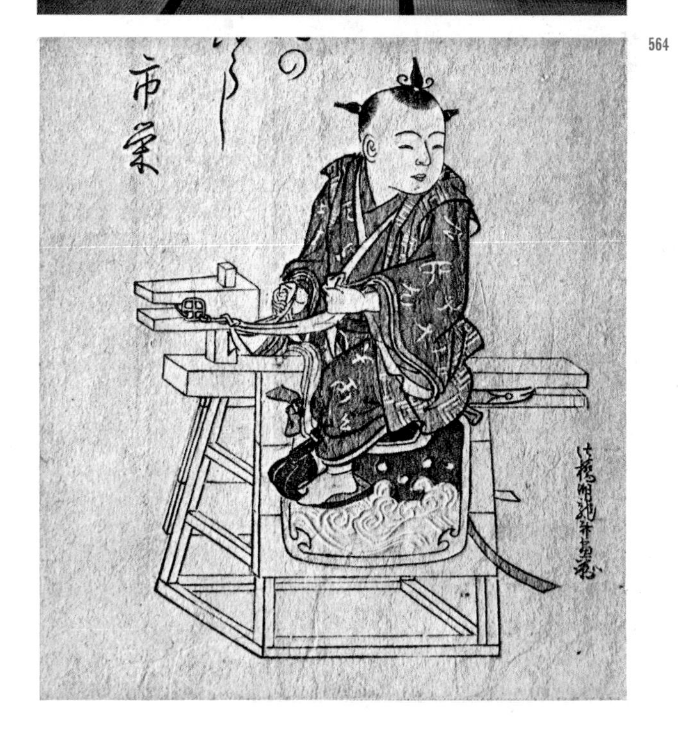

564

563

# The Geisha: a dream woman with all the talents, who can dance, sin

565

566

568

567

In the street, Kagi, the travelling salesman, is crying his wares, and women are coming out from their houses to buy his fresh noodles*. 565 The lovely O-Haru-san is in a hurry to go somewhere, tripping along in her wooden *geta* with a lantern in one hand and her parasol in the other*. 566 Her name means Mrs Spring, and she is probably on her way to some romantic assignation, for O-Haru-san is a geisha. Like all geishas she lives in the Yoshiwara on the outskirts of Yedo, the centre of the Ukiyo (the floating world), with its transient pleasures. Here are the theatres, restaurants, baths, and tea-houses.

These are patronised largely by the *chonin*, the wealthy merchants who, although they pay outward respect to the Samurai, are the real masters of the country; also by the sons of great families sowing their wild oats, and by a few Samurai whose numbers are increasing despite their adherence to the stern old moral code of Bushido (the way of the warrior).

Behind wooden grilles one can catch a glimpse of the *djyoro*, with their white-painted faces and red lips*. 567 In the great salon, while a storm rages outside, the *djyoro* are yawning with boredom, some of them picking at a bowl of crabs and one smoking a tiny metal pipe with a bamboo stem*. 568 Another is singing a high plaintive song and accompanying herself on the *samisen*, a three-string guitar. But the geishas are quite different people from these. They are in fact real artists and

573

569 571 570

they grace the tables of rich merchants with their dancing, singing, intelligent conversation and innumerable other talents. Theirs is a highly respectable profession, and they frequently end their careers with excellent marriages.

O-Haru-san is hardly home before she is out again, this time in a *kuruma*, a rickshaw drawn by a porter, to dine with her protector who is none other than the screen merchant, Hanabusa-san. After dinner she will display her skill as a dancer*. O-Haru-san entered the Yoshiwara at the age of seven on the death of her father. There she studied all the things a geisha must know, under a retired geisha for whom she worked until she had paid back the expenses of her training. Now she can sing, dance, play the *samisen* and the *koto* (a horizontal harp with ten strings), serve tea and make bouquets according to the rules, embroider and even write verse.

Also in the Yoshiwara are the theatres*. This is where the popular *kabuki** and the ancient *no* plays, a hieratic form of drama which is especially appreciated by the war lords, are performed. The puppet theatre is also in its heyday, and plays, called *joruri**, are written for the puppets by the best writers. The palace of the *shogun* differed little from the homes of ordinary citizens. It was built of precious woods and its many rooms opened onto spacious courtyards, but the same simplicity ruled everywhere*.

572

574 575

Towards the end of the eighteenth century, navigators sailed all over the world on long voyages, and once their mutual distrust was over they discovered that the savages they met were men like any others, and that their simple lives might even be better than the artificialities of civilisation. The memoirs of these explorers were read eagerly, and one of the most popular writers was an Englishman, James Cook, who had sailed round the world.

In 1769 Cook discovered two large islands, not far from the continent of Australia. They were given the name of New Zealand, and Cook was so charmed by the natives' beauty and gentleness that he returned there several times. Each time the outrigger canoes, laden with exotic fruit, came out to greet his ship, and the rest of the tribe waited among the tall coconut palms on the shore, drawn up in front of the council house*. This was a hut much larger than the rest, built like them of a wooden framework filled in with cane leaves. It was adorned with fine sculpture and on the roof-ridge stood a carved beam like a totem. Here the chiefs of the tribe met to discuss important affairs. The village itself stood further inland on the edge of a fast-flowing stream* with its groups of huts, called *whare*, and its education house, where the chiefs' sons learned orally from the *tohunga* (priest) the traditions, history, songs and legends of the tribe. The natives were mostly naked but were covered, sometimes over their whole face and body, with delicate and intricately tattooed patterns*. Acquiring this *moka*, or complete tattoo, was a very painful process, but they endured it bravely for it was an unmistakable sign of beauty among them. On some islands the people made a sort of garment out of prepared bark, called *tapa*, but the natives of Aotearoa (New Zealand) wore

576

577

ɔefore long, will be praising the freedom and dignity of the 'noble savage'.

578

grass skirts, wraps made of flax and kiwi feathers. In the twilight the men executed their *haka*, or war dance, as a sign of welcome to the travellers, and afterwards graceful young girls with flowers in their hair swayed to the motions of the *poi**. Afterwards the hospitable Maoris led the English sailors to a hut mounted on piles, in front of which was the giant, tattooed image of an ancestor. Here several families lived, sleeping on mats at night*. In the centre of the hut a dog was roasting on a stone hearth, for this, served with sweet potatoes and fern roots, was a favourite dish with the Maoris. There was a first course of sea-fish and sea-birds' eggs served on plates of woven green flax.

577

578

The next day, Cook and his companions witnessed a funeral and made an attempt to draw what they saw*. The body, daubed with red ochre, was carried solemnly to the sacred enclosure to the beating of drums, and laid out on a covered ledge or buried under a light covering of earth. Later the skeleton would be cleaned and the skull, or even the mummified head, carefully preserved. Cannibalism was still common in these islands, and the warriors ate the remains of conquered enemies in order to incorporate their victims' prowess into themselves. But with the exception of tribal wars leading to occasional war-sallies that were rarely very bloody, life in New Zealand was carefree and peaceful, and most of the people's needs were supplied from the earth or the sea.

579

It was for this reason that philosophers at the end of the eighteenth century held up the 'noble savage' as an example to their contemporaries. A veritable child of nature, upright, sincere and ignorant of all social distinctions, he was not, like civilised man, a slave who must constantly try to free himself from his bonds.

579

# Liberty. Equality. Fraternity. A new Republic is born and introduc

580

For twenty-six years, from 1789 to 1815, the eyes of Europe were turned towards France, where one society was dissolving as they watched and being replaced by a totally new one, based on the belief in Liberty, Equality and Fraternity. The years of the Revolution, with their many innovations, transformed the lives of everyone in the land, but progress in everyday life was brought about gradually; it came from evolution, not revolution, and as soon as life returned to normal, people were only too thankful to forget all that had happened. It was decided in the Assembly and in the clubs and cafés*, which were the centre of the new thought and where everybody was busy clamouring for reform, that the words Monsieur and Madame should be abolished and the terms Citizen and Citizeness used instead; that the familiar form of address, previously used only to inferiors or to one's family and most intimate friends, should be compulsory; and that a new era should commence, marked by the year One of the Republic. The year was to have only ten months of thirty days each, and Sundays and all religious festivals were abolished and replaced by patriotic holidays.

Reforms which might have proved more lasting were primary schools and free, compulsory education—but this lasted no more than a year—civil marriage and divorce, which did not outlast the Revolution, and the freedom of the Press which unleashed the enthusiasm of a crowd of patriots* all dressed fashionably in red and white striped breeches. This fashion too was soon to be a dead letter. In the upheaval, periwigs, paniers and all the frills and fancies of fashion went by the board and pantaloons began to carry the day over knee-breeches. But the armies of the tyrants were gathering along the frontiers and the young patriots sprang to the defence of the new Republic. A certain Doctor Guillotin, seen here with his family trying on his new uniform as a member of the *Garde Française**, recommended the use of a new invention from Italy for dealing with enemies within the Republic. It was a much swifter and more efficient means of execution than the axe.

581 582

vil marriage and compulsory education. But the reforms die young.

583

In 1793 another new measure turned French life upside down. This was the introduction of conscription, making national service compulsory. Wars had hitherto been fought by professional soldiers under the command of the nobility, but from now on almost the entire available manpower of France was in arms—and remained so for more than twenty years until the fall of Napoleon. Yet while the Napoleonic armies were spreading over the whole continent of Europe some ease and comfort began to return to the middle classes.

After the extravagances of the *Incroyables* and the *Merveilleuses*, fashionable people began to adopt the neat, almost severe English style of dress*. (583) This young man who has come to meet his pretty cousin from the stage-coach is wearing a tight-fitting coat in cinnamon colour with a high collar that rises above his intricately folded white cravat. His close-fitting nankeen breeches are tucked into the tops of his elegant riding-boots, and a cane and a curly brimmed beaver hat complete his outfit. The girl's dress is made of cambric, high-waisted, low-cut, and falling in straight, graceful lines. Her face is shaded by a bonnet made of the same material as her dress.

In 1805 the unprecedented measure of numbering houses was adopted, with odd numbers on one side of the street and even on the other, and proved extremely unpopular. The former great houses were now let out as apartments which, with their smaller rooms and lower ceilings, were much easier to keep warm. There was a large tiled hall, used as a dining-room, opening onto a sitting-room with mahogany furniture inlaid with bronze, in which the most impressive piece was the fine Erard pianoforte. Here the family gathered*: (584) father doing accounts at his desk, and mother playing with the children, who were at last beginning to be dressed in simple, practical clothes. Several interconnecting rooms gave onto the sitting-room, and there was even a bathroom, though its uses were varied. Social life was quieter than it used to be, although the theatre was enjoying a revival with artists such as Talma and Madame Georges, but contemporary plays were dreadful in the main. One might be invited to the Tuileries for one of the sumptuous but frigid official receptions*, which were organised (585) with almost military precision. French troops were at Leipzig, but in Paris people grumbled at the black bread and preferred cane sugar to the newly manufactured beet sugar. There were too many dead, too many war-wounded, and the country was tired of it. Then one fine day in 1814 there were cossacks bivouacked on the Champs Elysées and English and Prussian infantry buying a cup of cocoa* from an itinerant vendor. (586)

584

585

586

# In Germany students drink, dance and fight—and frighten their neighbours.

587

In Germany, the French invasion had at first been welcomed with open arms by all progressive and reforming spirits, but it soon revealed itself as a burden that roused a hitherto non-existent nationalism among the Germans. Students found in it a permanent excuse for rioting, and in the small university towns they took great delight in scaring the townsfolk by spectacular ceremonies which involved dressing up in military uniforms—a coloured cap, black tunic with a belt and sash—and plunging their swords into the fire swearing to defend their honour together*. But the scars 587

588

589

disfiguring their cheeks were not to be taken too seriously, for the *Mensur*, in which they acquired them, was only the caricature of duelling and the students, more rowdy than dangerous, had other outlets for their high spirits, including drinking parties where, at the command *Salamander reiben*, all beat their quart tankards three times on the table and then emptied them in three gulps. Here they are seen dancing in a beer garden among the drinkers who sit puffing on their long china pipes*. 588

590

During the vacations they strapped their knapsacks to their backs and set off on long tramps through the Black Forest or the Bavarian Alps, sketching and sightseeing*. On these occasions the great problem was to find somewhere to stay, for comfortable inns like the *Gros Coq* at Schopfheim were rare, dear and usually full. In other places one sometimes had to take one's own mattress; the rooms were minute, often had to be shared, and were more often than not dirty as well. The furniture was no more than a bed, a table and a few hooks on the wall for hanging clothes. In the main room, festooned with hams and sausages, a cauldron of coffee for the evening meal, which often consisted of plain bread and butter and nothing else, simmered on the fire. Yet, despite the discomfort, the bad roads and many accidents which they caused—broken axles, wheels sunk in the mud, arguments with postillions and innkeepers—Germany was a popular country for travellers.

589

Some went as far afield as Italy, but many looked for romantic landscapes in their own country. The Rhine and Main valleys were most popular with their picturesque bridges, old churches and medieval castles perched on the cliff tops*. Antiquities were fashionable, and the Germans rejected French taste and looked instead for the Gothic or even invented it for themselves. There were Renaissance town halls and Gothic churches built, and inside, everything was in the troubadour style, with stained-glass windows, oak chests, carved chairs and antique ewers and tankards. Even people's clothes began to reflect their passion for the archaic. Men wore doublets and ladies Medici collars, purses and chatelaines, but the fashion was almost entirely a fad of snobs and intellectuals. Among the nobility of the petty German courts the older people had retained almost intact the formality of the late eighteenth century. Old ladies were very dignified in lawn caps with lace frills round their faces*, and the younger generation on the whole preferred to follow English or French fashions.

590

591

591

Hallmark of the Romantic is a studied archaism.

# Travellers, following the sun, come upon the matadors and flamen

592

The Germans were not alone in their passion for travel. French and English, too, took to the roads in their post-chaises and barouches. And, as if they had some advance warning that with the coming of the railways a kind of uniformity would begin to spread everywhere and the picturesque vanish for ever, people set off in all directions. Some were drawn to Spain in the summer, and would stop to witness a bull-fight in some little Castilian town. Every vehicle in the neighbourhood was there, and before the *corrida** they paraded with the country- (592) women in their flowing dresses, frills and heavy gold bangles, sitting proudly in them. Then silence fell, the matadors entered the arena in a dazzling file, and the crowd acclaimed the first one to brave the bull*. Whenever possible, travellers went as (593) far south as Andalusia, where everything seemed to take on new richness of colour under the burning sun, and life was at the same time stark and sensuous. At Seville, all the men wore embroidered costumes, like toreadors, and odd, varnished conical hats with pom-poms. This girl with her street-stall and little pottery stove* has her hair (594) dressed like a great lady with a tall comb and kiss curls. Late at night the harsh voices of the flamenco singers echo down the *calles*.

594

596

But the great moment at Seville, even to this day, is Holy Week, when for days on end the streets are thronged with processions carrying the *pasos*, moving and impressive pieces of statuary decorated with flowers and lighted by torches or candles, which it takes several men to support. They advance very slowly, followed by a concourse of penitents and religious in long cloaks and tall hoods of different colours.

Not long after Holy Week is the *feria*, when the town is alive with cavaliers in Andalusian national dress and ladies in black mantillas, and there is singing and dancing and the click of castanets* on all sides among the throng of carriages and gaily harnessed horses. On the road again one meets the muleteers with their daggers and long firearms* taking their merchandise across the mountains,

595 596

593

597 598

for once away from the town the roads are very far from safe.

Italy too has her admirers who travel as far south as the Bay of Naples, to Capri and Ischia, despite the terrible reputation of Calabrian bandits with their heavy blunderbusses. But there is a special delight in the light sparkling wine when it is drunk under the trellis of an inn, watching the villages playing *mora**; and spaghetti, eaten with the fingers and held high above the head so that it drops into one's mouth, is a dish fit for a king when it is bought from a street-stall, to be eaten while it is hot, there and then*.

597 598

595

600

601

602

599

The countries in which German is the native language—Germany, Austria, and German-speaking Switzerland—have a folklore entirely their own. On the occasion of local festivals in the Tyrol, the young mountaineers, dressed in *lederhosen*—leather shorts and braces—and green felt hats with an edelweiss flower stuck in the band, 599 dance and yodel until the valleys ring*. In Switzerland, in the Bernese Oberland and Emmenthal the women wear full, dark skirts, with red borders, black silk or velvet bodices and long silver chains hanging to their waists. The peasant girls in the great wooden farmhouses on hillsides in the Black Forest wear tall, grey hats with long ribbons, and 600 the men a dress which was common in Alsace* until quite recent years. In the Grand Duchy of Baden the halo head-dresses, the long embroidered aprons and slashed breeches have remained un- 601 altered since the sixteenth century*. Even in a town such as Augsburg the townswomen have 602 adhered to their lace coifs and fichus*. Everything has the same old-fashioned simplicity. The dowry of a young peasant woman is made up not of money but of a bed, a cupboard, a cradle, a clock and household utensils, a spinning wheel and distaff. On winter evenings everyone takes turns in telling stories whose origins are as old as the hills. Old customs are carefully kept up; in Roman Catholic districts the Corpus Christi procession brings the whole village together, and the old pagan festivals, more or less christianised, like the traditional hobby horses and the Fires of St John's Eve, as well as the colourful rejoicings at harvest time and when the grapes are gathered, break the routine of peasant life.

Every family occasion has a patriarchal solemnity. This betrothed couple in a German village join their hands in front of the pastor*. The man wears 603 modern fashions, but the girl, like her sisters, clings to the traditional provincial costume: a long, pleated apron, a complicated head-dress of flowers and curly feathers, and on her bodice numerous necklaces and chains with a portrait of her fiancé prominently displayed in the centre.

## Not money but household utensils go to make the Tyrolese girl's dowry.



603 →

604 605

Brittany was the place where links with the past were perhaps strongest. The granite buildings, half-hidden in a clump of elms or hoary old oak trees, where the Bretons lived with their animals, contained only a single room*. The deep hearth was both the kitchen and the only refuge from the cold and draughts; one or two rough wooden shelves on the walls held some dishes and bowls in crude pottery, large painted cider jugs and a row of distaffs, ready for spinning, to make wool. Sliding shutters in the wall, with cunning fretwork rosettes for ventilation, concealed the family's beds, which were bunks placed one above the other. The large board on which the housewife kneaded the dough served both as a seat and a table, and barrels containing the store of cider lay on the floor which was simply earth, trampled hard. The roof was nothing more substantial than bundles of brushwood resting on beams, from which hung a collection of hams and baskets of cheeses and chestnuts. The cows, pigs and horses occupied the far end of the room, which was spread with bracken; they were separated from the human beings only by hurdles.

In the remoter districts local costumes persisted almost unchanged up to the 1914 war. The men* still wear the old-fashioned breeches, gaiters fastened by horn buttons, short, blue, cloth jackets, embroidered waistcoats and wide-brimmed, round hats whose black velvet bands are clasped with a silver buckle. It was at weddings that the finest costumes were to be seen. The bridal procession would make its way round the neighbourhood preceded by men playing fiddles or the Breton bagpipes*. Breton was the common language throughout the region, and there were traditional oaths of great antiquity, which were used to conclude any kind of bargain*.

606

607

# ocal customs, dress and folklore preserve the character of different regions.

608

610

These variations of local custom lent an added interest to travelling; they also did much towards compensating for the strain and weariness of the journey. Food, clothing and customs differed enormously from one place to the next. In Denmark, when couples went to church on Sunday, the wife rode pillion behind her husband*. (608) He smoked his long china pipe as they rode, and she wore her best clothes: a short, green jacket and yellow bodice with an odd little hat that hung down low at the back of the neck. A veil covered her mouth. The living-room of a Swedish farmhouse* (609) contained locally made tapestries with primitive pictures depicting biblical stories, coloured pottery and beer-mugs like animals, as well as ladles, spoons and salt-cellars all made of wood with finely chiselled decorations. Dutch sailors* (610) still clung to their wide trousers, which dated from the sixteenth century.

Poland, much of which was under Russian domination and was to remain so until the twentieth century, was still a feudal country. The people regarded hospitality as their first duty, and when the peasants went to the fields in the morning they left their cottages unbolted, so that passing travellers could stop and help themselves to the black bread, honey and vodka which were set out on the table for them. On holidays, the peasants would dance the *cracoviak* or the *mazurka* while the village fiddler played for them. Pedlars travelled from one farm to another selling illustrated almanacs, and itinerant tailors visited the houses, staying a few days in each and making new suits of clothes for the whole family. The stuff they used was usually woven from the wool of the farmer's own sheep. Another feature of the countryside was the travelling maker of sieves with his frogged overcoat, top hat and big, balloon-like pack*. (611)

609

611

# In Russia, rivers are blessed and fairs held on the ice.

612

We pass to Saint Petersburg during the winter of 1841. The thermometer reads twenty below zero, and the horses drawing the sledges and troikas are blowing out puffs of steam from their nostrils into the frosty air. In one of the suburbs of the city there is a strange scene of activity. Dead animals are lying in rigid heaps, and among them are a busy crowd of men in caftans and heavy 612 boots. This is the frozen meat market*, where the carcases of animals that have frozen to death in the intense cold are sold off very cheaply. As we make our way towards the river we pass a grim procession of about a hundred men, advancing slowly and painfully with iron chains round their legs, hemmed in by soldiers. They are a convoy of criminals, sentenced to deportation, on the first stage of the long journey whose goal, for those who survive it, is Siberia and exile. Russia abolished the death penalty in 1753, the first country to do so and much in advance of her time. In its place deportation became the supreme punishment, and although flogging was still common for less serious crimes, the use of the knout had been forbidden by Nicholas I.

At this moment, from a balcony in the Hermitage palace on the banks of the Neva, the Tsar is watching the picturesque ceremony of blessing the waters, which takes place on 6th January each year. A procession of priests with banners at its head advances towards a little pavilion built on the river itself*. There, among the sacred icons, a 613 bishop celebrates mass before a vast congregation, and then, while bells start ringing and the choir chants, he hurls a cross into a large hole in the ice.

614

613

615

# Lifelong exile in Siberia replaces the death penalty.

Some distance away, though still on the river, tall switchbacks rise above the skaters and sledges, and dozens of young people are rushing gaily down 614 their slopes*. Everywhere there are stalls selling nuts, hot *blinis* with cream, and fish pies. There are men with performing monkeys, others with *charmankas* (barrel organs), others reciting the old epic ballads, and all of them competing to attract the attention of the crowds. Today is a public 615 holiday, so the *traktirs*, where the coachmen* meet, are doing a roaring trade. Sitting in his smart barouche rattling through the streets of Saint 616 Petersburg is a young dandy with a monocle* whose name is Vassily Porphyrianovitch Zubin. He is dressed up to the nines and has nothing but contempt for all these common amusements. Like most of the high society of Saint Petersburg, he

616

617

pretends to speak no language but French and lives off the revenues of his estates, where he has several hundred serfs working for him. But today is his wedding day, and he is being married in the 617 traditional Russian way*. He is dressed in the old fashion with a gold crown, which a page boy has been holding above his head since the beginning of the service. Vassily stands in front of the *pope* and exchanges rings and kisses with his betrothed, then takes a cup of wine from the priest's hands, from which the couple drink three times in turn. After the ceremony there is a banquet for all the guests which includes all the specialities of Russian cooking. There are *zakouski* (*hors d'œuvre*), caviar, cucumber, little meat pies, sucking-pig with horse-radish, pullets, sturgeon from the Volga done in *zoubrovka* (an aromatic vodka) and, of course, the best French champagne, but this is served iced in the Russian manner.

618

Not long after his marriage Vassily Porphyrianovitch has to pay a visit to his estates, which are not far from Saint Petersburg, and he takes two friends along with him on the journey. They often make an excuse to stop and ask the way from young peasant girls, for they all look very pretty in their gay, coloured dresses called *sarafanes*, which are cut away at the neck and sleeves to show an embroidered blouse, in their flowered aprons and *kakochniks*, a red and blue diadem with glittering glass jewels*. At night the gentlemen have to break their journey at one of the posting stations, which serve as hotels. This is a big, rickety wooden building* with carved beams whose style of decoration has remained the same over hundreds of years.

At last the three young men reach their destination: a house with a pillared portico and a mass of red creeper covering its walls. Round it is a large garden running into a birch wood in the distance. Vassily's nurse runs the household and controls the army of serfs who complete the domestic staff. The reason for Vassily's journey is that Nastasia Fedorovna, his agent's daughter, is getting married. A wedding in the country means all kinds of formalities that are quite unknown in the city.

A few months earlier Nastasia's father, Fedor Ivanovitch, received a visit from the professional matchmaker (called the *svakha*) of the village. She came to propose an alliance with the Semenov family. The steaming samovar was brought into the room, and while the old woman drank her tea out of her saucer, they spent a long time discussing the conditions of the marriage. Nastasia was not told about the proposal until after the *svakha* had left the house, but the idea did not displease her, and ever since then she and her friends

619

Travelling is far from luxurious, but marriages mean wedding feas

had been busy sewing her trousseau, singing as they worked. Sometimes Mitrophane Sergeievitch came to his fiancée's house with its painted shutters* to spend the evening. The *dievitchnik*, the eve of the wedding, was traditionally a melancholy occasion. Nastasia was really as happy as a queen, but all the same she cried and moaned, as she was expected to do, while her mother took off the young girl's head-dress with its streamers of ribbon, called a *krasnaia krassota*. Next morning, after they had been blessed by her father with the family icon, the young couple went to the church with its onion-shaped bell-tower that glittered brightly in the sunshine; and then home to the big wooden house, where her new family were ready to greet the girl with teasing jokes*. This, however, did not worry Nastasia in the slightest, for she knew very well it was only the custom. Everybody, including the priest and the fine gentlemen from Saint Petersburg, sat down to a banquet which would continue more or less without a break for several days. In the intervals of eating, the

620

621

624

622

623

625

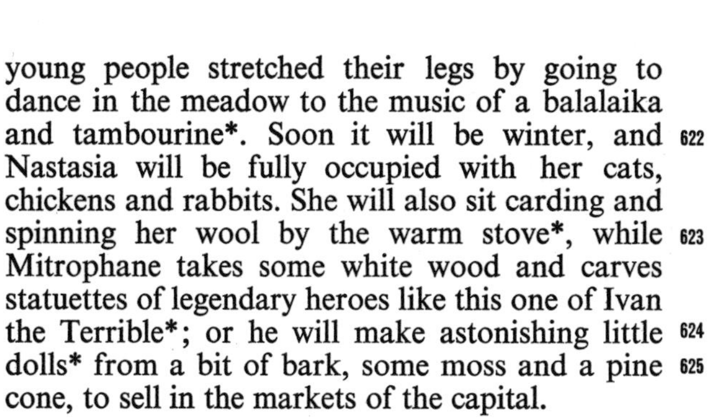

young people stretched their legs by going to dance in the meadow to the music of a balalaika and tambourine*. Soon it will be winter, and Nastasia will be fully occupied with her cats, chickens and rabbits. She will also sit carding and spinning her wool by the warm stove*, while Mitrophane takes some white wood and carves statuettes of legendary heroes like this one of Ivan the Terrible*; or he will make astonishing little dolls* from a bit of bark, some moss and a pine cone, to sell in the markets of the capital.

at go on for days with songs and dancing to the balalaika.

# Paris—1845: comfort and squalor rub shoulders.

626

627

Paris. 20th April, 1845

My dear Alfred,

Are you familiar with the houses built by our dear prefect, M. Rambuteau, two years ago and called after him? Nothing, I assure you, could be more fashionable and modern. A few months ago my cousins, the Ratinois—you know Jules Ratinois, the confectioner, who retired just recently—moved into a splendid new apartment building there* which has been built as an investment. To reach this temple dedicated to what the English call 'comfort' one has to negotiate a thoroughfare which is almost too broad—a seething mass of all kinds of traffic, from tilburies and gigs to drays and stage-coaches. You must have seen the powerful gas-jets which make the street almost as bright as day. What a contrast to my own wretched district, where there are still those terrible oil lanterns! Anyway, this is the building. A neat widow lives on the ground floor. She is never parted from her broom and keeps the place spick and span. My cousin lives on the first floor, and when we tiptoed very quietly into the elegant salon we found Monsieur and Madame waiting to receive their guests, and waiting with some impatience, if the truth be told, for it was already half-past five and dinner was ready. But my dear Alfred, consider the astonishing luxury and good taste of the apartment. The curtains hang in heavy folds of yellow velvet; there are soft carpets, graceful candelabra, and as if all this were not enough, you should see my cousin Julie's bathroom. There is even a bath-tub, fitted with an extraordinary contraption producing hot water.

626

628

# Trains are running, but impossibly fast. How can one enjoy the countryside?

We stole a look at the rest of the house. A respectable young couple called Dupont live on the second floor. Besides the husband and wife there are three children and the old mother. It was a peaceful scene, plain and homely; the little family had just finished dinner. M. Dupont had put on his frogged smoking jacket, tied with a silk girdle, and his velvet cap, and pushed his feet into his slippers embroidered by his wife. The grandmother was dozing over *the Constitutional*, but in a moment they planned to wake her up to suggest lime tea and the inevitable game of lotto. In the kitchen Marie, the cook, and Juliette, the maid, were spending the evening in their own way mend-
627 ing the children's clothes*. We continued our climb.

631

632

629

Further up, the picture was rather grimmer; we saw a bare room—everything in it had been pawned long ago and it was often full of angry creditors. It belongs to a journalist, and he is always in debt. The couple next door have little money, but they at least can afford to feed their dog.

On the fourth floor things could scarcely be worse. The tenants are penniless artists; a pathetic down-and-out on a straw mattress, and an unemployed worker and his family. But to return to the Ratinois: they are charming people with hearts of gold. They have no children of their own, so every year they give presents to their five nephews
628 and nieces*. Giving presents really is becoming more and more difficult these days. A little while ago I went into a sweet-shop* and they offered me 629 'medicinal salep chocolate' or 'anti-spasmodic orange flower chocolate'. I'm quite sure you have no such nonsense at Angoulême. Of course you haven't the *Bal Mabille* or the Musard concerts either*. I wonder if you have even heard of them? 630 The first is a company of ravishing little dancers, and at the second you can sit at a table and order ratafia or something while you spend the whole evening listening to ballads and patriotic songs. As for the theatre I would advise you to keep away from the 'Ambigu Comique', where there was such a crowd* trying to get seats the other day 631 that the police had to intervene.

630

You asked me whether I was coming to Angoulême soon; the answer is as soon as the railway* extends as far as that. That will be some 632 time, I think, because people are beginning to have second thoughts about this terrifying invention. Eleven miles an hour! It's madness! One can't see the countryside at all. Give Léontine a kiss from your affectionate friend,

Victor

633 →

# Big department stores have something for everybody—at a price.

634

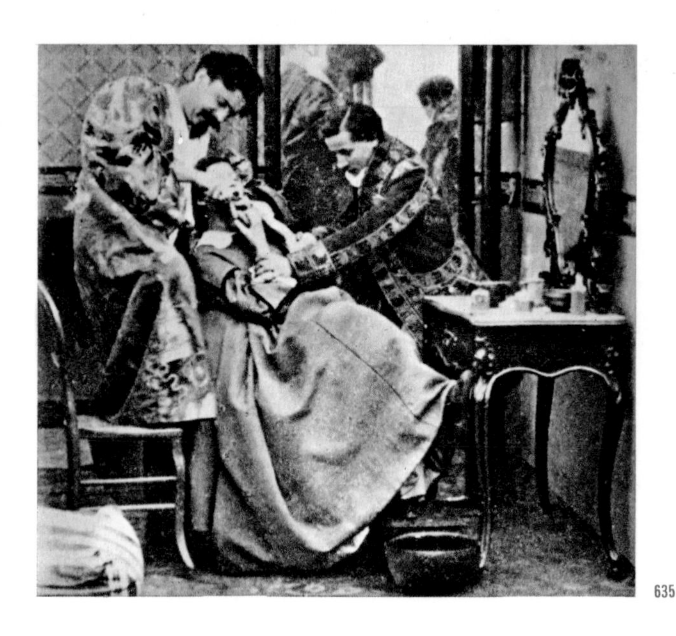
635

Paris. 6th June, 1854

My dear Alfred,

What's new in Paris? Well, the big stores to begin with. Eugénie dragged me round them for the first time in my life, and I found it exhausting but quite astonishing. We began at the Belle Jardinière, then we went to the Louvre and from there to the Magasins de la Chaussée d'Antin*. 633 Do you know, there is absolutely nothing they don't stock? There are eggs and books and shoes and saucepans, and we all bought ourselves new clothes from top to toe. I got a bottle-green frock-coat with a very tight waist, a white satin waistcoat, beige nankeen pantaloons, two stiff shirts, two pair of long drawers, an opera hat and patent-leather boots. In no time at all Eugénie was into a dashing new crinoline with a fine cashmere shawl and a little pink *crêpe* bonnet. We ran to earth some charming pantalettes with lace frills for Sophie and a big flowered straw hat*. 634 We looked so smart that we simply had to have our portraits taken by the Daguerreotype, although poor Eugénie still had rather a swelling in one cheek from having a tooth out. It had taken the combined efforts of two men to extract it*, 635 and it was partly as a reward for her bravery that I had suggested this visit to the shops. To make a day of it we had lunch in a restaurant first. We had soup, roast beef and peas, strawberries and cream and a whole bottle of wine, for 3 francs 95 per head. Of course the room was a trifle crowded and the service could perhaps have been improved*. 636

Write and tell me the latest news from Angoulême. Kiss Léontine and the children for me.

Your affectionate,

Victor

636

637

638

639

The United States in 1860 still seemed very provincial by comparison with Europe. Most Americans lived in the country, and the only city of any great size was New York, which, with a population of eight hundred thousand, was the third largest in the world. Yet it was still without any public drainage system. In summer New Yorkers migrated to Saratoga, a fashionable watering-place which, though eminently respectable, was not the most amusing place to stay. Young ladies wore crinolines and no make-up, carried parasols and never went out unaccompanied*. 637

Their mothers kept a strict eye on all their reading, and men surrounded them with respectful attentions, not even daring to utter their names in public. Most of the architecture of Saratoga was in the Palladian style, particularly favoured also in the South, with pediments and colonnaded balconies, but a movement in favour of neo-Gothic was beginning to gain ground, and there were occasional Swiss chalets, Norman manor houses and Florentine villas bearing witness to their owners' European travels. Most houses boasted a porch with climbing plants where the family sat in the evenings*. 638 Visitors were invariably amazed at the variety of American food. For breakfast, besides 'oatmeal' and eggs, there was meat, sausages, potatoes, cheese and pancakes with maple syrup. The two other meals of the day included different kinds of soup, hot leg of mutton or ham, poultry, puddings and tarts. After supper, which was generally eaten at about five or six o'clock, the grown-ups relaxed and watched the children playing. Everyone went to bed early. All reasonably prosperous households were well provided with servants, but nowhere were they as numerous as in the South, where a proportion of the Negro slaves were taken into domestic service. Their lot was much happier than that of the majority of slaves who were auctioned off like animals*. 639 They were half-starved, worked to death, sometimes for as long as eighteen hours a day, and totally at their owner's mercy. But slowly their condition began to arouse public

America has one great city—New York—and a great man, whose pl

640

641

642 643

opinion. One of the greatest contributions to their cause was the publication of *Uncle Tom's Cabin* in 1852.

However, this feudal society was almost entirely confined to the South. In other parts of America innovations were being made which in time were to revolutionise the American way of life. The McCormick harvester was already in use on some farms; factories began to use production lines, vulcanisation of rubber was discovered, and the success of the sewing-machine and the mechanical lift showed that this new era of machines would affect every aspect of daily life.

In 1859 the first oil well was bored in Pennsylvania. America was a growing country. Pioneers took the trails to the West in trains of covered wagons, heading for a new home in the virgin lands. This movement westwards received a great impetus with the discovery of gold in California. The gold rush was on. People swarmed to try their fortunes, from all over Europe as well as from inside America, and the city of Sacramento grew to become a crowded hell of speculation, gambling* and, for those who had staked everything and found nothing, abject poverty. (640) Meanwhile railways were being built, metal roads that would one day link together even the most isolated cities of America. Already the half-completed transcontinental line crossed the prairies where the first cowboys* were making their homes. (641)

At this time politics, which had hitherto been a matter for only a few, began to enter the lives of every citizen. Even local elections caused an uproar*, and henceforth the campaigns of presidential candidates would involve all the paraphernalia of banners, posters, gargantuan dinners and enormous public meetings. (642) In 1860 a single man, Abraham Lincoln, roused public opinion to a fury by preaching the abolition of slavery* and the end of the partition between slave-owning and anti-slavery states. (643) Within a few months of Lincoln's election as President, the Southern states seceded from the Union and America was plunged into a civil war that was to last for four years.

## abolish slavery leads to civil war between the North and South.

Benares, 1877. A wretched crowd of people huddle on the broad stone steps that descend in a gradual slope to the river Ganges*. A family is cooking *chapatis*, thin pancakes of unleavened bread, over a small fire of dried cow dung; old men sit on the ground talking and others are asleep on a bundle of rags. They are pilgrims who have travelled immense distances to see the Ganges and bathe in its sacred waters. On a terrace there are the remains of burnt-out fires where bodies are cremated so that the ashes can be thrown in the river. Further off, the wooden verandahs of the leper-houses give directly onto the road. A few thin white cows amble slowly through the crowd, looking for food among the rubbish. No one lays hands on them, for the cows are sacred animals. Hindus eat no meat, and even fish only rarely, and the undernourished, ownerless cattle produce hardly any milk. In 1877 the streets of Benares and Delhi are the same as they have been for centuries. English rule has changed little. Although it has apparently modernised the country, the expectation of human life is still about thirty years, and every year famine claims many thousands of

644

On the banks of the sacred Ganges: prayer and pover

646

647

victims. Diseases like malaria, tuberculosis, typhoid, bubonic plague, leprosy, cholera and smallpox, which have long ceased to be a menace in Europe, kill as many again.

One thing takes precedence above all others for the Hindu, and that is the performance of his innumerable religious duties*. Inside their temples, among the brilliantly colourful statues, there is always a line of devotees waiting to deposit their offerings and receive from the priest the sanctifying dab of red powder on their foreheads. In one court men, whose faces and bodies are daubed with stripes of white paint and ashes, are worshipping Kali*, to whom they sacrifice hundreds of goats and sheep. Even in the streets there are hairy and emaciated fakirs*, fasting for incredibly long periods in the hope of achieving a state of religious ecstasy. These two men, standing barefoot in a Bombay street*, wearing the usual Hindu dress, the *dhoti*, a long loin-cloth hanging low on the hips and pulled up in front, are untouchables. There are fifty million of them in India, amounting to one-sixth of the entire population, and they are only permitted to do the work which no one else is willing to do. All Hindus consider them unclean and repulsive and believe that anyone of a higher caste is contaminated if he touches them, looks at them or even allows the shadow of an untouchable to fall on him.

This delightful little girl with enormous eyes, standing in a carved stone doorway*, is eight years old and she has just been married to a man of forty. The young bride has to follow her husband everywhere, walking five steps behind him as a sign of respect, and she will be lucky if she does not become a widow while still a young woman. The British administration has forbidden the practice of widows committing suicide by throwing themselves on their husband's funeral pyre, but even if they survive him their lot is scarcely any better. They are put on one side and condemned to a life of solitude, dressed in rags and with shaven heads, or forced to become servants to their mothers-in-law.

645

648 649

d a land where death at an early age is all too frequent.

650

651

India is also the country of rajahs, of tiger-hunting from the backs of elephants, of fabulous treasures, of precious stones locked within great palaces of intricate design; such a palace might have wooden ceilings painted in dazzling colours, magnificent stonework floors* and vast honeycomb windows 650 made of marble* filtering the bright sunlight. The 651 raven-haired women of great beauty who live here are dressed in saris of the purest, most exquisitely patterned silk. At the courts of the rajahs it is also common for an old man to marry a child, and a woman of mature years a boy still in his teens*. But the vast majority of Hindus are 652 country people and live in villages which have usually only a few hundred inhabitants. The

652

houses are built of wood and dried mud and open onto a small courtyard. Few are more elaborate than one or two rooms with a verandah in front; but some have two floors, and these belong to the more important villagers. One of these is the moneylender, who lends money to the villagers at exorbitant rates of interest which keep them permanently in debt. Nearly all the people are farmers and belong to the same caste; the other trades which are necessary to the life of the village are carried on by people belonging by heredity to the artisan caste.

The only public buildings are a bazaar and a temple dedicated to Vishnu or Siva. Outside the village there is an uninhabited area which often contains the ruins of an ancient temple, where a few oxen rest among the stones*. 653

The Brahman's life is a closely woven texture of daily observances, all minutely worked out. Much of their religion is private and domestic, and their rites take place around the family hearth, in front of which is a clear space to serve as an altar. Here offerings are placed. Sometimes a cone is placed in the centre of a bowl to represent

ws wander at liberty through the villages, and every act is a ritual.

653

the *linga* of Siva and is sprinkled with fresh water 654 and decorated with flowers*. In the morning there is a ritual order for bathing in running water, cleaning the teeth, arranging the hair, reciting the holy words of Vedic texts, making oblations to the gods, to the demons and the *manes*, doing honour to the five domestic deities, and attending to the fire sacrifice. Before the midday meal, some food is thrown on the fire for the gods, and cooked rice is placed in little piles inside and outside the house for spirits and animals; not until this is done do the men squat down on the floor to eat while the women wait on them. In the evening there is another lengthy ritual to be performed in the same strict order as that of the morning.

The life of a practising Hindu is ruled from birth to death by the performance of his religious duties. When a Brahman's sons grow to manhood the holy thing for him to do is to abandon all his worldly goods and retire to a hermitage in the forest to wait for death to come to him. His 655 funeral rites* will transform him into one of the divine ancestors, to whom his descendants will offer the devotion due to the family *manes*.

654

655

Returning from a tour of duty in India in 1892, Lieutenant Richard Algernon White took his time over the journey. The voyage itself was by now a swift one, for, since the launching of the *Great* 656 *Eastern* in 1858, powerful steamers* were ploughing through the seas at greater and greater speeds. The lieutenant had often dreamed of the comfort- 657 able brick houses* of his native island during his five years in Bombay, but he was in no great hurry to reach home and broke his journey in several places on the way. The last halt was in 658 Paris, and from there he went to Boulogne*, where he boarded a ship with some English tourists who had been visiting the Continent under the auspices of Cook's agency. The first moment Lieutenant White felt that he was really back in England was when he leaned back on the studded 659 leather cushions of the London cab*. Twenty minutes later on the dot of four o'clock, he arrived at number ten St Thomas's Street in time for afternoon tea.

The whole family is assembled in the drawing- 660 room under the hanging gas-bracket*, and while Susie, the maid, is laying the table with muffins, butter, jam and cakes, Lieutenant White leans on the mantelpiece and surveys the scene of domestic bliss before him, warming himself at the coal fire and listening with half an ear to Dorothy playing an old Scottish air on the piano while her fiancé turns the pages of her music. Grandmother is sitting in an armchair with her embroidery frame, and Mr White is smoking a cigarette and reading the *Daily Mail*. The children are playing quietly, for English children in Victorian times were brought up to be seen and not heard. Edward is a bright boy and has been entered for Eton since he was a baby. When he is thirteen he will start to wear the uniform black jacket, waistcoat and trousers with a white shirt and broad white collar. But before this splendid life of ease and grandeur can be his there is the harsh reality of prep. school, to which he returns in a few days. After tea Richard hurries up to his bachelor room, where nothing has changed during the five years he has been away*. James, his batman, has taken advan- 661 tage of tea-time to unpack his luggage, light the oil-lamp and the gas-brackets, put the family

656

657

658

Home from the colonies, one may have muffins for tea, b

659

playing darts at the other end of the long bar. When Richard reaches the Thatched House Club and enters the dining-room, with its heavily brocaded walls and stern portraits, he is astonished to discover that his friends have organised a celebration dinner in his honour*. 662

With great dignity he takes his place under the huge, sparkling chandelier and eats his roast beef and green peas and potatoes, followed by pudding with raspberry sauce. His friend, David, rises to propose a toast, and then they settle down to enjoy their port and cigars.

660

661

photographs on the mantelshelf and Richard's pipes in the rack. His boxing gloves, hanging on the wall as a memento of his sporting prowess at Oxford, remind Richard that he had promised to dine at his club on the evening of his return home, and this is the more important because the next day is Sunday, and like all good Victorians Richard sentences himself to complete inactivity on the Sabbath, except for going to church. He rings for James and tells him to prepare the bath and lay out his evening clothes, then he takes off his uniform.

Not long afterwards, still tingling from a cold shower, Richard, resplendent in tail-coat, high collar and black tie, dons his top-hat, picks up his umbrella and sallies forth into St Thomas's Street. It is a fine, cool evening, and as it is still early Richard decides to walk to Pall Mall. His way takes him past the old pub called the *Voyage to Jerusalem*, supposed to have been there since the days of the Crusaders, and he pushes open the doors. Inside the pub, the atmosphere is full of the smell of beer and tobacco, and a few men are

662

ot darts at the pub or dinner at the club—if it is Sunday.

663

Life was not such an easy matter for everyone in Victorian England, the first nation to become an industrial power. After 1875 British agriculture began to suffer from foreign competition, for in future the country would have to depend largely on imported food to feed her growing population; but she held world trade in the hollow of her hand. Large numbers of people left the countryside to emigrate to the colonies or flooded into the towns to work in factories. Working conditions were appalling, especially in the mines*, where, despite the laws limiting the working day of women and children to ten hours, even the very young were still compelled to do hard and dangerous jobs. Yet not many years were to pass before laws were made for the protection of miners as a result of revelations in the Press, and the Government decreed that before going down the pit in the morning each man should be issued with a special safety lamp*. Also about this time people began to be concerned about the welfare of children, and in 1884, forty years after founding an animal welfare society, the admirable RSPCA, England embarked on the task of caring for her children. The NSPCC came into being. There was much work to be done by the new society; the works of Charles Dickens had already paved the way by showing the brutality of employers and the often criminal negligence of parents.

Houses in the slums were crowded from attic to basement with poor families whose children, barefoot, underclad and undernourished, ran wild in the streets, their lungs full of fog and smoke from the factories*. Thanks to a greater understanding of the rules of hygiene, infant mortality dropped considerably after 1870, and working-class parents were able to send their children to the new primary schools. Trade unions grew up to defend the rights of their members.

In the years just before and just after 1880 the appearance of American towns, too, began to alter radically. The first innovations of the machine age, made in the middle of the century, began to seem quite suddenly old-fashioned and picturesque, as can be seen in the contemporary drawings; this one, for instance, shows the New York Elevated Railway on Third Avenue, which continued to function until comparatively recently, straddling the road where a tram is hurtling past, scaring the horses of a sedate landau*.

664

665

For the majority work is hard, hours are long and wages meagre.

NEW YORK ELEVATED RY
63
NEW
HARLEM

# One new invention after another. Soon words travel by wire, a

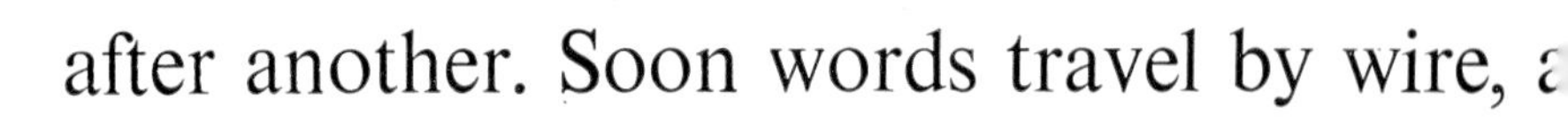

667

and replace it with another, quite different.

Invention followed invention, each one leading to the next. By applying electricity to Chappe's discovery of the telegraph*, Morse made it possible 667 to convey messages instantaneously over any distance. After 1870 the magic of electricity carried not merely messages but the actual human voice, thanks to Alexander Graham Bell, who invented the telephone. Twenty years later, by combining the work of a German (Hertz), a Russian (Popov), and a Frenchman (Branly), an

668

As the pace of material progress increased, and one invention gave rise to another, it could not fail to affect the lives of all civilised people. It was a colossal and far-reaching earthquake of which even today we have not heard the final reverberations. Yet it began quietly enough, and during the late nineteenth century no one, apart from a few Utopian writers such as H. G. Wells and Jules Verne, who developed a new literary genre that was to become science fiction, even suspected that it would destroy the world in which they lived.

Italian, Guglielmo Marconi, developed the wireless telegraph, to which the American Lee de Forest gave a practical application as radio. At first the public received the new invention with suspicion, then came amazement, and finally the new medium became so much a part of everyday life that people could hardly imagine what they had done without it.

Of all the developments whereby civilised man was increasing his power over his surroundings few excited such absolute wonder and stupefaction as

669

# ɔeople by the night express, or under their own power: by automobile.

670

that which led to the conquest of speed. From the very beginning of time until 1850 or thereabouts the maximum speed attainable by man had been that of his own legs or of the legs of a horse. Suddenly everything changed. The coming of the railways, with Stephenson's development of the steam-powered locomotive, provided a formidable rival to the old stage-coach*. Although it still survived for a time it had to compete against 668

671

trains* which, after 1880, were able to reach speeds of over sixty miles an hour. But even at this period travelling was still something of an adventure. People crowded eight or ten together on benches with neither arm- nor head-rests, and the only heating was supplied by foot-warmers which men were employed to refill every few hours. It was in America, where there were vast distances to be covered, that the sleeping-car was first developed. Europe followed the trend, and heated sleeping cars* and dining-cars* were in general 669 670 671

673

service after 1880. But these innovations benefited only the privileged few, and the same was true of the motor-car in its early stages. After 1885, when petrol came into use (the internal combustion engine dates from 1860) the first motor-driven vehicles* coughed and roared their way about the countryside, terrifying villagers; but such a means of transport was considered nothing more than an eccentric whim. By about 1895, however, the public were beginning to go car mad, and in the United States several million cars were sold between the years 1895 and 1915. Even before the 1914 war the motor bus had begun to replace the coach in places as remote as the Algerian desert*. 672 673

672

674

Step by step, the cities of the world began to change their appearance, but there was still no indication of where the problems presented by the overcrowding of industrial workers into the towns would end. A deadly growth of slum dwellings began to creep through the suburbs. Meanwhile *avant-garde* architects were building Renaissance-style mansions in New York*, and even the first skyscrapers (about 1910) were decorated with Gothic arches. The sudden expansion of the cities multiplied the distances people had to travel to their work, which was often on the other side of the city from their homes. More forms of public transport were essential. The first omnibus companies had started round about 1830; they had been reorganised in 1835 when the horse-drawn omnibus had made its appearance in Paris*.

In about 1871 the omnibus and the railway were combined to produce the tramway, and in 1895

675

As the cities grow it becomes more difficult to move about them.

676

677

679

676 the horses were replaced by steam*, but the new vehicles were hardly installed before they were faced by a new rival which had been in use in the United States since 1887. This was the electric 677 tramway, soon to be followed by the motor bus*, born in 1910 as a result of the progress in the motor industry. In 1900, the year of the World Fair in Paris, a peculiar underground railway was opened 678 for the first time: the metro*. At first people were very uneasy about it. They wondered how they would be able to breathe underground, or whether the Seine would flood the tunnels with water; but the railway soon proved to work very well and was imitated in other countries. The wave of modernisation even affected the old horse-drawn cabs. Certainly the traditional coachman in his caped greatcoat and leather hat was no more polite and obliging than he always had been—unless the reins were in the hands of a *coachwoman*—yet by 1905 it had become almost a pleasure to take a *sapin* in Paris* or a hansom in London with 679 their rubber-tyred wheels and taximeters. Soon, in all large cities, the horse-drawn cabs would be ousted by the new motorised taxis—like those at this taxi rank in Berlin*. 680

Already the streets were too narrow and the traffic was held up by solid jams, and already drivers were beginning to complain about the increasing number of two-wheelers on the road. After 1815, when the first experiments were made, there were many intermediate stages producing pedals and chain, ball-bearings and rubber-rimmed tyres, until gradually the velocipede ceased to be merely a curiosity and became commonly used. Then in 1888 an Irishman called John Dunlop discovered pneumatic tyres; these were followed by the free wheel, three-speed gears, brakes, and the bicycle was born*. A prophet of 681 1895 did not foresee a great future for it. 'Certainly bicycling will never gain great support among the generality of people. Can you picture a workman riding a bicycle with his tools on his back? Bicycles will vanish, with tennis and the belief in a flying machine.' Less than ten years later bicycles were part of everyday life.

678

680

Trams and motor buses appear—and Paris has the underground.

681

# Population growth means the rise of public services. Street cleaning is

One of the gravest problems produced by the rapid concentration of large numbers of people in cities was how to feed them. It had become vital to be able to preserve food and to be able to transport and distribute it easily. Early in the nineteenth century a Frenchman, Appert, had discovered the principle that food can be preserved by heat, but it was not until the introduction of canning that a new industry began to develop and was given a considerable impetus in America by the necessity to supply troops during the Civil War. In the fantastic canning factories established in Chicago five million pigs, two million head of cattle, and one and a half million sheep were 682 slaughtered in the year 1889. Huge goods yards* had to be built to enable food to be brought into

boots. The first motorised fire engines, introduced by 1889, aroused an understandable interest*. 683 One after another all public services were modernised. Automatic road-sweepers* 684 were already an old institution—they had been in service in Paris since 1863—and so were the heavy dust-carts which invariably spilled a good part of their contents out over the road*. 685 In Paris the task was greatly simplified by a civil administrator, M. Poubelle, who in 1884 made it compulsory for all householders to possess their own dust-bins. Dust-bins in France are still called by his name. There were even water-carts* 686—for in 1895 running water was a luxury very few could boast—which were soon to become museum pieces as their place was taken by motor-driven vehicles.

682

the very centre of cities; the development of central stores and markets was made easier by another new invention with many uses: refrigeration. Soon the first refrigerated ships were being used to transport fresh meat from one continent to another, and trains were carrying fish straight from the coast to the heart of the world's great cities.

Fire was another danger that had to be controlled. Public fire services were not generally organised until about 1850. Before that the work was done by volunteers who in America were dressed in red-flannel shirts, leather hats and

683

nicipal endeavour but in the States, firefighting a private enterprise.

684

But even in 1910 the old carts were still on the road, spreading the rubbish about without clearing it away, and watering the mud without cleaning the street, so that this woman in Berlin had to lift her long skirts to keep them dry as she crossed the street*. The pavement had become an essential feature about the middle of the century, because of the increase in traffic. It was a windy day and she was wearing a tight-fitting jacket into which were stuffed the great leg-of-mutton sleeves of her dress, and her hat was fastened on with a multitude of pins. By this time men had almost abandoned the top-hat in favour of the bowler, and an artist or a known eccentric could even get away with a soft hat, though it was usually ac-

685

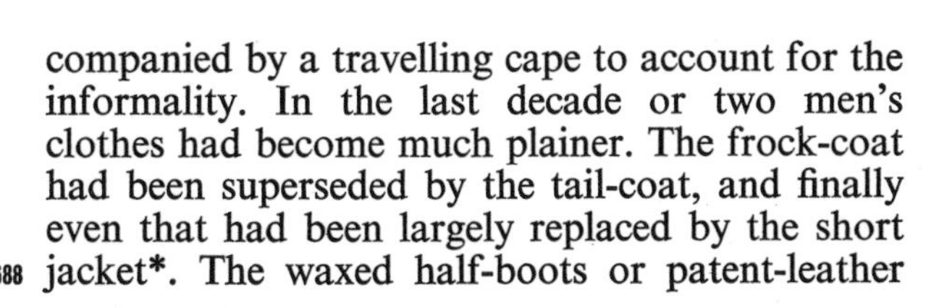

companied by a travelling cape to account for the informality. In the last decade or two men's clothes had become much plainer. The frock-coat had been superseded by the tail-coat, and finally even that had been largely replaced by the short jacket*. The waxed half-boots or patent-leather

686

boots of 1885 were replaced by button-boots* and later by lace-up shoes. The complicated black or white cravats gave way to loose bows or simple neckties, and shirt collars were less high and stiff. In 1900 pyjamas, which had originated in India, became accepted night-wear in England. But if England was the leader of men's fashions, in the field of women's clothes it was the Paris couturiers who set the tone for the whole of Europe. Women's clothes, round about 1910, also began to change, to become more practical and easier to wear. The era of the bustle (1882–1891) was followed by the Medici collar and leg-of-mutton sleeves (1890), by bell-skirts (1898) and by straight overskirts which

689

691

freed women from constricting corsetry. Huge hats, piled high with fruit, flowers and ostrich feathers, remained immensely popular*. In summer the capital cities of Europe filled with foreign tourists. The English visited Berlin on guided tours*, Germans made for Paris, all equipped with cameras, which, since the invention of the roll film in 1905, had emerged from the studio and become portable.

687

690

688

# The portable camera means snapshots and the family album

692

695

693

694

696

1900. It is a Thursday, and M. Lenoir, a man of comfortable private means, is out for a walk with Alice and Emile*. Alice is wearing a calf-length skirt, black stockings and a wide hat like her mother's while Emile has on his sailor suit, a navy blue overcoat and boots. On their way. M. Lenoir points out to the children one of the few remaining public letter-writers and explains gravely to them that with the spread of compulsory education all such relics of the past will disappear. When they reach the boulevards Papa stops for a moment to read the *Figaro* on the paper-stall*, and then has his shoes polished by the boot-black*. When he sees the jet of water spurting from the drinking fountain Emile announces that he feels thirsty, and luckily they have not gone much further before they come across the hot chocolate man*. Next door to his barrow there is a man selling iced wafers, a 'great novelty'. Both children are naturally tempted but two sous is a lot of money and how can they tell what will be inside? With the excuse that they might miss the show Papa hurries the children off to see the man with the performing bears*. The man comes from the Pyrenees and his two big, lumbering beasts will dance on their hind legs for him. Further off, among the stalls, between the shooting gallery and the lottery, where you can win prizes like Japanese vases and bags of lump sugar (which is replacing the old-fashioned loaf sugar), there is a new booth. M. Lenoir finds an opportunity to give his wife a nice little surprise; here is a 'photographic artist' who takes pictures on the spot for only six sous and no extra for glossy prints. They wait for a sweet little boy* in leather gaiters, whose nurse will not leave him alone however much the 'artist' begs her to, and then Alice and Emile take their turns in front of the camera*, both trying hard to catch a glimpse of the mysterious birdie. This evening two more photographs will be added to the big leather-covered family album with its silver clasps, where

692 693 694 695 696 697 698

## l reminders of how quickly hairstyles and fashion change.

698

697

699

they will join the other little Alices and Emiles rolling about on goat-skins with no clothes on, Uncle Adrian in his hussar's uniform and Aunt Adeline in her lace bonnet. As they walk on, they pass some women walking along with placards on 699 their shoulders*, and Papa tells them they are called sandwich women. The first lamp-lighters are already coming out, shouldering their long lighting 700 rods. In front of the big store*, selling everything anyone could possibly want to eat, from poultry and hams to fruit, vegetables, preserves and groceries, M. Lenoir waves his arm and says to Alice and Emile: 'Children, there is the future, you mark my words. Before you are grown up all the little grocery sellers, and cheese women, and strawberry women and water-carriers and the men who mend china and the chairs-to-mend men who fill the streets with their cries and their noises, all these will have vanished and in their place there will be big stores and shops where you are served by anonymous assistants.' Suddenly feeling very sad M. Lenoir goes into the shop and buys four bananas for dinner, for neither he nor Madame Lenoir, let alone the children, have ever tasted this exotic fruit brought at enormous expense from tropical countries.

700

# Lace curtains and aspidistras: world-wide trappings of the middle class.

It is seven o'clock in the evening and all the family 701 are gathered round the table in the dining-room*. At any moment cook will appear in her round cap, carrying the steaming soup-tureen as though it were a holy relic. The dining-room walls are covered in dark, leathery brown wall-paper, and there are a good many framed engravings and china plates displayed on them. A vast Henri II sideboard occupies almost the whole of one wall, its top part containing a large mirror, surrounded by columns and pediments of wood. There is a heavy stove in the fireplace and the chairs are typically ornate with stamped leather, silver studs and lots more little wooden columns. It takes the maid a good two hours to dust and polish them thoroughly in the morning. As well as net curtains and thick double curtains the windows are draped in a velvet pelmet trimmed with bits of leather and fringes, and the imitation wood linoleum of the floor is covered with a rug in the centre. This clutter and overfurnishing is what is known as comfort. The Lenoirs' dining-room is like hundreds and thousands of other dining-rooms, not only in France but, allowing for slight local variations, all over Europe. The Bergmanns in Munich, the Garofanos in Milan. the Fliets in Vienna, the Vallards in Geneva, the Van den Gindts in Amsterdam and the Sjörbergs in Copenhagen all have the same taste in curtains and carpets and table-cloths and potted plants. And they all of them sit in their overstuffed dining-rooms and eat too much and too richly and too often.

701

702

703

# Gas and electricity simplify the chores—but maids are still an institution.

Now let us take a look at the rest of the house. The Second Empire-style salon is dominated by the upright piano, draped in an oriental shawl, with its candles in little strawberry pink shades, embroidered piano-cover and revolving stool. In the bedroom* there is the immense wardrobe with a looking-glass that is the symbol of bourgeois prosperity; it could no more be spared than the host of other useless little bits of furniture: tables of all shapes and sizes, hold-alls and a mantel-piece complete with clock, candlesticks and figurines. Now for the bathroom*. There is no bath to be seen, for this is tucked away in a dark corner and only brought out on special occasions, but there is a prominent toilet-table with satin drapes and a marble top with a cloth on it. Here are arranged jug and basin, a sponge, china soap-dish and a host of powder-boxes, bottles and scent-sprays. On the floor is a tiny square of lino-leum. Washing is a delicate operation, since the room also serves the household as a lumber-room and space is limited. Yet there are unmistakable signs of progress; the brass hanging lamp in the dining-room works by electricity, and there is a gas-mantle in the bathroom. Even greater things are in store for the future; kitchen ranges, geysers, stoves, chandeliers and samovars will all be made to run on gas*. In 1900 nothing is impossible, however fantastic. The candles and oil-lamps of 1880 have been followed by paraffin-lamps, Swedish matches (about 1890), acetylene-lamps and finally electricity, though this is still

705

704

707

706

regarded with some distrust because people are afraid of the unpredictable short circuits that can easily cause fires. The sewing-machine*, first invented some fifty years previously, is now an accepted part of everyday life and there is one in most households. The other day Madame Lenoir even used a telephone. She held a little tube to her ear and heard a woman talking at the other end*. It was extremely impressive. People were even saying that soon one would be able to do without servants, though perhaps this was just another optimistic exaggeration. 'All the same,' thought Madame Lenoir, who knew the employment agency* only too well, 'it would be a relief.' But at the same time she wondered what would be-come of the 'gem' she still hoped to find.

708

The children of this halcyon period are already men and women between sixty and seventy years old. This may be your age; but if not, you can ask those who were children in 1900 what it was like and we will try not to tread too clumsily on their memories. The first thing they recall will probably be their nurse, a stern and awesome being, her face framed by a big starched collar and a halo of satin ribbons*. She was very proud as she pushed the new high baby-carriage, an innovation and not in general use before 1880. As for the baby, that was almost invisible underneath innumerable layers of embroidered lace and muslin. Older children wore padded coats with lace collars and bonnets, and their hair was allowed to grow long. Scientific baby-care was still in its very early stages, but it did exist. Incubators, sterilised milk, baby-scales, medical thermometers were all coming into use, though the great stand-bys in child-care were feeding, keeping out of draughts, cod-liver oil and castor oil. The luxury of bathing was not overdone. This little girl had better make the most of hers*, for before she is many years older she will have to wear a shift in it to preserve her modesty. That was the way children grew up strong and healthy.

Young children need toys and there were plenty of them: cut-outs, transfers, rocking-horses, lead soldiers, dolls and for the games-lovers the formidable diabolo* and shuttlecock. Those who wanted to be engineers when they grew up could begin with the brand-new toy railways* and the first scientific games. Most children could be sure that some of these would come their way at Christmas, which now had the added joy of a Christmas tree. This was a German custom that spread like wildfire through Europe and America. There were fairs, too, at frequent intervals, a never-failing source of joy, with rides on the painted wooden horses of the roundabout and the circuses of wild animals and clowns. But there was always an end to the holidays and the necessity to go back to school, for education had become compulsory in most civilised countries.

French education made a great stride forward in 1890 when it was made uniform over the whole country. Local differences gave way to conformity, and the dialects began to disappear slowly as soon as they were no longer taught in schools. The old village schoolmaster was replaced by a new qualified teacher in the *Ecole Normale*, and lessons became more formal and methodical.

711

710

709

Nannies wheel their prams in the park; children's games are elaborate.

712

Laws were passed regulating school attendance, and as greater and greater numbers of pupils took school certificates new schools had to be established even in remote country districts. In the *lycées*, the equivalent of the English grammar schools, an increasing number of pupils followed a modern, as opposed to classical, curriculum. More children studied foreign languages, and in some dusty schoolrooms they had their first lessons in gymnastics. School-life lost its military strictness, food improved and hygiene made its tentative appearance in the dormitories. The schoolboy's short blue jacket and *képi* were abandoned in favour of an overcoat with gold buttons and a peaked cap. There was plenty of latitude about what the day-boys wore*. (712) Girls were now eligible for secondary education and they wore an attractive uniform of long skirts, short capes and boaters in the summer*. (713) They were expected to wear their hair long, usually in plaits. Very few of these girls stayed at school longer than was necessary to pass a first examination. There was little point in their doing so while the professions demanding further study were still closed to women. All the same, a few bold spirits fought for higher education, and in 1870 a woman qualified as a doctor of medicine for the first time. In 1900 the first woman lawyer was called to the bar, and a few girls began to mingle with the crowd of students at the Sorbonne*. (714)

713

714

# Girls go to school in long skirts and boaters, and a few reach the universities.

# The rush to the sea is on, but modesty prescribes the bathing-machine a

715 716 717

It was a halcyon period for amusements too, though the ones that spring to mind most readily were the prerogative of a small, urbane and cosmopolitan society which at the turn of the century frequented the German spas, where they gambled for high stakes. Their favourite haunts were also the Riviera, Maxim's and the cabarets of Montmartre. The middle classes, many of them still living on private means, sought simpler and less expensive pleasures. They dined at home, and the men smoked cigars and played billiards, while in fine weather the ladies went into the garden for a game of croquet*. Golf, another descendant 715 of the same game, was especially popular in England, although even there it was not often played by women*. Tennis was the rage all over Europe. 716 This was really the old French *jeu de paume*, known in England as Court tennis and afterwards adapted and returned, scarcely recognisable, to the Continent, where it was considered smart to use the English vocabulary for the game. But these novelties did not oust the old sports which every well-bred man since the days of chivalry had been expected to master: riding and fencing.

In summer, crowds began to descend on the seaside. Sea-bathing was certainly nothing new for Margate and Brighton at the end of the eighteenth century, and Deauville, Trouville and Biarritz in the middle of the nineteenth had all had their illustrious patrons. But the turn of the century brought train-loads of middle-class people in search of sea-air and pleasure for the first time.

718

# ile the active turn to athletics, the sedentary choose the silver screen.

719

721

Little cabins in imitation peasant styles sprang up all along the cliffs to accommodate families for the summer months. Usually mother stayed there with the children and the servants, while father came down whenever he could be spared from his business, for as yet official holidays were only for school-children. Earlier, when town and country had still been to some extent inter-dependent, there had been a few weeks' holiday at harvest time, but industrialisation had put an end to that.

Families sat in deck-chairs on the beach and went down for a dip every now and again. Gentlemen plunged boldly into the waves in their striped bathing-suits, which left the lower parts of their legs and arms daringly exposed, and on their return draped themselves in thick beach-wraps*. (717) But for ladies bathing was much less simple. However elegant their costumes—they wore caps, laced sandals, sailor collars, short skirts and matching pantaloons peeping from beneath the frills—it was quite impossible for them to be seen walking about in them. They had to be pulled out to sea in little horse-drawn cabins. A door opened onto the waves, there was a short ladder going down to the water; a few moments splashing, and the cabin took the naiad back to the beach again. The seashore began to look as though a fantastic troop of little drunken houses was bobbing about on the waves*. (718) Children were privileged. Little boys were allowed to roll up their trousers and little girls to tuck up their skirts, though they still kept their elaborate hats on. Open-air lovers in England introduced camping as a sport. This did not yet involve any question of sleeping in tents, for people had comfortable furnished caravans*. (719) In Scandinavia and Germany many people grew passion-

720

722

ately interested in gymnastics. Then there was the terrifying sport of motor-racing, in which cars hurtled along at speeds well above sixty miles an hour*, (720) and since Pierre Coubertin inaugurated the new Olympic games in Athens in 1896 a small but growing public followed athletics*. (721) In America a traditional game called baseball had been gaining popularity since its beginnings in the middle of the eighteenth century, and now two new games, American football, derived in 1875 from the English rugby, and basket-ball, which began in 1892, made their appearance. A wonderful new entertainment began to appear in big cities: cinema, part illusion and part sheer magic, made its entry into modern life*. (722)

723

In 1900 there was still a number of occasions in France when people from different classes of society mingled freely, and one of these was 14th July*, which had always been a popular holiday 723 in every meaning of the word; but these occasions were becoming fewer and fewer. In the past there had been no dividing line between the homes of rich and poor in towns and cities; artisans' shops had been sandwiched in between noble mansions and sometimes even abutted onto their courtyards. More recently, the same apartment block had housed people of all degrees, and a great lady might pass a seamstress on the staircase, for there was not yet any such thing as a tradesman's entrance. But the growth of industry, the influx of country people into the cities in search of work and the enormous increase in the population of large cities had changed all that. The newcomers found themselves a lodging wherever they could, crowding into any vacant building, into disused barracks and overflowing at last into the nearby countryside, which gradually grew into working-class suburbs. Speculators made quick profits out of the desperate need for housing, and old houses were crammed with several times the number of people they had been designed to accommodate. To meet the demand, houses lacking not merely elementary comfort but light, space and air grew up like mushrooms. Smart houses were built in residential districts as far as possible from these slums. By scrimping and saving, foremen and some skilled workers just managed to keep up decent appearances*, but this was not the case 724 with the vast majority of working people. The working class was an altogether new social phenomenon. The apprentices and assistants of the old days had always had the hope of one day becoming masters and owners in their turn. The new worker knew he would remain a worker all his life; the only thing he could call his own was his capacity for work. He could be sacked without warning and compelled to spend weeks looking for another job*. The fate of the small clerk was 725 little better. For him, even more than for the

724

725

# social welfare and trade unions endeavour to improve conditions.

727

728

729

working man, keeping up appearances was a matter of pride, but in reality he was no more middle class than the manual labourer, and the growth of bureaucracy had reduced both classes to the status of a figure in a ledger or a cog in a wheel. The clerk's future was also menaced by the introduction of new machines, and it is understandable that copyists, whose livelihood threatened to become a thing of the past, were alarmed by the typewriter*. Slowly all these people who had at first been isolated by the disappearance of the old trade guilds began to combine to protect their own interests. All over Europe and in the United States unions were being formed in industry; soon these began trying to unite on an international level, and in 1913 the International Trades Union Movement was founded. At strikes and protest meetings the red flag* was often flown and the police and the army were called in. The common struggle nevertheless produced solidarity among the workers even when conditions for working people differed enormously from one country to another. In Russia, for example, they did not possess either the right to belong to a union or to go on strike. They were pitifully badly paid, many of them living in wretched free accommodation provided by the factories. Yet, advances were being made in social legislation: laws forbidding the employment of children under the age of twelve or the employment of women on night shifts, and laws limiting the working day to twelve hours. It now became recognised that the employer was responsible for accidents incurred during work, and that proper medical aid should be provided in large factories. Day-nurseries were set up to help working mothers*. The right to education was proclaimed, though in many places it was no more than a principle; not for long did the practice come of having a compulsory primary school whose classroom became a canteen at lunch time*. Peasants in Europe, still attached to their centuries-old traditional ways of farming, were reluctant to experiment with the new agricultural tools coming from America*.

726 727 728 729 730

730

731

The 1914 War, the first total war ever known on earth, interrupted these struggles towards progress and upset the lives of countless human beings. But, like all wars, it accelerated the pace of some innovations, although it was not until peace was restored that their permanent effect could be measured. One example is in the field of aviation, which before the war had been still in its experimental stage. As a war-weapon aeroplanes had taken a great stride forward, and the inauguration of the London–Paris flight in 1919 was the prelude to the installation of regular international passenger transport services. From 1930 onwards commercial aviation became an economic possibility, and the great international airlines came into being. Flying-boats and helicopters appeared on the scene. Aerodromes with their huge hangars and lighted runways became a regular feature of the landscape*. (731) Perishable goods could be flown from their country of origin to the consumer in a matter of hours, enormously increasing international trade and economic relations. Radio, too, was advanced by the war years, though the world's great radio stations were not set up until after 1920. Soon there were radios everywhere, even in this remote farm in Rumania*. (732) The first sets had individual headphones, then, as loud-speakers were installed, radio became companions for lonely people, fireside entertainment generously dispensing music, plays, news from all over the world and finally even advertisements. Immediately after the war, the cinema came into its own and crowds poured into darkened auditoriums to watch long films. Then, with the coming of talking films in 1927, the weekly ritual of the cinema, with its accompanying myth of the star, became a normal part of life. But a serious rival to the cinema was already making its first appearance. It combined the sound of radio and the picture of the cinema in the home. The first television demonstrations were no more than a curiosity in 1929*. (733)

The strong man* (734) still drew an audience with his dumb-bells and his rigid, heroic stance, as old as the hills and impervious to progress. But for how much longer?

732

733

# Air transport, radio and cinema cease to be miracles. Television is born.

# With the advances in medicine, doctors and dentists are less to be feared.

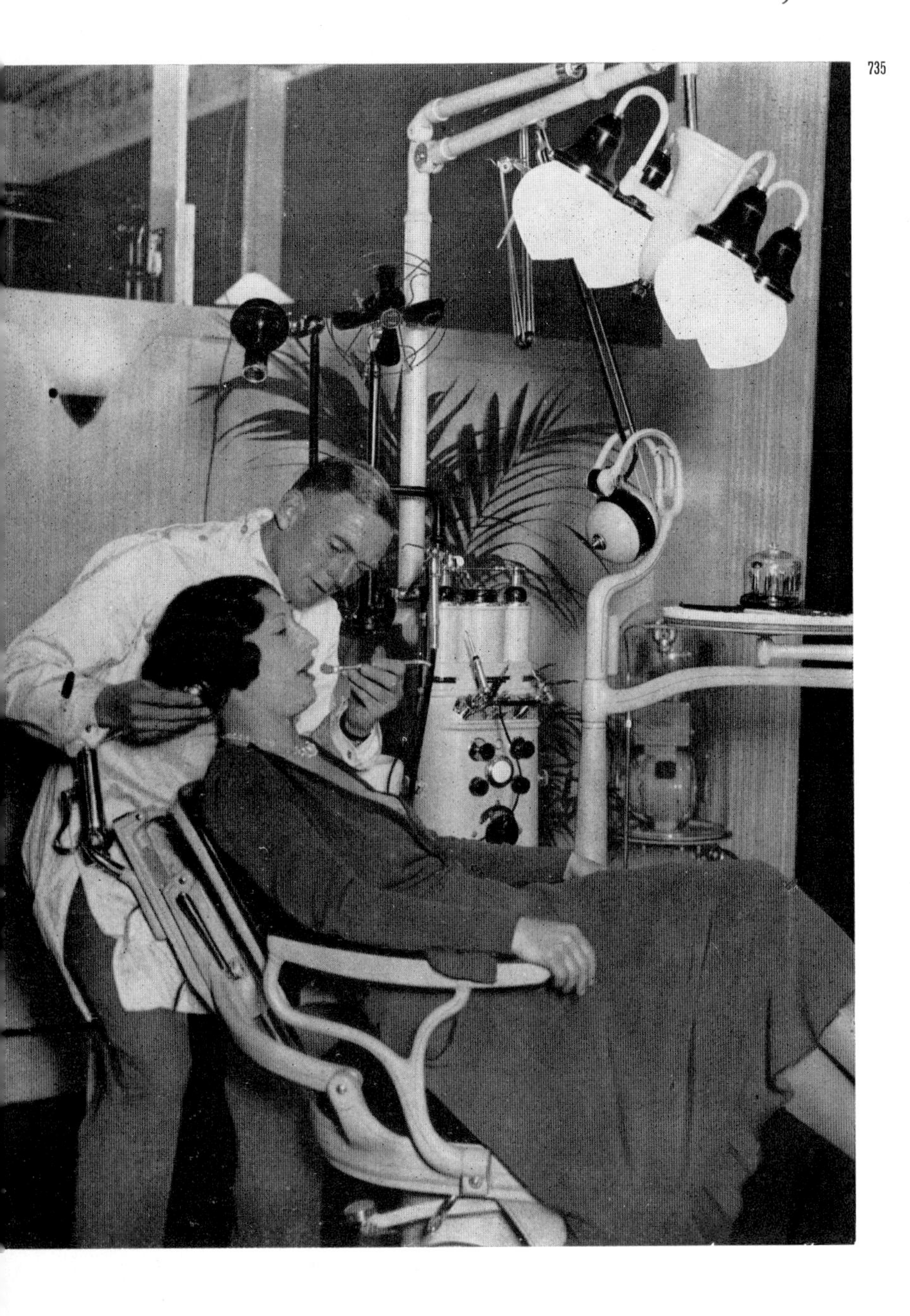

735

In the 1930's, some of the most obvious and startling advances in the development of daily life were made in the realm of medicine. The progress made by surgeons during the war was made infinitely more spectacular by the use of new antiseptic methods which had almost wiped out the gangrene which had formerly caused a large proportion of deaths. In a less dramatic but more commonplace field, dentistry had begun to lose many of its terrors, thanks to anaesthetics and the introduction of new precision tools. The old tooth-drawer had been transformed into the modern dental surgeon, and the dentist's surgery in 1930 had in some cases begun to look much as we know it today*. Hospitals were no longer an almost inevitable prelude to the graveyard. Sick people were beginning to be separated according to the kind of attention they needed and directed to the specialised departments with which all hospitals were equipped. Wherever physically possible the trend was towards replacing the single large ward by smaller ones containing fewer beds, or even individual rooms. Typical examples of the way in which many people in the more advanced nations were benefiting from the progress made between 1930 and 1935 were, among other things, the fresh impetus given to medical diagnosis by the use of radiography, the appearance of new drugs such as insulin and various vitamin preparations, and the development of preventive medicine. Many diseases disappeared altogether, and ways were found of dealing with others formerly regarded as incurable. Psychiatry evolved revolutionary new methods of treating nervous disorders as a result of the work of Freud in the early years of the century. Striking advances in gynaecology made childbirth much less dangerous. The deadly puerperal fever became a thing of the past; improved child care, and in particular the use of

736

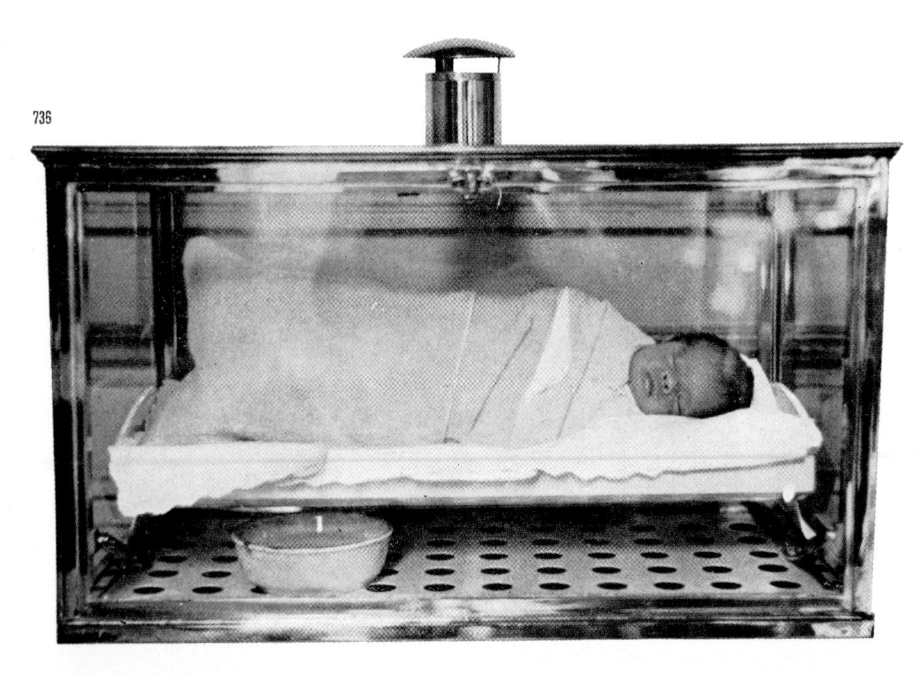

737

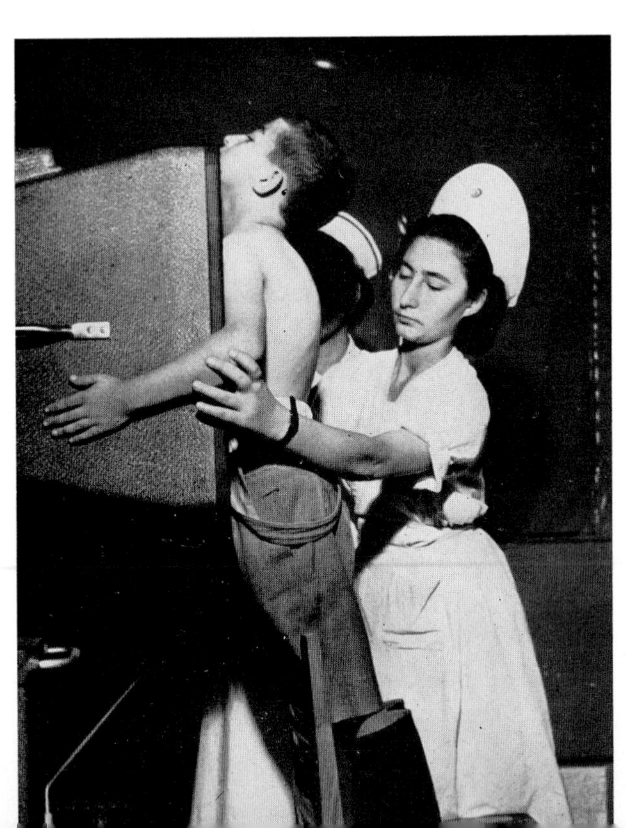

# A new subject is taught in the schools: gymnastics.

738 739

736 incubators* (first invented in 1880 but improved since), greatly reduced infant mortality. Whereas in 1900 a hundred and seventy children in every thousand died in their first year, by 1939 the number had been reduced to sixty. It was not only at home that children received the benefits of improved medical care. Their health was also closely 737 watched at school where X-ray examinations* made it possible to detect infectious diseases and take steps to prevent them. Sports and gymnastics were encouraged at school, and holiday camps offered town children the fresh country air they 738 needed*. In some instances, state intervention was 739 not altogether disinterested*. By this time the principles of hygiene were beginning to spread further than the most advanced countries, but still they only affected the upper levels of society.

The entirely Western cleanliness and comfort of this Hindu home* only stresses the contrast 740 between the comfortably off middle-class people who live in it and the untouchables dying of disease and malnutrition all around them.

But if in the West it was children who benefited most directly from the wave of progress, the condition of women also improved very rapidly. The lives of modern girls were very different from those of their mothers. The gulf between the middle- and working-class way of life was still wide, but it had begun to narrow. In a single generation, all the domestic equipment that could make the housewife's task easier and quicker underwent change. This American kitchen* may seem out of date to 741 us today, but it does possess the incalculable advantage of being light, clean and practical.

740 741

# Women are freed; they work. The new age brings other privileg

742

Women, even more than men, found it difficult to fit into the new society of the machine age. Before the industrial era they had scarcely left their own hearths, and although as industry began to develop many women were drawn into the factories, it was to be a long time before female labour was considered sufficiently useful to be employed on any but inferior, unpleasant and badly paid work. Laws were passed in England in the mid-nineteenth century designed to protect female workers from excessive exploitation. Their hours of work were limited and certain tasks forbidden, but all the same it was not until after the 1914 War that their conditions of work improved sufficiently to induce large numbers of women to enter factories. When they did, the majority of them went into the rapidly expanding textile and food industries.

The narrowing of the traditional gap between the conditions of men and women produced a demand for equal rights for women even in countries such as China*, where they had always been most sternly repressed. 742

Many women entered public services and there were women sweepers and bus-conductresses in all parts of the world, even Japan*. As public and commercial administration expanded, it attracted an increasing number of female office staff, and some jobs became almost entirely the prerogative of women. Among these were secretaries, shorthand-typists and telephonists. Post offices and telephone exchanges recruited almost only women, like these telephone operators in Poland*. 743 744

One of the most obvious and important changes brought about by the new living conditions was in women's clothes, which became much simpler and more practical. After 1920, clothes began to

743

ependence and the vote, short skirts and the changing hem line.

744

745 746

allow the female body a liberty it had not known for centuries, and the masses of petticoats and long, trailing skirts vanished for ever. Tight corseting was no longer necessary and underwear was reduced to a minimum. Tailored costumes were introduced that made women's clothes as much like men's as possible*. Special clothes such as divided skirts*, sweaters and tennis shoes, were designed to enable women to take exercise.

745 746

By contrast, beauty-care reached new heights of importance. In about 1930 the chemical industries began marketing mass-produced powder, creams, lipsticks and nail-varnish. Women in 1926 wore their hair short but wavy, and the invention of permanent waving in 1928 made the fortune of the hairdressing salon. At the same time Western woman started becoming less of a slave to housework. The market was flooded with domestic appliances, most of which had been invented long before but which had only now, through mass production and increased efficiency, become available to the bulk of the population. The 'Home Vacuum Cleaner' was first made in England and was on sale as early as 1910, but it was not in common use until 1930. Electric irons, which had been launched in the United States in 1906, also began to replace the old flat irons in about 1930. Even in 1939 refrigerators were still luxury objects in Europe, although they were common in the United States. Gas and electric ovens and many other gadgets such as potato peelers (1930) were making it increasingly easy to run a home.

Women were beginning to excel at a number of sports, such as swimming, and even hockey*, which had hitherto been considered the exclusive property of men. Women were now piloting not only cars but aircraft.

747

747

748

749

This rapid development in such a wide variety of fields was directly linked with the boom in industry. Between 1870 and 1938 the industrial output of the world increased tenfold. In the year 1910 American production reached a peak that equalled that of the whole of Europe put together; in later years it was considerably ahead of it. The reason was that the productivity of the individual worker had increased to an unbelievable degree. Equally amazing results were achieved by increased mechanisation, such as the assembly line installed in Ford factories in America*. Time and motion study, to obtain the maximum speed and efficiency with the minimum of effort, was evolved. 748

The immediate effect was the subordination of the worker to the machine, his reduction to the status of an automaton, such as Charlie Chaplin pilloried in the film *Modern Times*. But no one thought of remedying a situation which was justifying the arguments of the defenders of the past. The order of the day was 'produce and be damned', until the dreadful slump of 1929 spread sudden ruin and panic. At its height, unemployment in the

750

Production is the order of the day, and the worker becomes a cog i

752

United States rose as high as twenty-five per cent of the available labour, all of whom had to be maintained by the State*. 749

It was obvious that fundamental rethinking on the whole question of industry was essential, and among the consequences of this New Deal was an improvement in the status of the worker. Working hours were reduced, in some countries to as little as a forty-hour week. Age limits were imposed for starting work and retiring—people started work older and stopped sooner than ever before. From 1935 onwards, large American firms began to discover that the clock was not the key to production, and some even went to the lengths of declaring that 'a factory fulfils two main functions: the economic function of producing the goods, and the social function of ensuring the well-being of those who work in it.' This virtually amounted to a revolution in managerial outlook. Garden cities were built for the workers, to combat slum dwelling*; 750 as people began work later, more children attended primary school, and the percentage of illiteracy, which had been sixty per cent in France in 1830, in Belgium in 1850, in Italy in 1870 and in Russia in 1900, dropped to less than ten per cent in all the great nations of the world. Holidays were no longer the privilege of the middle classes. All summer, excursion trains carried huge numbers of working-class people to the seaside*, 751 a practice encouraged by paid holidays. The radio at home and the cinema round the corner were popular entertainments, and crowds of people flocked to motor-racing* 752 and the huge football stadiums for national and international rugger and soccer matches*. 753

A comparison of working-class conditions in 1930 with those of 1750 shows what a great stride forward had been made. In 1750 an average worker earned enough to buy one and a half pounds of bread per person per day, a bare subsistence level. Between 1830 and 1930, when it reached its peak, the amount of bread consumed increased by forty per cent, but at the same time consumption of richer foods, such as meat, milk and sugar, increased tenfold. Moreover, in 1830 food had accounted for eighty per cent of the family budget; this had dropped to thirty or forty per cent a hundred years later.

751

753

achine. But in 1929 there is the slump, and before long holidays with pay.

754

755

This era of astonishing material progress was rudely interrupted by a war more terrible in its effects than any humanity had ever known. The everyday life of countless millions of people sank to a lower state than anything known since the Middle Ages. The war itself was the worst anachronism of all. When life returned to normal, people realised that problems which had been shelved, or only temporarily solved before the war, had reached the point where only radical rethink-

756

ing could offer a hope of solution. One of the most pressing was the ever-increasing size of the world's cities.

An aerial view of almost any city in 1960 shows a tangled web of roads and buildings*. It is a cell 754 sending out tentacles in all directions, vertically as well as horizontally. Hitherto, with a very few exceptions, there had been no overall planning-control to limit the growth of cities; anyone had been free to build what he liked where he liked. The long-term results of this freedom were disastrous. The open spaces which allowed the urban population to breathe had vanished, one after the other; the spread of the motor-car industry made traffic circulation increasingly

# The modern metropol

757

759

758

difficult, and this was further complicated by parking in the streets. In the United States, where the problem was most serious, commuters driving into town to work formed the habit of leaving their cars in a parking lot in the morning and only picking them up in the evening for the drive home, relying on public transport during the day. Soon even car parks were overcrowded and spread over enormous areas. Two solutions presented themselves: one, the multi-floored garage with a car-lift to move the vehicles up and down* (755), and the other, the underground garage which was limited from the start by lack of basement space. Traffic jams* (756) were worst in the morning and evening rush-hours when pavements and streets filled as if by magic with people flooding out of factories and offices*. Buses and trains were packed to the doors (757) and long queues* (758) waited for hours before they could get home. Multi-level crossings and flyovers* (759) built in recent years have done little to reduce the congestion; they are already out of date. Numerous other threats are beginning at last to rouse public alarm. Among these are water and air pollution, the lack of sunshine and the nervous tension caused by noise, which are seriously affecting the health of those who live in cities. These and the ever-increasing pace and tension at which we live must take the blame for the many illnesses of modern man, nearly all of which are the result of overstrain.

760

762

761

A new science, town-planning, has emerged in recent years to attempt to lessen the evils which are threatening the health, stability and even the lives of people in modern cities. It aims at a fundamental reconsideration of the problems caused by the concentration of enormous numbers of human beings into cities, and to offer not merely temporary remedies but basic solutions. It is an attempt to introduce system and method into a domain until now ruled entirely by the needs of the moment. But while acknowledging the greatness of its aims we must also recognise that town planning can never be truly effective unless it is operating in cities which have been started completely from scratch, such as Chandigar in India or Brasilia in Brazil*. In existing towns, which have often grown up bit by bit over many centuries, a partial solution is all that can be attempted. 760

Schemes to improve the situation, put forward over the last few years, have all tended towards decentralisation. The city centre is reserved for shops, offices and entertainments, and in the larger residential areas individual houses are continually being replaced by large blocks of flats separated by open green spaces*. The first garden cities are by now nearly sixty years old; the formula did not gain widespread popularity until between the wars. Spreading at first to Holland and the Scandinavian countries, it became common in Europe only after 1945*. We know now that when cities become too large they cease to fulfil their functions and become instead one of the factors of social disintegration. Cities of today never sleep. In the past the hours of darkness were treated with respect, for people's safety depended on it, but the modern city is full of intense life all night. There is no lull in the traffic, no interval of silence, and the night is made bright by the perpetually shifting light of vast neon signs*. The sky above a city is full of the glow of a never-ending sunset. 761 762 763

## Broadway, where night becomes day and the mosaic costs millions.



763 →

Get satisfying flavor
So friendly to your taste!
PALL MALL

765

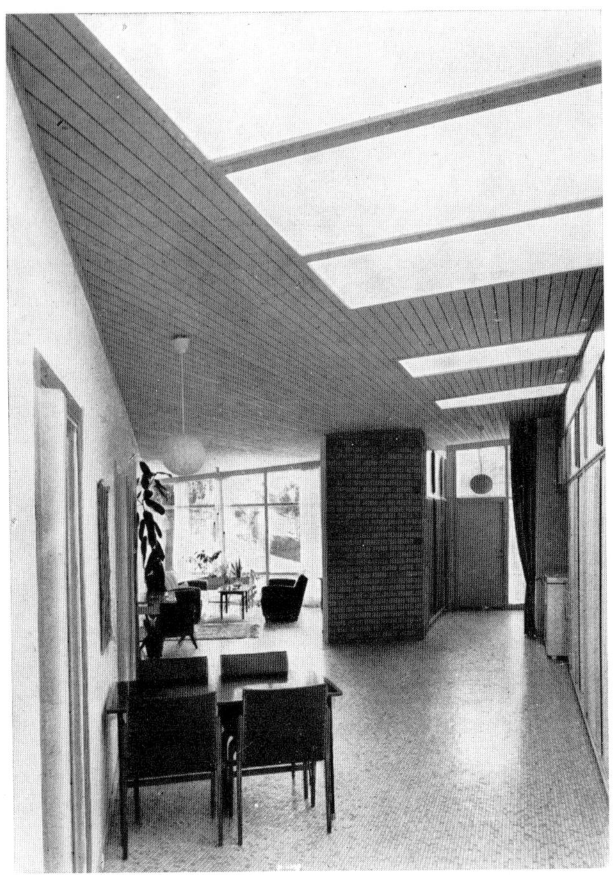

764

At the end of the nineteenth and beginning of the twentieth centuries the controlling factors in domestic architecture had been the building and not the individual apartment; the owner, not the tenant; the man who put up the money, not the man who paid to live in the building. Today the opposite is true and the family living unit is the basis of the whole design. Modern dwellings conform to a standard pattern, more or less effectively carried out*, and one of the most important ways in which they diverge from the traditional concept of housing is in the ability to maintain even temperatures indoors all the year round. This is the result of improvements in heating, insulation and new methods of air-conditioning and ventilation. Ideally, twentieth-century man can sit in his house and be totally unaware of weather conditions outside.

764

The largest room and the centre of a modern home is the living-room* in which are installed the radio, television and record-player. Its style varies with individual taste from the severity of Japanese design to the exaggerated comfort which so often results from the influence of magazines and the indiscriminate copying of Hollywood*. Separate dining-rooms are a derivation from banquet halls of earlier ages, but today the dining-room is on the way out. Now pared down to its basic essentials, it is more often than not simply a corner of the living-room within easy reach of the kitchen. People today feel an increasing need for privacy, everyone wants a bedroom to himself, and this is a

765

766

# abour-saving devices. Hollywood leaves a lavish mark on interior decoration.

767

768

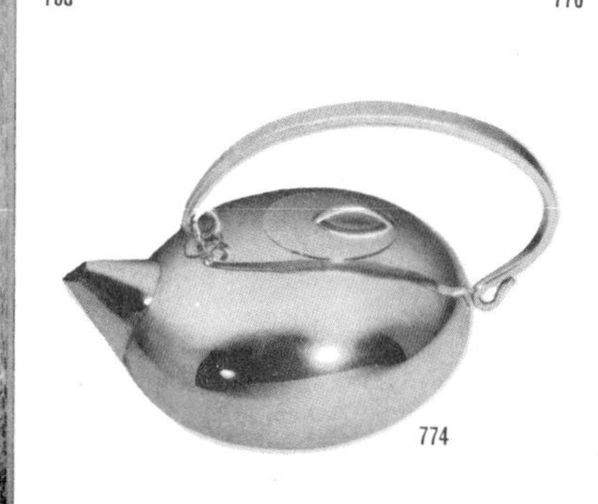

774

770

773

771

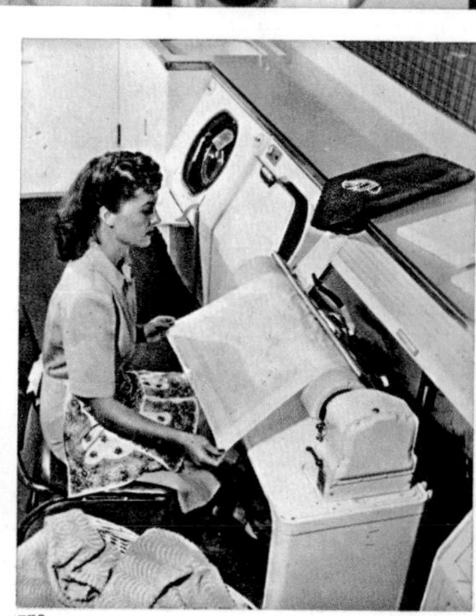

772

need to which old houses, where the whole household lived on top of one another, rarely conform. Twin beds, which have long been in use in England and America, are beginning to replace the old-fashioned double-bed in most countries. Whenever possible there are separate rooms for the children, furnished and decorated to suit a child's taste and requirements*. (767)

Showers are an increasingly popular feature of the modern bathroom, sometimes even replacing the bath* (768), and basic rethinking in kitchen design is aimed at obtaining the greatest possible efficiency in a small space and reducing domestic chores to a minimum. The kitchen has become a laboratory* (769) and the cook a dietician. Refrigerators* (770), washing-machines* and automatic ironers* (771 772) are a greater help to the housewife of the 1960's than a whole regiment of servants. Traditional household utensils, whose shape had remained unaltered for centuries, have not merely been radically re-designed* (773 774), they are being made of a whole new range of inexpensive, unbreakable materials which are playing an increasingly large part in modern living. Since the invention of celluloid in 1860 and bakelite in 1910, a large number of new plastic and synthetic materials have appeared, such as polythene and Plexiglas, which are cheap to produce and can be adapted to many different purposes.

769

# Packaged foods, supermarkets and department stores overwhelm the buyer.

775

This little Chinese boy* will be doing justice to **775** almost exactly the same meal whether his home is in Shanghai, Paris or San Francisco. He will still use chopsticks—those in the picture are made of plastic—and a traditional china spoon to eat his bowl of rice with chop suey, or chicken and bean sprouts. People cling to their basic national foods wherever they live, and the main difference between what this child is eating and what his ancestors would have had is in the variety of ingredients, for his peasant grandfather would have had to satisfy himself with a bowl of plain rice. In the past, a man's food depended directly on his social status. In modern nations the unskilled labourer eats roughly the same amount of meat, butter, milk and sugar as does his employer. An additional factor which has completely changed people's eating habits is the enormous development of the canning and preserving industries. Although the consumption of preserved foods varies greatly from one country to the next, they do not merely make meals easier to prepare but constitute against the perils of famine an insurance such as humanity has never before known. The increase in the amount, variety and

776

778

777

quality of food available is comparatively recent; so is the scientific study of food, which has determined the diet necessary to maintain health.

Only a few decades ago shopping was still an 776 exhausting task, but the modern self-service store*, originating in the United States, where all kinds of household goods are sold under one roof, does offer a solution to the problem. Foodstuffs are protected from germs by individual or family-size packs in cellophane or polythene which ensure that products are handled as little as possible. The same 777 self-service principle* has also been applied in restaurants, and the cafeteria idea, which was also American in origin, has now spread all over the world. Modern clothes can now be supremely elegant as well as practical, and one of the most characteristic aspects of modern fashion is in the 778 use of jewellery*. Women rely on originality of design and colour rather than on precious stones for individuality. Modern women possess a great amount of jewellery, but most of it is of little intrinsic value. The same is true of their clothes. In the past a woman might own one fabulously gorgeous and expensive dress which she would wear all her life and even hand on to her children;

780

now she can have an extensive wardrobe of dresses for all weathers and occasions. The clothing industry has adapted its methods to suit the enormous increase in ready-to-wear shops. The big stores of the 1960's, whether they are in London, New York, Berlin or Tokyo*, are equipped 779 with every possible service and offer an astonishingly wide range of garments*, catering to all 780 sizes and tastes. Women have managed to create fashions adapted to present-day requirements*, 781 borrowing to a greater and greater extent from the clothes worn by men. More and more women are wearing trousers, although there are still some places where they are frowned upon. The decline of commercial laundries in favour of automatic home appliances has hastened the simplification of underwear; it has also brought into existence synthetic fabrics which are cheap, easy to wash and quickly replaceable. Linen and cotton handkerchiefs have been almost entirely abandoned in favour of paper ones.

779

781

782

783

Modern man has every means of being in touch with all that goes on in the world. The fantastic development of the press*, with its daily papers and weekly illustrated magazines dispensing a never-ending stream of news and opinion, puts world events within the reach of people everywhere. Every event, whatever it is and wherever it happens, is written into the lives of all of us and becomes our concern. For years the press has provided fantastic news pictures, but now this purpose is increasingly served by the television*, which has been part of everyday life since 1945; for tens of thousands of people it is not merely the supreme home entertainment but a day-to-day source of visual information. In the future there will be an even greater role for television in dealing with the problem of leisure, which is becoming a fundamental hazard of an industrial civilisation. It has the power to form public taste and encourage people's interest in cultural activities. Never before have the peoples of the world possessed such opportunities to develop mutual knowledge and understanding.

Week-ends and, even more, summer holidays are a natural release for the psychological pressures resulting from the strain of modern city life. Every Sunday in summer the search for peace and quiet drives thousands of city-dwellers into the countryside; but these motorists* spend more of the day at the wheel than walking in the country. And it is in pursuit of something less constrained than their working lives that millions of people recapture the appearance of primitive ancestors and amuse themselves to the rhythm of age-old dances*. Camping sites* recall the settlements of savages, despite the plethora of equipment which would astonish any genuine cave man.

People in the 1960's want to go everywhere and see everything for themselves, and means of transport have been adapted to their requirements. Time and energy are saved by travelling at night, and if sleeping cars are not within the means of all, reclining seats offer a practical substitute. Air travel, already indispensable to overworked

786

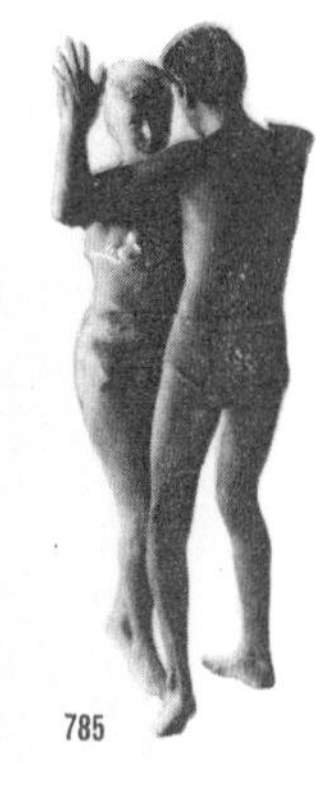

785

# The press, television and holiday travel lure modern man from h

787

784

arth. A new race is created : tourists.

789

businessmen, now provides normal eating and sleeping facilities*, and is becoming more and more used by tourists, especially for group travel. For besides the popularity of individual touring, for which increased camping facilities allow the maximum independence, a new trend has emerged over the last few years. This is the fashion for conducted tours which free the individual from all responsibility for making his own arrangements and ensure that he will not miss anything*. The passion for winter sports* is also a relatively new enthusiasm; its popularity will continue to spread as long as fresh air offers amusement and rosy cheeks. It is to be hoped that contemporary man will use his leisure to find a way out of the predicament into which a commercial and industrial society has led him, and that he will gradually regain not only his health but also a human dignity which he risks losing.

787 788 789

788

A huge, immensely wealthy country motivated by a spirit of fantastic energy, the United States of America has been for the last eighty years stressing material progress. Daily life is continuously changing. The population of the nation increased so rapidly in the 1920's that in order to accommodate their rising number of inhabitants cities were forced to build upwards*, producing the era of the skyscraper which, with a few exceptions, is already reaching its end. The tendency is now for people to move out of the centre of the cities where only the less prosperous now live. Like the majority of Americans the Wellers, who live in Milwaukee, Wisconsin, prefer a small house of their own, built on one or two floors, either of brick or, even more frequently, of prefabricated wood, with a garage and a small, carefully mown patch of lawn*. Their house contains a large, cheerfully furnished living-room, with deep armchairs and television, radio and record-player, as well as a dining-room, three bedrooms, kitchen, bathroom and a playroom for the children in the basement. In this little family world the children rule the roost. 790 791

It is six o'clock and the children are just having their supper. They are a large family even for America, where families are increasing in size. Mr and Mrs Weller are religious people, and in their house grace is always said before meals*. For supper this evening there is clam chowder, spaghetti and meat balls, a green salad with nuts and celery and, to finish with, the traditional apple pie and cheese. Afterwards there is time to watch television before the children go to bed, and from nine o'clock onwards the parents have some time to themselves. They take this opportunity to discuss family problems such as the children's education, for the parents pay for advanced education; the payments on loans, for they are buying both their house and their car on instalment payment plans; and what to do during the week-end. Mr and Mrs Weller have been asked to 792

790

791

In America the skyscraper is abandoned for the split-level. T

792

794

793

a party by some friends on Saturday evening and they will have to find a baby-sitter, who will probably be a student, to look after the children for the evening.

On Sunday if it is fine they will go for a picnic in the car, stopping at a special picnic-site* where the children can play baseball*. If it is wet, they will stop at home, and after morning church they will sit down to Sunday dinner, the only meal of the week for which Mrs Weller really cooks, making something traditional like southern fried chicken or baked Virginia ham and pineapple. Later they may go to a film.

793
794

But today is only Tuesday and tomorrow they have to get up early. Sam Weller is out of bed by seven o'clock, and he gets dressed and gets his own breakfast: a glass of orange juice, a plate of cornflakes, bacon and eggs, toast and coffee. By the time Mrs Weller calls the children for their breakfast at eight, he is ready to leave the house. Mrs Weller packs up the children's lunch, which they eat at school, giving them sandwiches with alternate layers of cold meat, mayonnaise and lettuce, some fruit and a thermos of milk, and then drives them to school in the car. From there she goes straight to the suburban shopping centre to do her shopping. Here there are the few essential shops, including the supermarket which is butcher, baker, dairy, grocer and greengrocer all rolled into one, and the drug store, part-chemist part-general shop, where there is a soda fountain. Meanwhile Sam Weller, who like 34% of Americans, including a notable number of women*, is a white collar worker, puts his feet up during his office break*. He leaves his office early, and is usually home before six o'clock.

795
796

795

796

mmuter takes over the suburbs—where children rule the roost.

# Leisure becomes an industry. Swimming-pools, slot-machines and drive

The Wellers of Milwaukee, Wisconsin, are not the only people who are wondering what to do at the week-end, for the satisfactory use of those two precious days' leisure presents all sorts of problems. Saturday is the day for Mr Weller to repair the chair or mow the lawn and for the family to shop for clothes or new records. They spend time window-shopping*, for there is always something new prominently displayed that was unheard of the week before but is now indispensable. It is one of hundreds of ingenious new gadgets which appear on the market every year. For many Americans a free Saturday is also the chance to learn something new and useful, and there are numerous courses to choose from. Adult education classes are plentiful and well attended, providing everything from elementary to advanced courses in all business

797 798 799

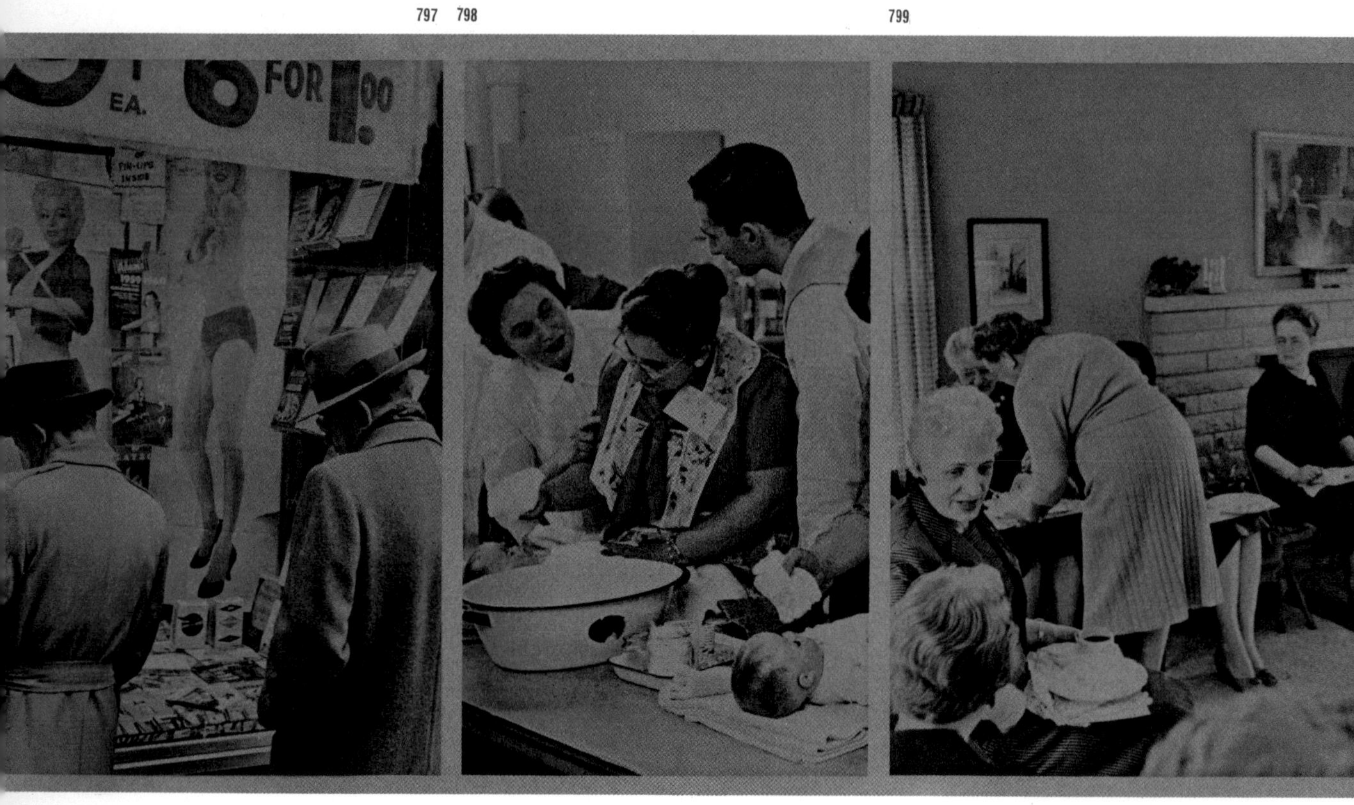


subjects, as well as teaching all aspects of the American way of life, of which this baby-care class is an example*. In addition there are many active voluntary associations undertaking charitable, educational or cultural works for the good of the people. Women's clubs* are among the most energetic of them. Finally, there is entertainment in its narrower sense.

A whole section of New York is given over to the entertainment industry and Broadway is famous the world over. Here, as well as theatres and cinemas, there are amusement arcades, called playlands, with rows of pin-tables*. The streets are crowded with sightseers gazing at the flickering neon signs and eating popcorn. In the evenings out of town, there are the drive-in cinemas* where motorists park their cars in the open air and watch the film without getting out, for independent amplifiers between each parking space transmit the sound-track. Independence Day, the Fourth of July, is the great occasion of the summer and it is celebrated by parades in which drum majorettes, in boots, shakos and very short skirts, lead school bands and old regimental associations. People who live within reach of the sea flock to the coast on Saturdays and Sundays, and in summer the beaches near New York are always full of people.

800

ıemas sprout like mushrooms. That mixed blessing, the week-end, is born.

802 Coney Island*, where there is a vast amusement park, is the most popular of all.

American holidays are usually short, generally not more than two weeks, and those, such as students, who do have long vacations often take temporary jobs. Many students mix work and pleasure by hitch-hiking cheaply across the continent and taking jobs as waiters or messengers in summer hotels. For their parents the most essential part of a holiday is the car, and instead of staying in one place they tour through a number of states, 803 going from one motel* to another—a motel is a hotel made up of individual chalets with parking spaces. Motels seldom have restaurants since roadside eating places are readily available. It is true that those wanting to get to know their country have plenty to keep them busy. The

802

801

distances between the Atlantic and Pacific coasts, and from the Mexican border to Canada are immense and there is no lack of tourist attractions. They can take pictures of cowboys in Texas, of Indians on their reservations, and visit huge nature reserves like Yellowstone National Park, the Everglades in Florida and the Grand Canyon in Colorado where wild animals of every kind are allowed to roam at liberty among the magnificent natural surroundings.

803

Impatient Russia struggles to learn, to advance, to surpass. But for the citiz

804
805
806

807

daily needs are the same: subway, department store and television set.

For twenty-five years Theodore Gabrielovitch Agapian has been a Communist Party member and manager of a state bazaar* in a small village near Erivan, the capital of Soviet Armenia. In return for his service, the Government of the Armenian Republic have offered him at long last the chance to visit Moscow, and for the first time in his life Comrade Agapian goes up in an aeroplane. On landing he is taken charge of by an Intourist guide who speaks his own language and shepherded to a hotel with a group of others from the same country. Agapian's first visit the next morning is to the Mausoleum where Lenin and Stalin lie in state, but to get in, the Armenians have to queue for nearly two hours with a number of other delegations in Red Square*. The square faces the Kremlin and Saint Basil's Cathedral.

Agapian thinks of the enormous difference the Soviet regime has made in the everyday lives of all these people. Since the revolution of 1917, there have been attempts to produce a single social class. It is questionable to what degree these attempts have been successful. There have been years of privation, but at last the standard of living is slowly rising and people are beginning to acquire some of the things they have wanted for so long. As a party leader, Agapian bought a television set in 1958, and in 1959 the state provided him with a car called a *Pobieda*, the only one in his village, although there are three of the cheaper model called a *Moskvitch*.

On the second day Agapian visits the University, and in front of it he meets a group of *Uzbeks**. Students are the future of any country. In all there are over two million university students in the U.S.S.R., and fifty million Soviet citizens, adults as well as children, or one-fifth of the whole population, are said to be attending some form of educational institution. Not only does the state attempt to provide education for all, it also claims to ensure a higher standard of living for those with higher intellectual qualifications and university degrees. After leaving the University, Agapian goes towards the Moskva river, where there are tall, recently completed blocks of flats*. Behind the big new buildings one can get a glimpse of the little wooden *isbas* which still give to parts of Moscow a rural appearance.

Next, our Armenian tourist turns into the nearest underground* station to go back to Red Square. At first his oriental imagination makes him think he has stumbled into a palace out of the *Arabian Nights*, but it really is the underground, and Agapian gets out near the large store called GUM*. His wife has given him a long list of things to buy there. In the evening Agapian and his fellow countrymen are invited to dinner at a *kolkhoz*, and from the top of a hill crowned by farm buildings and the homes of the workers the tourists are shown the newly reclaimed land. Nearby some children of the *kolkhoz* are getting ready for a picnic with their school-mistress*.

808

809

810

811

812

814

813

Agapian has yet to fulfil the most important commission given by his wife. The day after his arrival, Theodore Gabrielovitch goes to one of the fashion houses and takes a look at their latest models*. 811 Agapian's wife is rather stout and he is frightened he will not find anything to fit her, but he need not have worried. He sees the dress he wants and is determined to have it right away, whatever the price. People explain to him that the dresses themselves are not for sale, only the paper patterns for making them, and Agapian finds himself out on the pavement again with his piece of paper clutched in his hand. His guide takes pity on him and shows him a shop where they find the material they want, though not without a certain amount of difficulty. Now it will be up to his wife to cope with it. Before leaving the shop he and the guide linger in the furniture department where there is such an ingenious piece of furniture on show that the salesman has to demonstrate three times the way it works. It is for a child's bedroom, and it can become a bed, or a table or a cupboard at will*. 812 Agapian will not yet have stopped talking about it by the time he gets home to Erivan. But the guide is getting impatient. It is time they went to visit a 'park of rest and culture'*. 813 Among the woods where children are playing, they find exhibition halls, reading rooms, a chess club, a restaurant and a bar where they are serving orange sodas. Not far away are sports grounds and a dance floor. The next morning they have to catch the plane back to Erivan, but a long three-day stop-over has been arranged at a Crimean seaside town* 814 with its palm trees and oleanders.

## Leisure is a government project.

815

817

China in 1949 was still living an eighteenth-century form of life, but already there has been an astonishing transformation. For hundreds of years it had been accepted that thousands of Chinese people would die every year from starvation or floods. People still die, but now agrarian reform, collective farming and the regrouping of the rural population into communes, organised along the lines of military camps, have radically transformed the life of the nation. A hundred and fifty million peasants clad in dungarees* and fed in canteens have altered the face of the Chinese landscape. The commune provides for the needs of the whole country. In 1960 the number of children attending primary school* was one hundred million, or a sixth of the population. In 1950 there was little industry, but today factories are springing up by the hundreds. In the near future China, a country traditionally dependent on agriculture and commerce, may become a third great industrial region of the world, after the United States and Europe. China is a world where so much changes from one year to the next that it is impossible to draw an accurate picture of daily life, for facts that are true today will be out of date by tomorrow. The youthful processions* which march past the nation's leaders in Peking, on the threshold of the old forbidden city of the Emperors, are filled with enthusiasm that is more than duty. China's development into the nation she is today presents a fantastic example to other under-developed countries in showing what under-nourishment, under-employment and degradation can drive nations to accomplish in the space of a single generation. Students learn modern dances* with the same vigour as they learn about the modern world in their studies, and it is they who will constitute the professional classes of the future.

816

818

China, no longer patient, joins in the quickened pace.

819

821

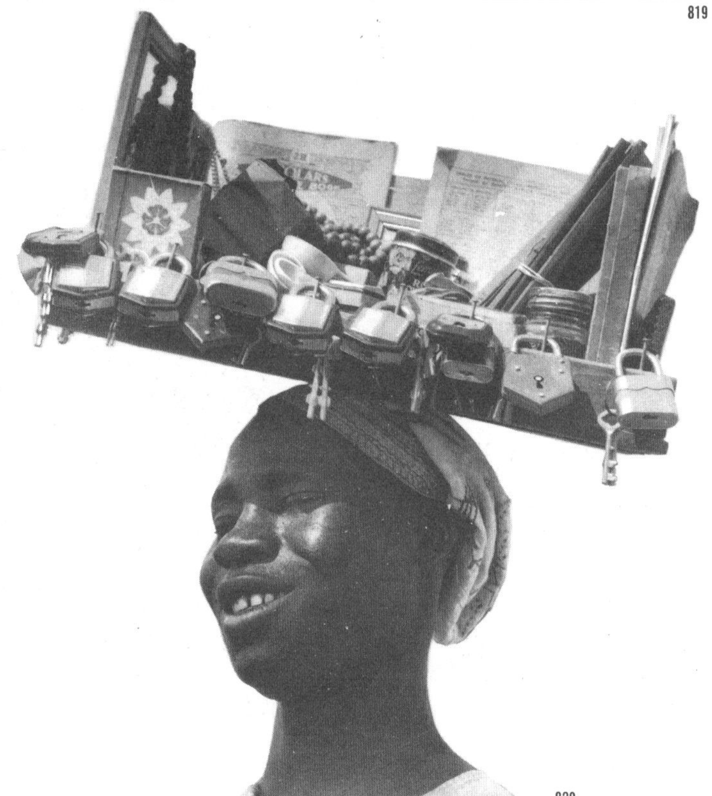

820

Beyond the huge areas of the world where our complicated modern civilisation has grown and spread, there are still vast stretches of the world where civilisation is only beginning to penetrate. There are still two thousand six hundred million human beings living at well below starvation level: seventy per cent of the world's population get less than the minimum of two thousand five hundred calories of nourishment per day, below which the morbid symptoms of malnutrition generally appear. Among these hundreds of millions of people there are some who are heirs to the remains of what in the past have been brilliant and progressive civilisations; others have simply ceased to keep pace with the development of the rest of humanity. In most cases they have been ignorant of the existence of other civilisations. These African women* are only beginning to reap one of the greatest benefits of civilisation—education; and to discover with delighted wonder the simplest objects which are in daily use elsewhere*. The arrival of European slave traders did nothing to alleviate the abject poverty which has been the unhappy lot of Africans for centuries. For all its ills, later colonisation did provide the beginnings of benefits to the governed.

819 820

But civilisation plays tricks and progress seems

822

823

821 If the Indians of North and South America* had not been suppressed by European invaders and their descendants confined to reservations, their civilisation might have continued its natural evolution through today. In Peru and Bolivia the descendants of the Incas, though they still cling
822 stubbornly to the ancient dress* and customs of their people, are now little more than a starving rabble.

People like this are scattered over the earth's surface; they are a proportion of the population of some Latin-American states, almost the whole of black Africa, the majority of the Muslim populations of the Middle East, the four hundred million inhabitants of India and, up till very recently, the six hundred million people of China.

Japan has imitated the technological progress of the western nations without achieving their same social enlightenment, but as mass education
823 spreads* there is a chance that this too will come. All these different peoples are the victims of a phenomenon which international experts are only beginning to study: under-development. It is a problem which mankind must face during the last forty years of the twentieth century.

-pass the once-great. Passive Incas pose for tourists.

824

825

827

An under-developed country is first and foremost an under-nourished country, and a place where the population is under-employed. As long as political power in these countries rests in the hands of a minority of feudal landowners, and as long as economic necessities are subject to foreign pressures, national efforts towards building up industry are doomed to failure. Characteristic of the present situation is the fact that the under-developed countries themselves are acutely aware of their problems. If these countries are to develop further, the first essential is the speedy growth of an educated minority* able to furnish from among themselves the specialists they need in every field of modern life. Europeans long believed that men whose skin was black or yellow must be the intellectual inferiors of those whose skin was white, and it has only recently been acknowledged that they are fully as capable of assimilating education* as white men, and using it probably more keenly in their eagerness for knowledge. Rapid population expansion has necessitated immense projects for reclaiming land, irrigation and soil improvement. The population of the world has doubled in a little over half a century, and by the year 2000 the under-developed countries of Asia, Africa and South America will account for eighty per cent of the world's population. In certain lands the desert is already producing harvests*, but if they are to achieve results, the cultivators must know that they are working for themselves and their children. In most countries there are resources, especially of minerals, which have been insufficiently exploited or exploited by foreigners; for example, almost all the oil of Iraq and Saudi Arabia is

826

And where progress is slowest, birthrate is highest. The earth giv

830-831
➛

828

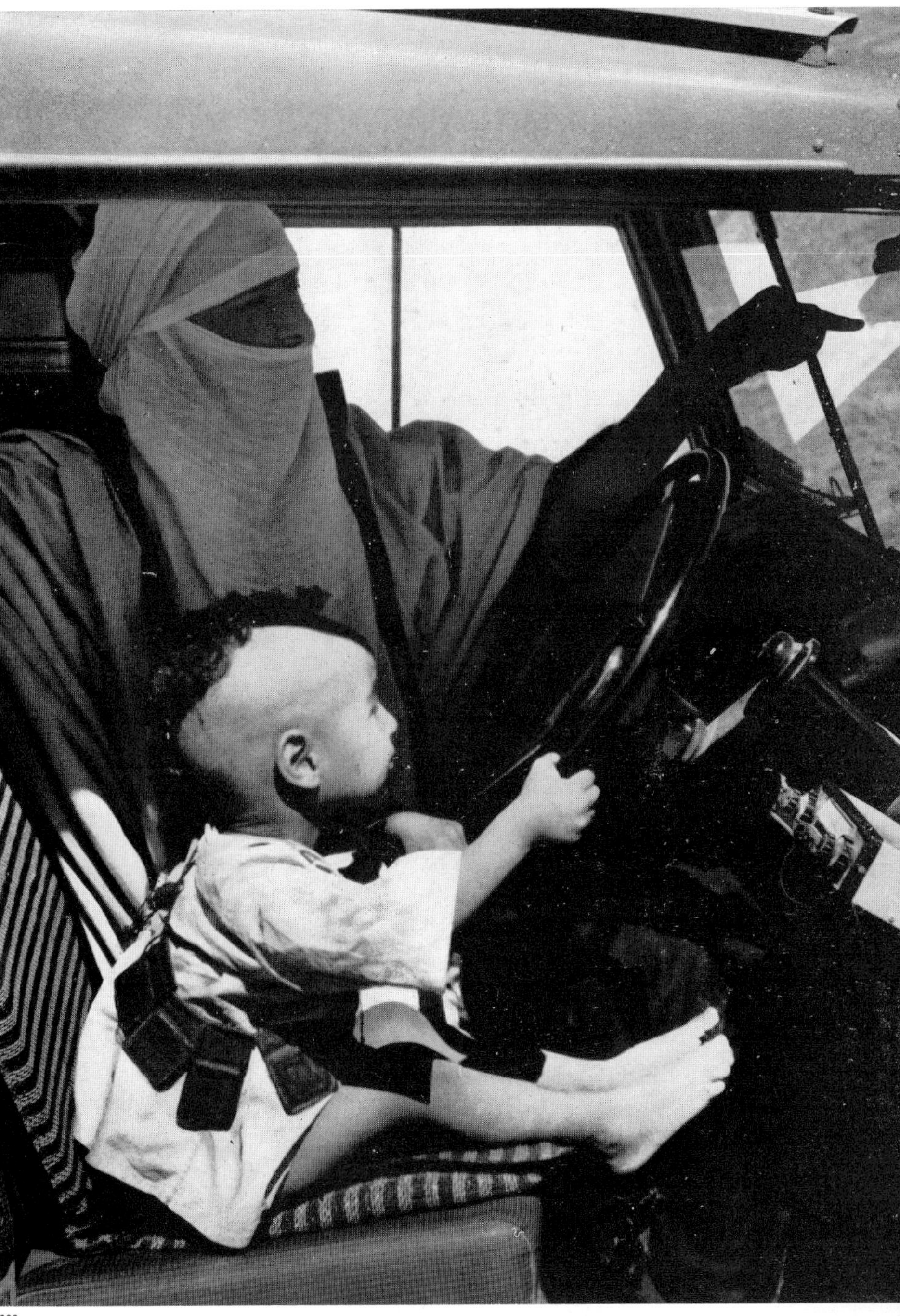

829

exported for lack of native industry. They need tools which only industry can provide. Only industry can absorb the surplus labour which concentrates on the outskirts of large cities and forms a mass of unemployed, living from hand to mouth in shanty towns. These disorganised, underfed masses, among whom disease spreads unchecked, need doctors and proper medical supplies*; decent houses must be built for them. This negro in a Brazilian shipyard is using an adze, an implement as useful today as it was several thousand years ago*. Furthermore, a network of communications must be constructed to combat the economic isolation of different regions, so that trade connections can be established. This desert Bedouin may be the first of his tribe to drive a truck instead of a camel, but his son will have been accustomed to it from birth*.

827 828 829

It is in these countries that we can find the most striking and significant contrasts of our time. Veiled Pakistani women squat on the ground near the buildings of Chandigar, one of the world's most modern cities*, and smiling African women carrying bundles on their heads walk in single file past the mechanical giant shifting the red earth of their native land*.

830 831

ʼhat it has, but a new means is exploited for survival: education.

# But the past often crops up unexpectedly—in church, in monarchy, in custo

832

833

But this contrast between the ways of the old world and the new is not confined to backward countries. It exists everywhere, but is now such a recognised part of our daily lives that we do not notice it. 832 This uniformed beadle* is a Swiss guard, the direct successor of the soldiers of Swiss regiments who guarded the palaces and persons of the kings of France and stood at the gates of noble mansions; today he walks at the head of a procession of first communicants, whose dresses and veils have been the same since their great-grandmothers' time.

Little family ceremonies date back to beliefs whose origins have long since been forgotten. In country places in France a young bride still cuts a white ribbon, stretched across her path, with a pair of scissors*. The old, horse-drawn carriage is only 833 used today on state occasions or, in some parts of Europe, as a hearse*. It is in the Church and in the 834 ceremonial surrounding royalty that the old customs have most often been preserved unaltered. In Catholic and Orthodox countries, monks and priests still wear the robes that men wore in the

834

835

836

ıd in costumes. Gypsies have been touched by no age and no country.

837 838

Middle Ages. Wherever monarchies survive, the changing of the guard is still a colourful ceremony that attracts spectators to watch the bear-skins and 835 bright uniforms*. In the streets of Seville during Holy Week there are still the processions of 836 penitents* who seem to have emerged from a childhood nightmare. Secretive and indomitable, 837 coming from no one knows where, the gypsies* still keep up their perpetual wandering across Europe. Centuries ago they may have come from India. In modern Japan men in Western clothes sit in tea-houses and are entertained by geishas* 838 in traditional costume while they eat. From south-east Asia to north-west Europe, age-old prayers and devotions are kept up. The burning incense this Vietnamese woman holds above her head* 839 and the candle flame lighted by a Russian peasant in Zagorsk* are equally links with the shreds of 840 history. This Danish postman*, on his bicycle, 841 wears a uniform from the era of Hans Christian Andersen, but then Santa Claus himself belongs to no particular time or place.

839 841

840

842

of the earth. Among them are the Sardinian woman spinning the wool from her own sheep*, 842 the Egyptian fellah working the *shaduf* to empty buckets of water into his irrigation ditches, the Mexican peasant pounding maize with a stone and the Eskimo piling up blocks of snow to build his igloo*. The Indian hunter of the Amazon basin 843 will see the spaces which are his livelihood slowly

845

Such things as rituals, ceremonies and even local costumes are likely to survive in the world of the future, for these are essentially traditional; but the actions and activities which have been a familiar part of men's lives for thousands of years are already being remorselessly wiped off the face

disappearing as the land is reclaimed and turned into plantations. The nomadic tribes of the Sahara will be forced, willingly or unwillingly, to abandon their camel-hair tents* and adapt their age-old 844 way of life to the oil wells springing up around them. Adaptation to modern life is primarily

843

844

## ...at the tourist finds convenient to overlook.

achieved by imitation. During this period there will be Kanakas in pyjamas, Polynesians in print dresses and Bantus in football jerseys. Later, once the barriers have been broken down, it is likely that some local habits will return, simply because they suit the climate, the peoples' temperament or the local resources better than those imported wholesale from the West. Some things that seem to us curious and picturesque are merely one aspect of poverty. As they are preserved only at the cost of famine, disease and despair, we must look forward to their disappearance.

Before long, even the darkest corners of the world will be enjoying the fruits of other continents, just as the West does today. We have only to think of our daily meals without the potatoes, beans and tomatoes which came from the South American Indians, the peaches, apricots, oranges, bananas and, above all, the tea which came from Asia, the olives, apples, pears, cherries, dates, almonds and figs from the Mediterranean. It was not in the West that corn was first cultivated, or sheep, poultry and cattle domesticated, giving us milk, butter and eggs. Coffee, though today's comes mostly from Brazil, originated in Ethiopia. The groundnuts and bananas of Africa were originally products of central Asia, and the cotton grown in the United States and in Egypt came first from India.

Looked at in the light of its history, our daily life seems to have been formed by elements from every corner of the earth. It is a bridge connecting different nations and continents and gives an underlying continuity to apparently unconnected areas of history. It is the most substantial bond of brotherhood between all men, for it is every human being's struggle towards a better life on earth, and in that struggle the exploitation of some has not necessarily led to the lasting good of others.

Let us look once more at some scenes from a way of life that was hard and dangerous but free and full of adventure too, before these have become only memories. Expectation of life was much shorter than it commonly is today, but it may have been lived at a much greater intensity, for every moment was a bitter struggle. In this Bolivian village the street sweeper's costume goes back to the Middle Ages*. Siamese peasants are 845

846

holding back their fierce fighting cocks before the combat*. In a hut somewhere in Laos there is a 846 scene of witchcraft from a bygone era*, and on the 847 verandah of a house built on piles, deep in the jungle, an old Dayak is squatting, gazing into the distance and thinking of the past*. 848

847

848

849 851

850

Among these people, direct communion with nature, contact with the supernatural, surrender to the powerful undercurrents flowing strongly in all human beings and finding their release in music, rhythm and song* are still a part of day-to-day reality. For this native* of New Guinea his ornaments are still, as they have always been, the symbols of a fundamental change. We may be surprised and even shocked at these primitive survivals, but we must acknowledge that they reflect an ancient wisdom. Lost in their anonymous cities, jostled by the panting life of today and lonely among the crowds, the people of Western countries sometimes find themselves yearning for a brief return to the life of the savage. Perhaps there is much we could still learn from such savages as remain. We need not go the extremes of imitating the head-shrinking techniques of the Jivaros* of Ecuador; the fashion for this is already dying out, but we can at least learn again the value of silence, peace, patience, manual dexterity, lack of worry, ingenuity and observation.

849 850 851

But whether we live in the jungle of nature or of machines we a

852

By following the general trends of this history of daily life we may try to lift a small corner of the veil drawn across the life of the future. If some of the pressures on modern life are not resolved, we may, in these three pictures, make a guess at the outlines of the life of a woman at the end of the twentieth century. In the first there is complete isolation at work*: the individual becoming absorbed into more and more abstract tasks, entrenched behind a battery of filing cabinets, calculating machines and electronic brains, a work only interrupted by frequent, necessary rests. In the second, the extreme simplification of all domestic chores: with a push-button kitchen* in which an electronic brain coordinates an ever-more complex range of precision instruments. Lastly, there will be the need for medical cures to induce relaxation*, made necessary by constant wear and tear on the nerves. This is a caricature of course, but the fact that it is even a remotely conceivable picture of life in the near future should make us pause and think.

853

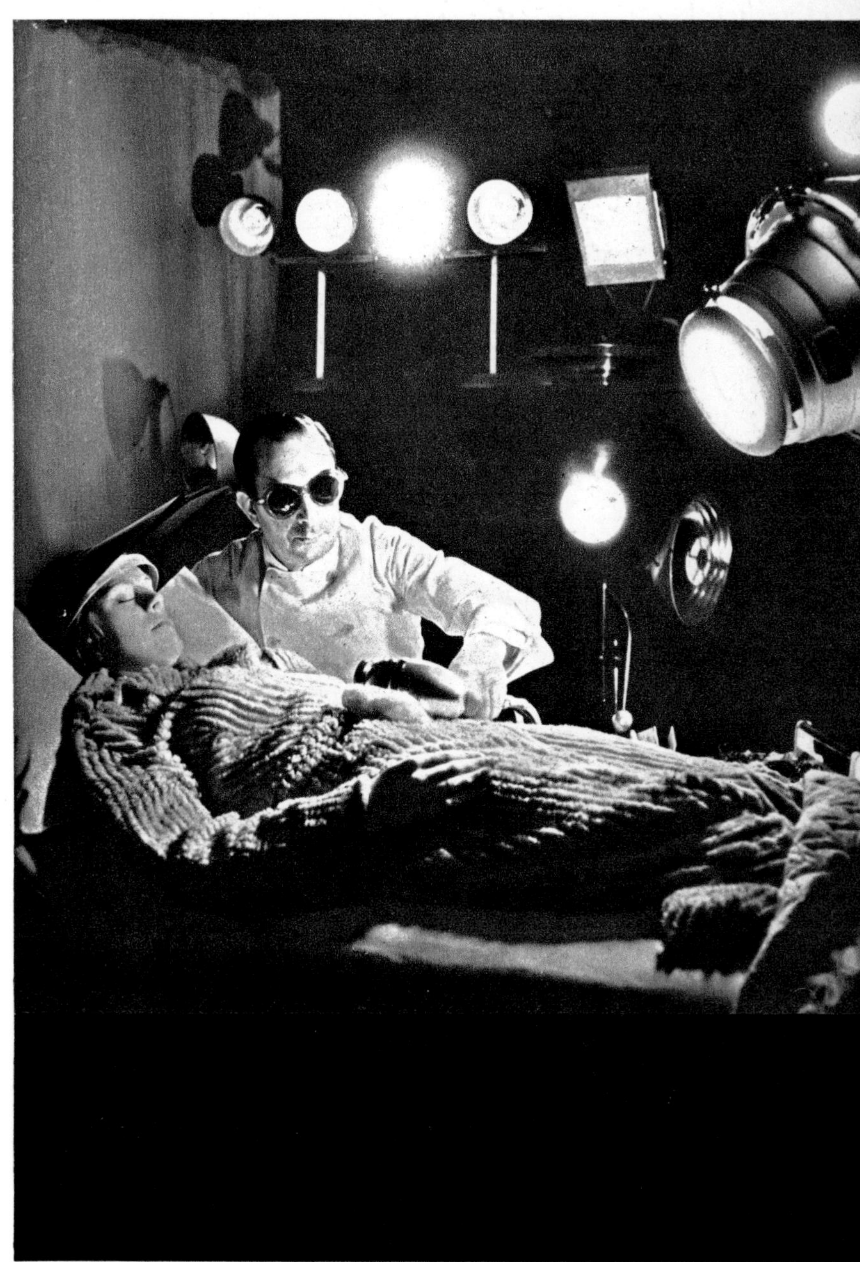

854

und together by what we share in common: our humanity.

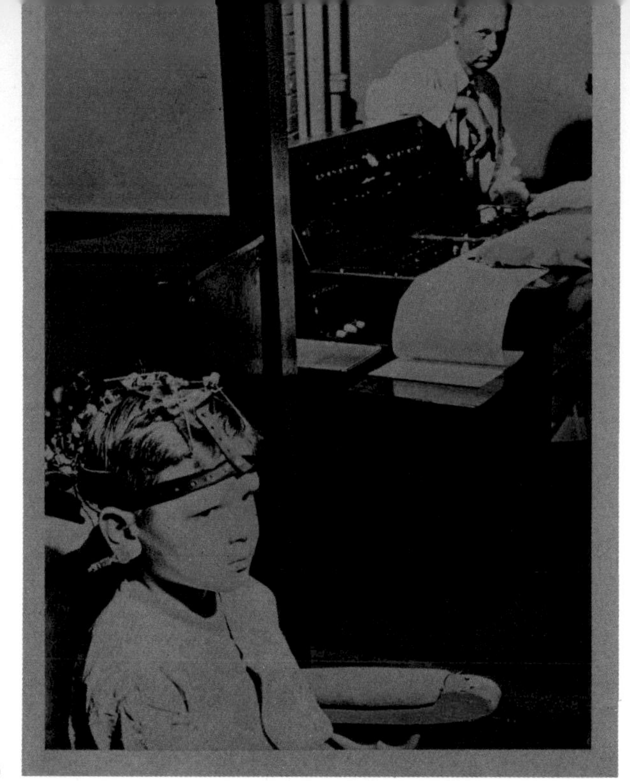

855

tion of the population. In remoter areas in Europe, which have for so long existed only on the fringe of the general progress, basic changes must be made if they are to wave aside the dead hand of traditionalism. One of the tasks of the years to come will be the creation of a new rural culture to meet the need for fewer hands and more brains in modern farming.

As these countries develop, it is to education that they must turn the full force of their efforts. All of them now have primary education, but this is no longer sufficient equipment for the times in which we are living. It is to secondary education for everybody, and higher education within the reach of all who can benefit from it, that the most advanced nations of the world look for the means of exploiting their resources to the full. The essential factor in human progress is not simply raising output at all costs but increasing productivity. Before 1850 the Western world already

856

Modern science has produced wonderful treatments for nervous disorders; doctors are able to 855 watch the brain working* and fathom its troubles, sometimes even to cure them. But there is still more to be done. We must eliminate the primary cause of the trouble. It is a long and difficult task, but there are indications to show that it is within the bounds of possibility and that, in some directions, the work has even been begun. In the great industrial countries nation-wide planning schemes are being formulated, tending towards the decentralisation of industry and culture and redistribu-

857

An over-populated world must plan together to survive.

needed more food than it could provide; for a hundred years it was starved of manufactured goods; now, in the 1960's, these needs are satisfied or very nearly so. In the foreseeable future, much closer at hand than public opinion in general is aware, automation* and the peaceful use of atomic energy* may reduce the length of the working day even further and eliminate unpleasant jobs altogether. In the world of tomorrow there may be no more labourers, only skilled workers, engineers and administrators. In consequence the social strata which exist today would be radically altered or even eliminated. It cannot be expected that rich and poor nations will respond to this development at the same pace, but ultimately the extremes between wealth and poverty are bound to be reduced and no longer will the rich get richer and the poor get poorer. Another hitherto insuperable obstacle which time will remove in the world of the future is the existence side by side of

856 857

858

859

860

overcrowded slums and empty deserts. Nature, too, is about to undergo great changes: reclamation and reallotment, so that the day should come when every corner of the earth may be equally inhabitable*. 858

Man has conquered the earth. Now it is his task to set it in order, and he owes it to himself to master his own nature as well as he has mastered the world. This can only happen if his physical needs are satisfied, his work related to his abilities, his life passed in congenial surroundings* and his home facilitated for him by modern methods*. 859 860

One great source of hope: the peaceful uses of the atom.

861

862

Future historians of daily life may well look back on the period in which we live as a decisive moment in human history. Probably for the first time in the history of the world scientists, technicians, economists and designers are working together, making fundamental reappraisals of life and proposing radical solutions. The great question today is whether we shall have the wisdom to listen to their findings and the courage to follow them, or if we shall be content with the half-measures that are so often no more than an excuse for lack of faith. Undoubtedly some conceptions* may seem 861 too bold, but Gothic art, printing, railways and electricity were also in their time stigmatised as eccentricities with no future. Man has already travelled far and fast in his march forward; now he is ready to voyage into space*, but still he must 862 learn to control the earth before the moon will be any use to him.

For this it is not enough to open new shipyards and build new cities*; a cure must be found for 863 the devastation already created on earth by lawless and irresponsible exploitation. Having struggled against nature for thousands of years, man must now learn to cooperate with it. The enjoyment of natural beauty must not be allowed to become a thing of the past; it must belong as much to the life of the man of tomorrow* and become an 864 integral part of urban living. We live in an era of opportunity. If we are to confront it with imagination, we need to know the real history of mankind: it does not lie in catalogues of kings and their battles but in people's daily lives.

864

On the vast threshold of a new era, Space; the horizon is where we put it.

Then there will be the earth, faithful friend,

and man,

whose long and wayward journey

of daily life will have led him at last to . . .

THE END

# Tables and Index of Illustrations

# GEOGRAPHICAL SURVEY OF THE ELEMENTS OF DAILY LIFE

| | | SHELTER | | |
|---|---|---|---|---|
| | | BUILDING | INTERIORS | VEGETABLE F |
| EUROPE | North | igloo | | rye, chicory<br>cabbage, turni<br>beet, bilberry<br>whortleberry |
| | West | cement<br>reinforced<br>concrete<br>pointed arch | oak<br>walnut<br>rushes<br>fireplace<br>glass windows | lettuce, salsify, c<br>celery, truffles, sc<br>carrot, chestnu<br>hazelnut, strawb<br>raspberry, blackcu<br>gooseberry |
| | East | isba | stove | hops, sauerkra<br>bortsch, nuts |
| | Mediterranean | round arch | mosaic | olive, pea<br>artichoke, cele<br>asparagus, lee<br>parsley, grape<br>rhubarb |
| ASIA | West | mud<br>brick<br>arch<br>flat roof | | wheat, barley, ra<br>spinach, onion, a<br>pear, plum, cherry,<br>fig, date, pistac<br>pomegranate, o |
| | Central | yurt | | saracen-corn, ry<br>apricot |
| | East<br>(China, Japan) | peaked roof<br>paper houses | thuya<br>lacquer<br>sliding walls<br>screens<br>blinds | rice, bamboo-sh<br>soya, sea-weed, p<br>orange, lemon, ma<br>litchi, Chinese arti |
| | South<br>(India, Malaya<br>Indonesia) | | teak<br>sandalwood<br>bamboo<br>cane | rice, millet, auber<br>cucumber, gher<br>groundnuts, sugar<br>banana, coconut, gr |
| AFRICA | North<br>(including Egypt<br>and Ethiopia) | column | | cabbage, beans, arti<br>melon, watermelon, |
| | Central<br>and South | mud huts | | sorghum |
| AMERICA | North<br>and Central | tents, huts | | maize, Jerusalem ar<br>pumpkin, melon, wat |
| | South | huts | mahogany<br>rosewood<br>hammock | manioc, tomato, m<br>beans, potato, sweet<br>pineapple, guava, a<br>pumpkin |
| AUSTRALASIA | | houses built<br>on piles | | taro, yam<br>tetragonia |

| OD AND DRINK | | | WASHING AND DRESSING | | TRANSPORT | |
|---|---|---|---|---|---|---|
| NIMAL FOODS | DRINK | SPICES, DRUGS MEDICINES | HYGIENE | MATERIALS AND DYES | DRAUGHT ANIMALS | MEANS |
| seal<br>whale<br>cod | | chives | sauna<br>ambergris | | reindeer | kayak<br>skis |
| rabbit<br>herring<br>sardine<br>oysters<br>mussels | cider<br>cognac<br>gin<br>whisky | mustard<br>digitalis<br>valerian | soap | | | |
| caviar<br>sturgeon<br>*kefir*<br>yoghurt | *kwass*<br>vodka | tarragon<br>horseradish<br>paprika | | | | |
| tunnyfish | | thyme<br>rosemary<br>savory<br>hyssop<br>garlic | lavender | purple | | |
| mutton<br>goat<br>beef | wine<br>beer | poppy<br>capers<br>hashish<br>myrrh<br>balsam<br>gum arabic | hammam<br>kohl<br>henna<br>attar of roses<br>incense | wool<br>linen | | cart |
| | *koumys* | | musk | hemp<br>felt | yak<br>camel<br>horse | snow-shoes<br>sledge |
| dog<br>birds' nest<br>sharks' fin | palm wine<br>tea<br>*saké* | aniseed<br>opium | | silk | | rickshaw |
| beef<br>buffalo<br>pork<br>chicken<br>pheasant | | cinnamon<br>betel<br>benzoin<br>pepper | sandalwood | cotton<br>jute<br>grass cloth<br>indigo | elephant<br>ox<br>humped ox<br>buffalo | |
| | coffee | senna | civet | | donkey<br>dromedary | sailing boat |
| guinea fowl | | castor oil | | | | |
| turkey | | tobacco<br>chewing gum<br>peyotl, aloes | castor | sisal<br>cochineal | | |
| guinea pig | cocoa<br>*maté*<br>chicha | vanilla, pimento<br>cocaine<br>quinine<br>ipecacuana<br>friars balsam | | alpaca wool<br>vicuna wool<br>rubber | llama | |
| | | cloves, nutmeg | | | | outrigger-<br>canoe |

# HISTORY OF THE ELEMENTS OF DAILY LIFE

| | TECHNOLOGY | | HOUSING | | FO |
|---|---|---|---|---|---|
| | TOOLS AND MATERIALS | TECHNIQUES AND DISCOVERIES | STRUCTURE | DECORATION | INGREDIE |
| **PREHISTORY** | | | | | |
| **Neanderthal Man** | stone tools<br>axe-heads<br>sticks for digging | scavenging<br>hunting<br>fire | wind-breaks | | roots, ber<br>game |
| **Homo sapiens: Aurignacian Solutrian** | elaboration of tools<br>knives, scrapers<br>javelin, bow(?) | oil lamp<br>torch<br>game traps | cave<br>brushwood hut | cave paintings | smoked m<br>shellfis |
| **Homo sapiens: Magdalenian** | bone and horn tools: fish-hooks<br>harpoons, needles<br>catapults, boomerangs | sewing<br>domestication of dogs | | fresco-decorated sanctuaries | fish<br>honey |
| **Neolithic** | polished stone tools, hoe, sickle<br>millstone, spindle<br>distaff, loom<br>gridiron | agriculture and domestication of sheep, goats<br>cattle, threshing<br>pottery, weaving | thatched hut<br>house on piles<br>granaries<br>tents | woven mats<br>braziers | cereals:<br>meal, porri<br>bread, cak<br>milk, cheese |
| **ANCIENT HISTORY** | | | | | |
| **First urban civilisations East Mediterranean 4000–1000 B.C.** | metal tools:<br>plough, spade<br>cart wheel<br>potter's wheel<br>saw, square, bellows | irrigation<br>metal-working:<br>copper, bronze<br>iron, decorated<br>pottery, glass | houses of brick, mud, wattle<br>whitewashed walls<br>flat roofs<br>temples, arches | bed clothes, chest<br>stool, bench<br>chair<br>table, lock | butcher's m<br>cultivated f<br>and vegeta<br>olive oi<br>wine, be |
| **Classical period 1000 B.C.–500 A.D.** | trowel, plane(?)<br>pincers, nail, screw | welding, mortar<br>coinage | bridges, aqueducts<br>theatres, baths<br>amphitheatres<br>vaulted roofs<br>tiles | oiled-parchment window-covering<br>key, hanging lamp | gruel<br>cultivated ca<br>salt foo<br>cured me<br>garum (fish s<br>botargo |
| **MIDDLE AGES** | | | | | |
| **The Far East 100–1200** | spinning wheel<br>telescope | artesian wells<br>coal, gunpowder<br>porcelain, printing<br>paper-money | peaked roofs<br>glazed tiles | lacquered furniture<br>brick oven | cane sug<br>noodles<br>ginger |
| **The West 500–1200** | collar-harness<br>horseshoes<br>stirrups | windmills<br>water-wheels<br>alcohol, tapers<br>wax candles | slates<br>fireplaces<br>stained glass | bin, chest<br>tiled floor<br>rush-strewn floor | sweetmeats, r<br>sugared alm<br>starch foods<br>canary bre |
| **The West 1200–1500** | scissors, hinges | cast iron<br>majolica ware<br>faience ware | houses with exposed beams and jutting upper storey | sideboard, dresser<br>tapestries<br>glazed tile stove | cultivated stra<br>raspberri<br>pickled her<br>waffles, wa<br>sparkling |
| **MODERN TIMES** | | | | | |
| **The West XVIth Century** | cobalt | microscope<br>machine-knitted stockings | parquet floors<br>latticed windows | upholstered chairs<br>cupboard, cabinet<br>panelling<br>wall fountain | cauliflow<br>asparagus, fra<br>macaroons, b<br>chocolate, dri |
| **XVIIth Century** | crystal | pressure cooker<br>barometer<br>astronomical telescope<br>clock springs<br>air pump | ashlar<br>glazed windows | tapestry-covered arm-chairs<br>console table<br>commodes<br>warming pans<br>cast-iron stove | sausage<br>meat pie<br>crème Char<br>béchamel, cro<br>ices, tea, c<br>marc (liqu |
| **XVIIIth Century (before 1780)** | galvanised iron,<br>tin, nickel<br>bleach | thermometer<br>lightning conductor<br>steam engine | apartment buildings<br>wrought iron | chaise-longue<br>easy chair<br>chiffonier<br>dressing-table<br>wallpaper, desk | various m<br>pâté de foie<br>mayonnaise,<br>meringues, p<br>increased u<br>potato |

| UTENSILS | PERSONAL HABITS<br>CLOTHES | ADORNMENT, HEALTH AND HYGIENE | TRANSPORT | EDUCATION ENTERTAINMENT RECORDING OF TIME |
|---|---|---|---|---|
| griddle<br>barbecue pit | skins | body-painting | | |
| stone oven<br>cooking by hot stones thrown into water | | rouge, ochre<br>cosmetic palettes, tattooing<br>stone and bone necklaces<br>trepanning | raft | sculpture<br>painting, engraving<br>magic, dancing<br>initiation ceremonies |
| pots made of hide and of bark(?) | skins sewn together | bone pins<br>flint razors | canoe | |
| terracotta vessels<br>cauldron<br>cooking pot<br>millstone | loin cloth<br>woollen robe<br>codpiece | combs | pack animals | |
| hard stone jars<br>stoppered jars<br>metal buckets<br>spoons | linen garments<br>sandles, buckles, wig | ornaments of gold and precious stones<br>metal mirrors<br>perfumes, cosmetics<br>medicine | solid wheel:<br>4-wheel<br>horse-drawn chariot<br>sailing ship<br>spoked wheel:<br>2-wheeled chariot<br>decked ships | writing<br>clay tablets, papyrus<br>draughts, dice<br>sundial<br>lunar year, Sothic calendar<br>school of scribes |
| casserole, stove<br>sieves, brick oven<br>barrel | draped garments<br>toga, chiton<br>silk<br>breeches, hood | thermal baths<br>Hippocratic medicine<br>lavatories, dental powder<br>soap<br>spas, cupping | saddle horses<br>litter<br>road-building<br>galley, anchor | parchment<br>theatre<br>athletics, circus games<br>schools<br>hourglass, water clocks<br>sundials<br>Julian calendar |
| china vessels | silk clothes | acupuncture | wheelbarrow<br>compass | printing, newspaper<br>polo, kites<br>mah-jong<br>shadow puppets |
| table-cloth<br>chalice<br>ewer, trencher | breeches<br>hooded cloak<br>buttons, furs | hospital<br>cauterisation<br>medicinal alcohol<br>tub baths | horse collar<br>shoeing, stirrups<br>rudder | chess, football<br>tournament, quintain<br>handball |
| napkin, tankard<br>pewter vessels<br>aquamanile | velvet<br>underwear<br>shirt, tunic<br>surcoat, doublet<br>and hose, tabard<br>hennin | spectacles<br>mercury-backed mirrors<br>commode | wheelbarrow<br>canals<br>sluice gates<br>post horses | hockey, golf, playing cards<br>pendulum clock<br>printing<br>woodblock engraving |
| spit<br>use of forks<br>drinking glasses | serge, muslin<br>cap, farthingale<br>fan, muff, doublet | study of anatomy<br>lancing of boils<br>tourniquets | coach | court tennis<br>bowls, skittles<br>watches<br>Gregorian calendar |
| silverware<br>coffee mill<br>teapot, coffeepot<br>corks, corkscrew<br>sugar-tongs<br>glass decanters | periwig<br>fitted coat<br>waistcoat<br>knee breeches<br>cravat | quinine<br>calomel, forceps<br>gradual elimination of principal epidemics<br>blood-circulation discovered<br>intravenous injections<br>establishment of big hospitals<br>blood transfusions | carriage<br>sedan chair | lead pencils<br>billiards<br>backgammon, whist<br>wall clocks |
| rolling-pin<br>four-pronged fork<br>cast-iron kitchen range | hoops, corsets<br>umbrella | disappearance of famine in the West<br>bidet<br>flush-lavatory | covered barges<br>windjammers<br>packet boats<br>cabs, stage coaches<br>macadam roads<br>iron bridges<br>steam drays | steel nibs<br>boxing<br>water-polo<br>cricket<br>rowing<br>baseball<br>eraser |

# SCIENTIFIC DISCOVERIES AND DAILY LIFE FROM THE END OF T

| | SCIENTIFIC AND TECHNOLOGICAL DISCOVERIES | PREPARATION AND PRESERVATION OF FOOD | DOMESTIC IMPROVEMENTS | HEALTH AND HYGIENE |
|---|---|---|---|---|
| 1780 | birth of modern chemistry<br>mechanical loom | cognac | eiderdown<br>coal gas<br>argand lamp | household bleach<br>water closet<br>wooden legs |
| 1790 | Chappe's telegraph<br>metric system | beet sugar | cement | smallpox vaccinations |
| 1800 | Volta's battery<br>nitrous oxide<br>matches | | main drainage | |
| 1810 | | preserved foods | | iodine, stethoscope<br>morphine, quinine |
| 1820 | electrodynamics<br>mechanical harvester<br>beginning of photography | | composite candle | hydrogen peroxide<br>false teeth |
| 1830 | paraffin, electric telegraph<br>electric motor<br>electroplating | ice cream (U.S.A.) | phosphorus matches<br>aneroid barometer | lorgnette, monocle<br>homeopathic medicine |
| 1840 | transformer<br>vulcanite<br>pneumatics | gas cooker | plywood | elastic bandage<br>rubber hospital mattresses<br>ether and chloroform anaesthe |
| 1850 | aluminium<br>petroleum | endives<br>condensed milk<br>percolator | laundry machine<br>gas lighting | bone-setting plaster<br>cocaine |
| 1860 | celluloid<br>ammonia refrigeration<br>reinforced concrete | margarine<br>cold storage | linoleum<br>oil lamp | |
| 1870 | Mendel's law, roller, flour-mill<br>telephone, microphone<br>gramophone, electric light bulb | white bread | hydraulic lift<br>central heating | digitaline, thermometer<br>pasteurisation, pills<br>antisepsis, sterilisation |
| 1880 | arc lamps, internal combustion engine<br>liquid gas, fluorine<br>ironing machine, petrol engine | patent foods | gas mantle<br>electric lift<br>electric bell | incubator, sanatoria<br>iron lung, baby carriages<br>anti-rabies vaccine |
| 1890 | Ader's aeroplane, cinema, radio<br>Hertzian waves, X-rays<br>ultra-violet rays | chocolate bars<br>lump sugar<br>thermos flask | fitted carpets<br>Swedish matches | blood-pressure gauge<br>flushing lavatory, running wat<br>toilet paper, suppositories |
| 1900 | radium, radio-activity<br>argon, helium, liquid air | | | anti-diphtheria serum<br>radiotherapy |
| 1905 | theory of relativity<br>first hydro-electric plants | | electric iron | X-rays |
| 1910 | bakelite<br>vitamins | thermostat-controlled<br>electric ovens | home vacuum cleaner<br>pocket torch | skin grafting |
| 1915 | | | | chlorinated water |
| 1920 | splitting the atom | | | insulin<br>psychoanalysis |
| 1925 | penicillin | | | |
| 1930 | nylon<br>glycerine, alizaric resins<br>neon lighting | dietetics<br>yoghurt<br>electric percolator | sound-proofing | |
| 1935 | synthetic rubber<br>polythene | frigidaire | insulation, asbestos | ascorbic acid (vitamin C)<br>D.D.T.<br>plastic surgery, penicillin |
| 1940 | use of atomic energy<br>vinylite, silicones | | fluorescent lighting<br>air conditioning | sulphonamids, artificial limbs<br>electric razor, hearing aids<br>contact lenses |
| 1945 | | deep freeze<br>pressure cooker<br>frozen food | solar ray heating<br>washing machine | nylon toothbrush<br>streptomycin, cortisone<br>aureomycin |
| 1950 | | packet soups<br>electric coffee mill<br>automatic mixer | prefabricated houses | polio vaccine<br>isotopes<br>heart-surgery |
| 1955 | atoms-for-peace | | | chemical treatment of<br>nervous diseases |
| 1960 | | | | cancer and leukemia research |

# VIIIth CENTURY TO THE PRESENT

| DRESS AND FASHION | TRANSPORT AND COMMUNICATIONS | PUBLIC SERVICES | SOCIAL ADVANCES | INTELLECTUAL LIFE | SPORTS | |
|---|---|---|---|---|---|---|
| frock-coat | macadam roads<br>balloon, parachute | | | | | 1780 |
| | early form of bicycle | | Declaration of Rights of Man (Fr.) | lithography | | 1790 |
| trousers<br>top-hat<br>heavy coats | steamboat | street-numbering | | | | 1800 |
| | | | | | | 1810 |
| waterproofs, snowboots<br>opera-hat<br>mackintosh | locomotive<br>Stockton–Darlington Railway<br>first Atlantic steamship crossing | omnibus | Napoleonic Code | steam printing press | | 1820 |
| sewing-machine | postal service<br>tubular boiler, propeller | penny postage (Brit.) | | | rodeo (U.S.A.)<br>horse racing<br>sea bathing | 1830 |
| ready-made clothes | Morse code | | freedom of the press | daguerreotype | rugby<br>football | 1840 |
| crinoline<br>multiple stores | refrigerator cars<br>marine cable | | suppression of the knout (Russ.) | development of journalism<br>rotary press | baseball<br>canoeing<br>football | 1850 |
| synthetic dyes | clipper ships<br>internal combustion engine<br>Westinghouse brakes | electric lighthouse | abolition of slavery (U.S.A.) | wood-pulp paper | tennis | 1860 |
| black evening wear for men | sleeper and restaurant car<br>Suez canal<br>transcontinental railway, U.S.A. | mechanical streetsweeper<br>electric | | colour photos | summer mountaineering<br>bridge | 1870 |
| bowler hat | ball bearings, refrigerator ships<br>electric tram, telephone<br>Daimler cars, bicycle | street-light<br>dustbins | divorce | typewriter | | 1880 |
| mass-produced ready-made clothes, pyjamas | airships, submarines<br>corridor trains (60 m.p.h.) | long-distance telephone | | linotype | basket ball<br>Olympic Games | 1890 |
| suspenders, shoe-trees<br>men's low-quarter shoes | pneumatic tyres, Diesel engine<br>motor-cycle, Zeppelin<br>Ford production | | Boy Scout movement<br>65-hour week | cinema | Davis cup<br>Tour de France | 1900 |
| press-studs<br>soft hats | electric trains<br>aeroplane, speedometer | Paris Metro | votes for women (Brit.) | Nobel prize<br>radio | motor racing<br>International | 1905 |
| dinner jacket | helicopter, taxicab<br>Channel crossing by air<br>motorbus | | votes for women (U.S.A.) | roll-film | ski champs. | 1910 |
| coloured neckties | liners (30 knots) | | 60-hour week | | | 1915 |
| crepe- and rubber-soles | | nursery schools<br>garden cities | 45-hour week | | | 1920 |
| | aeroplane (180 m.p.h.) | | | | winter sports | 1925 |
| | Atlantic crossing by air<br>motorways<br>seaplanes, airmail | neon lighting | youth hostels | talking cinema | | 1930 |
| | Golden Gate Bridge (U.S.A.)<br>radar | | paid holidays<br>social security | television | skin diving<br>water skiing | 1935 |
| nylon stockings<br>synthetic fabrics | | self-service | | | | 1940 |
| blue jeans | motor scooters<br>jet aircraft | restaurant<br>launderette<br>supermarket | penal reform | spread of television | | 1945 |
| | | | movement against capital punishment | long-play records | | 1950 |
| | | | 40-hour week | | | 1955 |
| | sputnik, lunik | anti-air-pollution drives | | | | 1960 |

# Index of Illustrations

**ABBREVIATIONS**

| | |
|---|---|
| **Arch. Nat.** | Archives Nationales, Paris. |
| **B.N.** | Bibliothèque Nationale, Paris. |
| **Doc. Franc.** | Documentation Française. |
| **E.N.I.T.** | Ente Nazionale Industrie Turistiche. |
| **U.S.I.S.** | United States Information Service. |
| **Ph.** | Photograph. |

121 Egyptian potters, nr. Luxor. (*Ph. E. Erwhitt. Magnum.*)

122 Offering a jar. Detail of relief on the Sarcophagus of Khaouit. 11th dynasty. Cairo Mus. (*Ph. Hassia.*)

123 Potter's kiln, nr. Luxor. (*Ph. E. Erwhitt. Magnum.*)

124 Launderers. Detail of fresco from the tomb of Ipouy. 19th dynasty. Deir-el-Medineh. (*Ph. Hassia.*)

125 Bas relief of a cabinet maker. Old Kingdom. Cairo Mus. (*Ph. E. Sved.*)

126 Treating a headache. Detail of fresco from the tomb of Ousirhat. New Kingdom. Cheikh-abd-el-Qourna. (*Ph. E. Erwhitt. Magnum.*)

127 Doorway of a Nubian house. Aswan. (*Ph. Hassia.*)

128 Relief of a door from the Sarcophagus of Khaouit. 11th dynasty. Cairo Mus. (*Ph. Hassia.*)

129 A: Villa and garden. Fresco from the tomb of Minnakht. B: Garden pool. Fresco from the tomb of Sebekhotep. New Kingdom. Cheikh-abd-el-Qourna. (*Ph. Hassia.*)

130 Woman eating. Detail of the Sarcophagus of Khaouit. 11th dynasty. Cairo Mus. (*Ph. Hassia.*)

131–132 Coloured glass vases. New Kingdom. Cairo Mus. (*Ph. Hassia.*)

133 Papyrus sandals. Cairo Mus. (*Ph. Hassia.*)

134 Painted ebony and ivory head-rest. Tutankhamen's tomb. Cairo Mus. (*Ph. Hassia.*)

135 Woman at her toilet. Detail of relief from the Sarcophagus of Khaouit. 11th dynasty. Cairo Mus. (*Ph. Hassia.*)

136 Head of a woman in a wig. Wood plated with gold. 12th dynasty. Cairo Mus. (*Ph. Hassia.*)

137 Hippopotamus jar for cosmetics. Middle Kingdom. Mus. St-Germain-en-Laye. (*Ph. Giraudon.*)

138 Carved cedarwood and glass coffer. New Kingdom. Cairo Mus. (*Ph. Hassia.*)

139 Amulet representing the eye of Horus. Louvre. (*Ph. Giraudon.*)

140 The family of Anhour Khaou. Detail from fresco. 19th dynasty. Deir-el-Medineh. (*Ph. Hassia.*)

141 Statuette of a harpist. New Kingdom. Cairo Mus. (*Ph. Hassia.*)

142 Detail of sarcophagus painting of Sennedjem. 20th dynasty. Cairo Mus. (*Ph. Hassia.*)

143 Making funeral furnishings. Fresco from the tomb of Ipouy. 19th dynasty. Deir-el-Medineh. (*Ph. Hassia.*)

144 Glass ushabti. New Kingdom. Cairo Mus. (*Ph. Hassia.*)

145 Nubian house modelled on ancient tomb. Aswan. (*Ph. Hassia.*)

146 Anubis embalming a corpse. Interior of painted wood coffin. New Kingdom. Cairo Mus. (*Ph. Hassia.*)

147 Covered vases. Ramesid period. Louvre Mus. (*Ph. Giraudon.*)

148 Funeral procession. Fresco from the tomb of Ramose, governor and vizier. (Amenophis IV). 18th dynasty. Cheikh-abd-el-Qourna. (*Ph. Hassia.*)

149 Woman mourning at her husband's tomb. Detail of a stele, Lybian period. Cairo Mus. (*Ph. Hassia.*)

150 Palace of Minos at Knossos, Crete. (*Ph. L. Frederic. Rapho.*)

151 Hall of the Double Axe, Knossos. (*Ph. L. Frederic. Rapho.*)

152 Gateway of the palace at Knossos with a view of Cretan Landscape. (*Ph. R. Zuber. Multiphoto.*)

153 Baby's bath. Knossos. (*Ph. L. Frederic. Rapho.*)

154 Rhyton in shape of cart drawn by three oxen. (*Ph. Zervos.*)

155 Women in blue. Fresco. Knossos. (*Ph. R. Viollet.*)

156 Relief pattern on vase known as 'The Harvesters'. Phaistos. Heraklion Mus. (*Ph. Giraudon.*)

157 Washerwomen. Terracotta group. Cyprus. *c.* 3000 B.C. Louvre. (*Ph. A. Vigneau. Ed. Tel.*)

158 Harp player. Cyclades. Nat. Mus., Athens. (*Ph. L. Frederic. Rapho.*)

159 Sardinian woman making bread. (*Ph. G. Viollon.*)

160 Carver. Detail from a wine bowl. 7th c. B.C. Corinth. Louvre. (*Ph. A. Vigneau. Ed. Tel.*)

161 Potter. Painted terracotta plaque. 6th c. B.C. Attica. Louvre. (*Ph. Percheron.*)

162 Archaic terracotta of woman selling bread. 6th c. B.C. Bœotia. Louvre. (*Ph. Percheron.*)

163 Street on the island of Mykonos, Greece. (*Ph. G. Viollon.*)

164 Model of the House of the Trident. Delos. 2nd c. B.C. *Domestic Life in Greece and Rome* exhib. Louvre. (*Ph. Franceschi.*)

165 Small terracotta bed from Myrina, Asia Minor. 2nd c. B.C. *Domestic Life in Greece and Rome* exhib. Louvre. (*Ph. Franceschi.*)

166 Two washerwomen. Attic red figure vase, Athens. Late 5th c. B.C. *Domestic Life in Greece and Rome* exhib. Louvre. (*Ph. M. Chuzeville.*)

167 Young woman at her toilet. Terracotta from Milo. 5th c. B.C. *Domestic Life in Greece and Rome* exhib. Louvre. (*Ph. Franceschi.*)

168 Kneeling girl wearing a *chiton.* Terracotta. *Domestic Life in Greece and Rome* exhib. Louvre. (*Ph. Franceschi.*)

169 Head of a woman. Syracusan coin. 5th c. B.C. (*Ph. J. Roubier.*)

170 Greek woman wearing antique jewellery. (*Ph. D. Seymour. Magnum.*)

171 Scenes from the women's quarters. Design from a terracotta chest. 5th c. B.C. Louvre. (*Ph. Valbert.*)

172 Woman reading. Attic red figure vase. Athens 5th c. B.C. *Domestic Life in Greece and Rome* exhib. Louvre. (*Ph. Franceschi.*)

173 Seated girl, in bronze. *Domestic Life in Greece and Rome* exhib. B.N. (*Ph. Franceschi.*)

174 Maenad. Brygos cup. Staatliche Antikensammlungen, Munich. (*Ph. M. Hirmer.*)

175 Old woman with a baby on her knee. Terracotta. 1st c. B.C. *Domestic Life in Greece and Rome* exhib. Louvre. (*Ph. Franceschi.*)

176 Woman seated playing with a baby. Interior of a cup. Late 5th c. B.C. Mus. du Cinquantenaire, Brussels. (*Ph. Percheron.*)

177 Boy having a music lesson. *c.* 510 B.C. (*Ph. M. Hirmer.*)

178 A young ephebe. Cup. 6th c. B.C. Staatliche Antikensammlungen, Munich. (*Ph. M. Hirmer.*)

179 Man at a banquet. Amphora of Andokides. *c.* 510 B.C. Staatliche Antikensammlungen, Munich. (*Ph. M. Hirmer.*)

180 Houses at Santorin, Greece. (*Ph. G. Viollon.*)

181 Modern production of a classical play at Delphi. (*Ph. D. Seymour. Magnum.*)

182 Girl and ephebe. Attic red figure vase. 5th c. B.C. *Domestic Life in Greece and Rome* exhib. Louvre. (*Ph. Franceschi.*)

183 Boxer binding his fists. Amphora of the painter of Cleophrades. *c.* 500 B.C. Staatliche Antikensammlungen, Munich. (*Ph. M. Hirmer.*)

184 COLOUR PLATE: Banqueting scene. Detail from the Tomb of the Leopards at Tarquinia, Italy. 5th c. B.C. (*Ektachrome Arte e Colore.*)

185 Burial chamber, Tomb of the Reliefs. Necropolis of Cerveteri. (*Ph. Trincano. Ed. Arthaud.*)

186 Etruscan coffer from Palestrina. 5th c. B.C. Nat. Mus. of the Villa Giulia, Rome. (*Ph. Franceschi, Ed. Arthaud.*)

187 Etruscan brazier from Chiusi. 6th c. B.C. Louvre. (*Ph. Franceschi, Ed. Arthaud.*)

188 Dancer. Central figure of bronze candelabra. Etruscan. Louvre. (*Ph. Franceschi, Ed. Arthaud.*)

189 Roman key with four prongs. Bronze-covered iron. *Domestic Life in Greece and Rome* exhib. Louvre. (*Ph. Franceschi.*)

190 Vestibule seen from the street. House of the tragic poet at Pompeii. Model from *Domestic Life in Greece and Rome* exhib. Louvre. (*Ph. Franceschi.*)

191 Birds' eye view of the atrium and surroundings. House of the tragic poet, Pompeii. Model from *Domestic Life in Greece and Rome* exhib. Louvre. (*Ph. Franceschi.*)

192 House of the happy lovers, Pompeii. Actual condition. (*Ph. J. Roubier.*)

193 Man in a toga. Lateran Mus. (*Ph. Giraudon.*)

194 Bas relief showing a wine shop. 2nd–3rd c. A.D. Arch. Mus., Dijon. (*Ph. Alinari. Giraudon.*)

195 Fountain, Street of Plenty. Pompeii. (*Ph. J. Roubier.*)

196 Man knocked down by a mule. Relief. Tebessa, Algeria. (*Ph. M. Bovis.*)

197 Millstones at Pompeii. (*Ph. J. Roubier.*)

198 Wine cellar at Herculaneum. (*Ph. E.N.I.T.*)

199 Oil merchant. Bas relief. Cherchell, Algeria. (*Ph. N. Bovis.*)

200 Roman bronze scales. *Domestic Life in Greece and Rome* exhib. Louvre. (*Ph. Franceschi.*)

201 Sign of the shop of Vecilius Verecundus. Street of Plenty, Pompeii. (*Ph. Alinari, Giraudon.*)

202 Bas relief of a cobbler and shoemaker from a sarcophagus at Ostia. Nat. Mus., Rome. (*Ph. Alinari, Giraudon.*)

203 Amphorae in a dyeworks. Pompeii. (*Ph. J. Roubier.*)

204 Money changer. Bas relief from a sarcophagus in the Salviati palace, Rome. (*Ph. Alinari, Giraudon.*)

205 COLOUR PLATE: A street in Pompeii, showing the temple of Fortune. (*Ektachrome Scala.*)

206 A banquet. Detail of a bas relief. 3rd c. A.D. Mus. de Trèves. (*Ph. Alinari. Giraudon.*)

207 Roman lamp and stand. *Domestic Life in Greece and Rome* exhib. Louvre. (*Ph. Franceschi.*)

208 Relief of a game of dice. Mus. Tebessa, Algeria. (*Ph. M. Bovis.*)

209 Bronze kitchen utensils. Roman. *Domestic Life in Greece and Rome* exhib. Louvre. (*Ph. Franceschi.*)

210 Clear glass saucepan. Roman. *Domestic Life in Greece and Rome* exhib. Louvre. (*Ph. Franceschi.*)

211 Roman kitchen. Detail from a bas relief. 3rd c. A.D. Mus. de Trèves. (*Ph. Alinari. Giraudon.*)

212 Terracotta feeding bottle. Tebessa, Algeria. (*Ph. M. Bovis.*)

213 Interior of the Baths of Caracalla, Rome. (*Ph. E. Erwhitt. Magnum.*)

214 Consulting a doctor at the baths. Detail of a mosaic. Mus. Gsell, Algiers. (*Ph. M. Bovis.*)

215 Actors. Detail of ivory dyptich of Anastasius. B.N. Paris. (*Ph. Giraudon.*)

216 Post wagon. Roman relief. Mus. de Trèves. (*Ph. H. Retzlaff.*)

217 Woman pouring a drink. Romano-Gallic bas relief. Autun Mus. (*Ph. I Bandy.*)

218 Watermen. Detail of Romano-Gallic bas relief. Avignon Mus. (*Ph. I. Bandy.*)

219 Barrel on a cart. Romano-Gallic bas relief. Langres Mus. (*Ph. I. Bandy.*)

220 Bas relief of a draper's shop. Mus. de Trèves. (*Ph. J. Roubier.*)

221 Shoemaker. Bas relief. Arch. Mus., Rheims. (*Ph. J. Roubier.*)

222 Portrait of a woman from a funeral stele. Autun Mus. (*Ph. I. Bandy.*)

223 COLOUR PLATE: Terracotta bed. Romano-Gallic. Mus. St-Germain-en-Laye. (*Ektachrome Franceschi.*)

224 Model of a Romano-Gallic villa. Montmaurin. (*Ph. Yan, Rapho.*)

225 Entrance to a house. Romano-Gallic fresco. Mus. de Trèves. (*Ph. J. Roubier.*)

226 Birdscarer. Detail from a terracotta lamp. Mus. G. Mercier, Constantine. (*Ph. M. Bovis.*)

227 Mosaic of a fisherman. Bardo Mus., Tunis. (*Ed. Plon.*)

228 Market at Oulan Bator, Mongolia. (*Ph. C. Arthaud. F. Hébert-Stevens.*)

229 Inside a yurt. Oulan Bator, Mongolia. (*Ph. D. Darbois.*)
230 Pin decorated with an axe and various animals. Caucasus. Mus. St-Germain-en-Laye. (*Ph. Giraudon.*)
231 Shepherd and his flock in the steppe near Oulan Bator, Mongolia. (*Ph. C. Arthaud. F. Hébert-Stevens.*)
232 Harnessed camels in the Gobi desert. (*Ph. C. Arthaud. F. Hébert-Stevens.*)
233 Mongol horseman. (*Ph. C. Arthaud. F. Hébert-Stevens.*)
234 Setting up camp in Mongolia. (*Ph. C. Arthaud. F. Hébert-Stevens.*)
235 Viking helmet from Vilero. Nat. Mus., Copenhagen. (*Ph. Nat. Mus.*)
236 Iron age circlet. Nat. Mus., Copenhagen. (*Ph. Michaelides.*)
237 Drakkar. 12th c. bestiary. Brit. Mus. MS. (*Ph. Brit. Mus.*)
238 Lindholm burial ground, Denmark. Nat. Mus., Copenhagen. (*Ph. Nat. Mus.*)
239 Fragment of a Merovingian sarcophagus. Garin. France. (*Ph. Dumas-Satigny.*)
240 Bone pin. Mus. St-Roch d'Issoudin. Buckles and clasp of torque. Mus. des Beaux Arts de Troyes. Merovingian 5th c. (*Ph. Giraudon.*)
241 Carolingian horseman. 6th c. mosaic. Brit. Mus. (*Ph. Brit. Mus.*)
242 Part of a MS. showing Carolingian nobles. Brit. Mus. Library. (*Ph. Brit. Mus.*)
243 Carolingian builders at work. From a MS. copy of the Utrecht Psalter. Brit. Mus. Library. (*Ph. Brit. Mus.*)
244 Working in the fields. From a MS. copy of the Utrecht Psalter. Brit. Mus. Library. (*Ph. Brit. Mus.*)
245 Scene from rural life. From a MS. copy of the Utrecht Psalter. Brit. Mus. Library. (*Ph. Brit. Mus.*)
246 Carolingian banquet. From a MS. Brit. Mus. Library. (*Ph. Brit. Mus.*)
247 Temple of the Inscriptions. 629 A.D. Chiapas. (*Ph. D. Darbois.*)
248 Yellow clay statuette from Jaina, Yucatan. Nat. Mus., Mexico. (*Ph. Freund.*)
249 Terracotta whistle representing an old woman seated. Jaina style, Yucatan. Coll. Stendhal, Hollywood. (*Ph. Franceschi.*)
250 Painted anthropomorphic pot, from Casas Grandes, Chihuahua. Archaic. Nat. Mus., Mexico. (*Ph. G. Freund.*)
251 Maya toy in terracotta. Jaina style. Yucatan. Coll. Stendhal, Hollywood. (*Ph. Franceschi.*)
252 View from the Great Pyramid. Below: pelota. Chichen Itza, Yucatan, Mexico. (*Ph. D. Darbois.*)
253 Detail from the Dresden Codex. (*Ph. Mus. de l'Homme.*)
254 Seated figure with tattooed face. Terracotta. Jaina style. Campeche, Yucatan. Coll. Stendhal. Hollywood. (*Ph. Franceschi.*)
255 Head of a woman. Encaustic funeral portrait. Romano-Egyptian. Fayoum. Cairo Mus. (*Ph. Hassia.*)
256 Detail from a mosaic of the story of Noah. 13th c. San Marco, Venice. (*Ph. O. Böhm.*)
257 Head of a man. Encaustic funeral portrait. Romano-Egyptian. Fayoum. Cairo Mus. (*Ph. Hassia.*)
258 Egyptian bronze incense burner. 8th c. Louvre. (*Ph. Giraudon.*)
259 COLOUR PLATE: High Byzantine officials. Miniature from a Greek MS. B.N. (*Ektachrome Doc. Franc.*)
260 Building the tower of Babel. Detail of a mosaic. San Marco, Venice. (*Ph. O. Böhm.*)
261 Chariot racing in the Hippodrome at Byzantium. Dyptich of the Lampadii. Ivroy, 5th c. Christian Mus., Brescia. (*Ph. Giraudon.*)
262 Icon. The Monastery of Mount Sinai. (*Ph. Hassia.*)
263 Bronze key. Viking period. Nat. Mus., Copenhagen. (*Ph. Michaelides.*)
264 The meal. From *The Story of the Leper*. MS. Escurial Library. Spain. (*Ph. Giraudon.*)
265 Harp player. Detail from the *Tropaire de Saint-Martial*, Limoges. 11th c. (*Ph. Dumas-Satigny.*)
266 Draughts piece depicting Judith and Holofernes. Ivory. 12th c. Louvre. (*Ph. Dumas-Satigny.*)
267 Bathing. Detail from *The Life of St Radegonde*. MS. 11th c. Poitiers Library. (*Ph. Dumas-Satigny.*)
268 The grape harvest. Capital from Moutiers-St-Jean, France. 12th c. Louvre. (*Ph. Dumas-Satigny.*)
269 Tree felling. Detail from the Bayeux Tapestry. (*Ph. Giraudon.*)
270 The harvest. Tympanum of St Ursin, Bourges. (*Ph. M. Bovis.*)
271 Whaling. Seal. Fontarabia. 1335. Arch. Nat. (*Ph. Pont Royal.*)
272 Treating polypus. Medical and Herbal Treatise. English MS. 12th c. Brit. Mus. (*Ph. Brit. Mus.*)
273 Treating piles. Medical and Herbal Treatise. English MS. 12th c. Brit. Mus. (*Ph. Brit. Mus.*)
274 Reliquary head of St-Bodime. 12th c. Church of St Nectaire, France. (*Ph. Franceschi.*)
275 Fishing. Bas relief. Exterior of temple of Bayon. Angkor. Khmer. 13th c. (*Ph. Cauchetier.*)
276 Woman selling fish. Bas relief. Exterior of temple of Bayon, Angkor, Khmer, 13th c. (*Ph. Cauchetier.*)
277 Royal cooks preparing food for labourers. Bas relief. Exterior of temple of Bayon. Angkor. Khmer, 13th c. (*Ph. Cauchetier.*)
278 A cart. Bas relief. Exterior of temple of Bayon. Angkor. Khmer, 13th c. (*Ph. Cauchetier.*)
279 A visit from the doctor. Bas relief. Exterior of temple of Bayon, Angkor. Khmer, 13th c. (*Ph. Cauchetier.*)
280 Chess players. Bas relief. Exterior of temple of Bayon, Angkor, Khmer, 13th c. (*Ph. Cauchetier.*)
281 Sword swallower. Bas relief. Terrace of the Leper King. Angkor-Thom. Khmer, 13th c. (*Ph. Cauchetier.*)
282 High officials seated. Detail from a screen painted over gold leaf by Sumiyoshi Gukei. (*Priv. Coll. of Dr Durix.*)
283 A lord's kago with escort in a street of Kyoto. Detail of a screen painted over gold leaf by Sumiyoshi Gukei. (*Priv. coll. of Dr Durix.*)
284 Official procession travelling from Kyoto to Nijo-Jo. Detail of a screen painted over gold leaf by Sumiyoshi Gukei. (*Priv. coll. of Dr Durix.*)
285 Travelling salesmen in the streets of Kyoto. Detail of a screen painted over gold leaf by Sumiyoshi Gukei. (*Priv. coll. of Dr Durix.*)
286 Juggler in a street of Kyoto. Detail of a screen painted over gold leaf by Sumiyoshi Gukei. (*Priv. coll. of Dr Durix.*)
287 Pilgrims at the temple of Mount Hiei near Kyoto. (*Ph. W. Bishof. Magnum.*)
288 Women in a street in Kyoto. Detail from a screen painted over gold leaf by Sumiyoshi Gukei. (*Priv. coll. of Dr Durix.*)
289 House cleaning in Kyoto. Detail of a screen painted over gold leaf by Sumiyoshi Gukei. (*Priv. coll. of Dr Durix.*)
290 Gardens at Kyoto today. (*Ph. W. Bishof. Magnum.*)
291 Alfresco meal in a garden near Kyoto. Detail from a screen painted over gold leaf by Sumiyoshi Gukei. (*Priv. coll. of Dr Durix.*)
292 COLOUR PLATE: Slave market at Zabid, Yemen. 13th c. Arab MS. B.N. (*Ektachrome Doc. Franc.*)
293 Street in old Cairo. (*Ph. Hassia.*)
294 Ladies on an excursion in old Cairo. (*Coll. Ringart.*)
295 Men bathing in Iran. (*Ph. G. Bourdelon.*)
296 A hammam. 15th c. Arab MS. Brit. Mus. (*Ph. Brit. Mus.*)
297 Muezzin calling from a mosque in Cairo. (*Ph. E. Erwitt. Magnum.*)
298 Sermon in the mosque at Samarkand. 13th c. Arab MS. B.N. (*Ph. B.N.*)
299 Pupils learning the Koran at the mosque of Al Azhar, Cairo. (*Ph. E. Erwitt. Magnum.*)
300 Mosque lamp in coloured glass. Mus. of Arab Art, Cairo. (*Ph. Hassia.*)
301 Woman spinning at Laghouat, Sahara. (*Ph. M. Broutta.*)
302 Courtyard in the convent of Bektachis, Mokkatan, Cairo. (*Ph. Hassia.*)
303 Marble fountain. Mus. of Arab Art, Cairo. (*Ph. Hassia.*)
304 Bronze ewer. Mus. of Arab Art, Cairo. (*Ph. Hassia.*)
305 View of Carcassone, France. (*Lapie, aerial photo service.*)
306 Distributing shoes. Register of College of Hersant. 14th c. (*Ph. Doc. Franc.*)
307 Distributing clothes. Register of College of Hersant 14th c. (*Ph. Doc. Franc.*)
308 SS. Savin and Cyprian broken on the wheel. Fresco in the crypt of St-Savin-sur-Gartempe (Vienne). (*Ph. Giraudon.*)
309 Burgesses at dinner. Miniature from MS. in Arsenal Lib., Paris. (*Ph. Doc. Franc.*)
310 Noah asleep. Miniature from a MS. in Leyden Univ. Lib., Holland. (*Ph. Univ. Lib.*)
311 John I of France. Effigy from the Basilica of Saint-Denis. (*Ph. P. Jahan.*)
312 Man on stilts. Miniature from the Luttrell Psalter. 14th c. Brit. Mus. (*Ph. Brit. Mus.*)
313 Archery. Miniature from the Luttrell Psalter. 14th c. Brit. Mus. (*Ph. Brit. Mus.*)
314 Merton College Library, Oxford. (*Radio Times Hulton Pic. Lib.*)
315 New College, Oxford, *c.* 1453. Woodcut. New College Lib. (*Ph. Radio Times Hulton Pic. Lib.*)
316 Small bellows organ. Miniature from the Luttrell Psalter. 14th c. Brit. Mus. (*Ph. Brit. Mus,*)
317 The Prioress. Engraving from the 1493 edition of *The Canterbury Tales*. (*Ph. Radio Times Hulton Pic. Lib.*)
318 Fortified town. Miniature from the Luttrell Psalter. 14th c. Brit. Mus. (*Ph. Brit. Mus.*)
319 Small Kentish town. (*Ph. Black Star. Rapho.*)
320 Pilgrims eating. Engraving from the 1493 edition of *The Canterbury Tales*. (*Ph. Radio Times Hulton Pic. Lib.*)
321 Woman disembarking after a sea voyage. 15th c. MS. (*Ph. Radio Times Hulton Pic. Lib.*)
322 Sickroom. 15th c. miniature. Brit. Mus. (*Ph. Radio Times Hulton Pic. Lib.*)
323 Woodcut of a doctor and patient. (*Ph. Radio Times Hulton Pic. Lib.*)
324 Walled city. *Deposizione* by Fra Angelico. Detail. Mus. San Marco, Florence. (*Ph. Alinari.*)
325 Man with a mule. Detail from a fresco by Ambrogio Lorenzetti. Siena. (*Ph. Alinari. Giraudon.*)
326 Old peasant at Oliena, Sardina. (*Ph. G. Viollon.*)
327 Butcher's stall. Detail from a 14th c. miniature. Veronese school. B.N. (*Ph. Pont Royal.*)
328 Election of councillors at Pisa. State Archives, Pisa. (*Ph. E.N.I.T.*)
329 Moneylenders. School of San Maffeo. Venice. (*Ph. O. Böhm.*)
330 COLOUR PLATE: Banqueting scene. Miniature from *The History of Alexander the Great*. 15th c. MS. Petit Palais. Paris. (*Ektachrome Michaelides.*)
331 Woman with a flask. From 14th c. illuminated MS. by Cecco d'Ascoli. Laurentian Lib., Florence. (*Ph. E.N.I.T.*)
332 Servants. Detail from *The Birth of the Virgin* by Pietro Lorenzetti. Siena, Cathedral Treasury. (*Ph. Anderson. Giraudon.*)
333 At the draper's shop. Miniature from a 14th c. MS. Veronese school. B.N. (*Ph. Pont Royal.*)
334 Terracotta head of a young man. Carving from Machisan Caves, China. (*Ph. D. Darbois.*)

335 Planting rice in China. (*Ph. D. Darbois.*)
336 Mandarin making an offering. Painting on silk. 10th c. Touen-Hang, China. Mus. Guimet. (*Ph. Giraudon.*)
337 Fashionable ladies entering a carriage. Detail from a fresco in the Touen-Hang caves, China. (*Ph. D. Darbois.*)
338 Little boy chasing butterflies. Detail from a 10th c. painting. Han style. Langweill coll. (*Ph. Giraudon.*)
339 Children bathing. Detail from a 10th c. painting. Han style. Langweill coll. (*Ph. Giraudon.*)
340 Woman in ceremonial dress. Detail from a votive painting. 983 A.D. Mus. Guimet. (*Ph. Giraudon.*)
341–342 Characters from a fresco in the caves of Touen-Hang, China. (*Ph. D. Darbois.*)
343 Scale model of a pleasure house. Funeral pottery. Han era. Mus. Cernuschi. (*Ph. Giraudon.*)
344 View of the summer palace, Pekin. (*Ph. D. Darbois.*)
345 House of the phoenix. Detail of fresco in the caves of Touen-Hang, China. (*Ph. D. Darbois.*)
346 View of a Chinese village. Fresco from the caves of Touen-Hang, China. (*Ph. D. Darbois.*)
347 Scale model of a pleasure tower in a bowl. Funeral pottery. Han era. Mus. Cernuschi. (*Ph. Giraudon.*)
348 *Kin* player in pinkish grey limestone, from Yun-Kang. Wei period. 6th c. Mus. Guimet. (*Ph. Giraudon.*)
349 Terracotta polo player. Mus. Cernuschi. (*Ph. Giraudon.*)
350 Convent at Louvain, Belgium. (*Ph. Roubier. Rapho.*)
351 Street in Bruges. (*Ph. L. Henri. Rapho.*)
352 Flemish town in the 15th c. Detail of the Mérode altarpiece by the Master of Flémalle. (*Ph. Marburg.*)
353 Main square of a town. From an illustrated Flemish MS. 15th c. Brit. Mus. (*Ph. Brit. Mus.*)
354 Carpenter. Wood carving. 15th c. Mus. de Cluny. (*Ph. Franceschi.*)
355 Tailor. Wood carving. 15th c. Mus. de Cluny. (*Ph. Franceschi.*)
356 Pig-killing. Wood carving. 15th c. Vendôme. (*Ph. Roubier. Rapho.*)
357 The Mint. Miniature from Aristotle's *Ethics*. 15th c. Municip. Lib., Rouen. (*Ph. Giraudon.*)
358 Mirror with ivory frame and cover. 15th c. Mus. de Cluny. (*Ph. Franceschi.*)
359 Ivory-handled knife inscribed with music. 15th c. Mus. de Cluny. (*Ph. Franceschi.*)
360 A public bath house. Miniature from *Les Faits et Paroles mémorables de Valère Maxime*. 15th c. MS. Municip. Lib., Leipzig. (*Ph. Giraudon.*)
361 Drawing of monks putting out a fire. Late 15th c. Mus. des Arts décoratifs, Paris. (*Ph. Giraudon.*)
362 The dowry. Miniature from a 15th c. French MS. B.N. (*Ph. Doc. Franc.*)
363 The blessing. *The marriage of Guibert and the Lady of Narbonne*. From the Lib. of decorative arts. (*Ph. Giraudon.*)
364 Dance with trumpets. *The Marriage of Renaud de Montauban*. Miniature. Arsenal Lib. (*Ph. Giraudon.*)
365 Colour Plate: Saint Barbara (Master of Flémalle.) Prado, Madrid. (*Ektachrome Giraudon.*)
366 The quarrel. Miniature from *The History of Renaud de Montauban*. 15th c. MS Arsenal Lib. (*Ph. Giraudon.*)
367 By the fireside. Miniature from *The Hours of Charles d'Angoulême*. 15th c. B.N. (*Ph. Doc. Franc.*)
368 Doctor examining urine. Illustration from 15th c. MS. of *The Epistle of Othea* by Christine de Pisan. Royal Lib., Brussels. (*Ph. Giraudon.*)
369 Extreme unction. Miniature from a French 15th c. MS. B.N. (*Ph. Doc. Franc.*)
370 Detail from *The Miracle of Saint Nicolas of Bari*. Florentine school. 15th c. Louvre. (*Ph. Giraudon.*)
371 Detail from *The Birth of the Virgin*, by Carpaccio. Accademia Carrara, Bergamo. (*Ph. Anderson. Giraudon.*)
372 Detail from *The Road to Emmaus*, by Carpaccio. San Salvatore, Venice. (*Ph. Anderson. Giraudon.*)
373 15th c. forks. Carrand. coll. Nat. Mus., Florence. (*Ph. Alinari. Giraudon.*)
374 *The Wedding of Boccaccio Andinari*. Ancient and Mod. gallery, Florence. (*Ph. Giraudon.*)
375 *Tournament on the Piazza Santa Croce*, by Stradano. Fresco from Palazzo Vecchio. Florence. (*Ph. Alinari. Giraudon.*)
376 Venice. An outdoor scene. 16th c. engraving. (*Doc. Pont Royal.*)
377 *Miracle of the Cross at campo San Lio*, by Giovanni Mansueti. Accademia, Venice. (*Ph. O. Böhm.*)
378 Hunting scene. Florentine school, 15th c. Mus. des Augustins, Toulouse. (*Ph. Giraudon.*)
379 Alfresco concert. Enamel by Léonard Limousin. Louvre. (*Ph. Giraudon.*)
380 Colour Plate: Detail from *The Miracle of the Cross*, by Carpaccio. Accademia, Venice. (*Ektachrome Scala.*)
381 Mining village in Lorraine. Drawing in silverpoint. Lib. Ecole des Beaux Arts, Paris. (*Ph. Giraudon.*)
382 Street in a small village near Hamburg. (*Atlas-Photo.*)
383 German dining-room with dresser. (*Ph. S. Weiss. Rapho.*)
384 *Woman spinning and entertaining a visitor*. Engraving by van Mecheln. B.N. (*Ph. Pont Royal.*)
385 *Saint Elizabeth tending plague victims*. Laufer a.d. Salzach. (*Ph. Marburg.*)
386 *Birth of John the Baptist*. German school. Mus. Unterlinden, Colmar. (*Ph. Giraudon.*)
387 The Fuggerei, Augsburg. Ehem, Staatl. Bildstelle.
388 *Market-place at Eger*. Pen drawing, 1480. German Nat. Mus., Nuremberg. (*Ph. Nat. Mus.*)
389 German inn. (*Ph. S. Weiss. Rapho.*)
390 *Inn parlour in winter*. Drawing by J. Breu the elder. Ecole des Beaux Arts, Paris. (*Ph. Giraudon.*)
391 Clock maker. Engraving, 1641. B.N. (*Ph. Roche. Pont Royal.*)
392 Washerwomen. Miniature from a 16th c. German treatise on alchemy. B.N. (*Ph. Pont Royal.*)
393 Bavarian peasants in holiday dress. (*Ph. H. Hubmann. Rapho.*)
394 Pedlar. Engraving, 1641. B.N. (*Ph. Roche. Pont Royal.*)
395 Children's toys. 16th c. German Nat. Mus., Nuremberg. (*Ph. Nat. Mus.*)
396 Colour Plate: *Tournament at Nuremberg, 3rd March, 1561*, by J. Ammam. Bavarian Nat. Mus., Munich. (*Ektachrome Nat. Mus.*)
397 *Philip II*, by S. Coello. Priv. coll., Paris. (*Ph. Giraudon.*)
398 *Portrait of a Woman*, by S. Coello. Priv. coll., Buenos Aires. (*Ph. Giraudon.*)
399 *The Kitchen*, by Velasquez. Detail. Château de Villandry. France. (*Ph. Giraudon.*)
400 Spanish ceremonial dress. Late 16th c. Engraving by Sebastian Vranex. B.N. (*Ph. Giraudon.*)
401 Detail from *Saint James feeding the Poor*, by Murillo. Academy of San Fernando, Madrid. (*Ph. Anderson. Giraudon.*)
402 Procession of heretics to the autodafé. Detail from an engraving. B.N. (*Ph. Giraudon.*)
403 Caravels arriving in the West Indies. Engraving from a work by Th. De Bry. (*Ph. Desmarteaux. Ed. Pont Royal.*)
404 Old Indian woman at Chichicastenango. (*Ph. F. Patellani. Dalmas.*)
405 Aztec peasant woman carrying a child. From *Codex Borbonicus*. Aztec civilisation. Palais Bourbon Lib., Paris. (*Ph. P. Espagne.*)
406 Small terracotta model of house. Nayarit. North-west civilisation. Stendhal coll., Hollywood. (*Ph. Franceschi.*)
407 Small terracotta model of house: close-up of upper storey. Nayarit. North-west civilisation. Stendhal coll., Hollywood. (*Ph. Franceschi.*)
408 Seated infant with malformed head. Yellow clay. Olmeque civilisation. Coll. Franz Feuchtwanger, Mexico. (*Ph. G. Freund.*)
409 Chief Taculpotzin. From *Codex Ixtlixochitl*. Mexican MS. B.N. (*Ph. B. N.*)
410 Funeral procession. Terracotta. Nayarit. North-west civilisation. Stendhal coll., Hollywood. (*Ph. Franceschi.*)
411 Sun pyramid at Teotihuacan, near Mexico City. (*Ph. G. Freund.*)
412 Priests in ritual costume. From *Codex Borbonicus*. Aztec civilisation. Palais Bourbon Lib., Paris. (*Ph. P. Espagne.*)
413 Human sacrifice. From *Codex Vaticanus A*. Vatican Lib. (*Ph. Mus. de l'Homme.*)
414 Colour Plate: Bottleneck in form of a portrait head with a ring in the nose. Fragment of anthropomorphic pot. Coloured terracotta. Late Mochica. Cummings coll., Chicago. (*Ektachrome Giraudon.*)
415 Peasant woman on an old Inca road. (*Ph. C. Arthaud.*)
416 Anthropomorphic jar. Mochica art, Peru. Petit Palais, Paris. (*Ph. Bulloz.*)
417 Modern dwellings built in Inca style. Pisac, Peru. (*Ph. F. Hébert-Stevens.*)
418 Inca meal. Drawing from the *Nueva Coronica y Buen Gobierno* of Poma de Ayala. Late 16th c. (*Ph. P. Espagne.*)
419 Inca peasant with llama. Drawing from the *Nueva Coronica y Buen Gobierno* of Pomo de Ayala. Late 16th c. (*Ph. P. Espagne.*)
420 Anthropomorphic vase. Recuay art, Peru. Petit Palais, Paris. (*Ph. Bulloz.*)
421 Alcades from the Altiplano. Pisac, Peru. (*Ph. C. Arthaud.*)
422 Old inn at Exeter. (*Ph. Black Star. Rapho.*)
423 Gosworth Hall, Cheshire. (*Ph. Radio Times Hulton Pic. Lib.*)
424 Preparations for a banquet. Engraving by Justus Sodeler after Antonio Tempesta (1555–1630). (*Ph. Radio Times Hulton Pic. Lib.*)
425 The classroom. Engraving *c.* 1600. (*Ph. Radio Times Hulton Pic. Lib.*)
426 The Globe Theatre. Engraving by Hollar. (*Ph. Radio Times Hulton Pic. Lib.*)
427 Hallway of a 16th c. farmhouse in Herefordshire. (*P. Popper. Atlas-Photo.*)
428 Maidservant swatting flies. Engraving from Heywood's *The Spider and the Fly*, 1556. (*Ph. Radio Times Hulton Pic. Lib.*)
429 Game of table bowls. Engraving from *Deliciarum Libellus*, by Crispin de Passe. (1550–1643). (*Ph. Radio Times Hulton Pic. Lib.*)
430 Colour Plate: Children's Games (Pieter Brueghel the Elder). Detail. Kunsthistoriches Mus., Vienna. (*Ektachrome E. Meyer.*)
431 Men playing bowls. Drawing by Van Ostade. Louvre. (*Ph. Giraudon.*)
432 Village bath house. Treating a corn. (Brouwer). Detail. Bavarian. State Mus., Munich. (*Ph. Stat. Mus.*)
433 Peasant interior at Oktops, Holland. (*Ph. Rapho.*)
434 *Village store*, by Gerard Dou. Louvre. (*Ph. Giraudon.*)
435 *Stock Exchange at Amsterdam*, by Berckheyde. Detail. Stadel Mus., Frankfurt. (*Ph. Marburg.*)
436 *View of the Spaarne at Haarlem*, by Berckheyde. Detail. Douai Mus. (*Ph. Giraudon.*)
437 Interior of Rubens' house at Antwerp. (*Ph. Rapho.*)
438 *Woman and child*, by Brekelenkam. Brunswick, Gemäldegalerie. (*Ph. Brückmann. Giraudon.*)
439 Duel between the Chevalier de Guise and the Baron de Luz. Drawing. B.N. (*Ph. Doc. Franc.*)

440 The Barber. Engraving by Abraham Bosse. Detail. (*Ph. Bulloz.*)
441 Lady at her toilet. Engraving by Abraham Bosse. Detail. (*Ph. Bulloz.*)
442 The shoemaker. Engraving by Abraham Bosse. Detail. (*Ph. Bulloz.*)
443 The newborn baby. Engraving by Abraham Bosse. Detail. (*Ph. Bulloz.*)
444 Childhood. Engraving by Abraham Bosse. Detail. (*Ph. Bulloz.*)
445 Making fritters. Engraving by Abraham Bosse. Detail. (*Ph. Bulloz.*)
446 *The Banqueting Table*. Detail. French school. 17th c. Strasbourg Mus. (*Ph. Giraudon.*)
447 An At Home in a bourgeois household of the 17th c. Engraving by Abraham Bosse. Detail. (*Ph. Bulloz.*)
448 Scene at the theatre. Drawing attrib. to Abraham Bosse. B.N. (*Ph. Doc. Franc.*)
449 Gallantry. Engraving by Abraham Bosse. Detail. (*Ph. Bulloz.*)
450 Staging a farce. Anon. engraving. B.N. (*Ph. Doc. Franc.*)
451 The apothecary and his patient. Engraving by Abraham Bosse. Detail. (*Ph. Bulloz.*)
452 Nuns nursing in the hospital, Paris. B.N. (*Ph. Doc. Franc.*)
453 The funeral. Engraving by Abraham Bosse. Detail. (*Ph. Bulloz.*)
454 Russian peasant in winter costume. Engraving. Lib. of Dec. Arts, Paris. (*Ph. P. Brossé.*)
455 Muscovite girl's dress. Engraving. Lib. of Dec. Arts, Paris. (*Ph. P. Brossé.*)
456 Man plaiting sandals. Popular Russian engraving. Mme Ehrenbourg and M. P-L. Duchartre. (*Ph. Fr. Nat. Pedagog. Inst.*)
457 Steam baths. Woodcut. Mme Ehrenbourg and M. P-L. Duchartre. (*Ph. Fr. Nat. Pedagog. Inst.*)
458 Palm Sunday procession outside the Kremlin, Moscow. Engraving from *la Galerie du Monde*. B.N. (*Doc. Pont Royal.*)
459 Celebration of office in Moscow church. (*Ph. Tikhomiroff. Rapho.*)
460 Muscovite baptism. Engraving. Lib. of Dec. Arts, Paris. (*Ph. P. Brossé.*)
461 Father's birthday. Popular Russian engraving. Mme Ehrenbourg and M. P-L. Duchartre. (*Ph. Fr. Nat. Pedagog. Inst.*)
462 Muscovite floggings. Engraving. Detail. Lib. of Dec. Arts, Paris. (*Ph. P. Brossé.*)
463 Husband beating his wife. Popular Russian engraving. Mme Erhenbourg and M. P-L. Duchartre. (*Ph. Fr. Nat. Pedagog. Inst.*)
463a Colour Plate: A Gathering of Ladies. French school, 17th c. (*Ektachrome Michaelides.*)
464 Market-place. Brussels. Anon painting, Brussels. (*Ph. Marburg.*)
465 Carriage. Anon engraving. 17th c. Detail. (*Ph. Bulloz.*)
466 Fashionable people listening to a sermon. Detail from an engraving, 1693. B.N. (*Ph. Bulloz.*)
467 Carved wooden snuff grater. 17th c. Louvre. (*Ph. Giraudon.*)
468 Seller of gold fringes. Detail from an engraving, late 17th c. (*Ph. Jacques Boudet coll.*)
469 *The baptism*, by Antonio Viladomat. Detail. Mus. of Catalan Art, Barcelona. (*Ph. Mus. of Cat. Art.*)
470 Hot chocolate. Detail of a ceiling made of blue and white tiles called *azulejos*. Catalan School, 17th c. Mus. of Art, Barcelona. (*Ph. Mus. of Art.*)
471 The carpenter's shop. 17th c. engraving. B.N. (*Ph. Doc. Franc.*)
472 The innkeeper. 17th c. engraving. B.N. (*Ph. Roche. Pont Royal.*)
473 Haberdasher. Engraving by Bonnart. B.N. (*Ph. Pont Royal.*)
474 Coalman. Engraving by Bonnart. B.N. (*Ph. Doc. Franc.*)
475 Public letter-writer. 17th c. engraving. B.N. (*Ph. Doc. Franc.*)
476 Iman reading the Koran. (*Ph. Hassia.*)
477 Portrait of Fatih Mehmed II. Istanbul Mus. (*Ph. Giraudon.*)
478 Festival of guilds at the hippodrome. Osman miniature. Book of the Sultan Mourad III. Lib. of palace of Topkapu Saray, Istanbul. (*Doc. Pont Royal.*)
479 Pair of lovers surprised by Janissaries. Miniature from album of Sultan Ahmet I. Lib. of palace of Topkapu Saray. Istanbul. (*Doc. Pont Royal.*)
480 Public baths at Brousse, Turkey. Miniature from album of Sultan Ahmet I. Lib. of palace of Topkapu Saray, Istanbul. (*Doc. Pont Royal.*)
481 A musician. Turkish miniature. 18th c. (*Ph. Giraudon.*)
482 Colour Plate: Portrait of a noble lord in his garden. Miniature, Dekkan school, 18th c. Mus. Guimet. (*Ektachrome Giraudon.*)
483 The shah and his vizier. Persian. Mus. des Arts Dec. (*Ph. Giraudon.*)
484 Preparations for a meal. Persian miniature. Louvre. (*Ph. Giraudon.*)
485 Theological school. Mosque of the shah's mother. Isfahan. (*Ph. G. Bourdelon.*)
486 In the bazaar at Isfahan. (*Ph. G. Bourdelon.*)
487 Hunting scene. Detail of Persian tapestry. Louvre. (*Ph. Giraudon.*)
488 *The Feria on the Plaza de la Cebada, Madrid*, by Manuel de la Cruz. Municipal Mus., Madrid. (*Ph. Virgilio Muro.*)
489 Street in Vienna. Austrian engraving. 18th c. (*Ph. Roche. Pont Royal.*)
490 Carnival in the streets of Paris. B.N. (*Ph. Pont Royal.*)
491 The vinegar seller. Statuette. (*Ph. Bulloz.*)
492 The porter. Engraving by Bouchardon. B.N. (*Ph. Pont Royal.*)
493 The fair of St-Ovid, Place Vendôme, 1763. Engraving by Poisson. B.N. (*Ph. Bulloz.*)
494 Bavarian village. (*Atlas-Photo.*)
495 The arrival of the players at Le Mans. Engraving after J. B. Pater, B.N. (*Ph. Doc. Franc.*)
496 *Breakfast*, by François Boucher. Louvre. (*Ph. Giraudon.*)
497 Silver coffee pot. 18th c. Exhib.: Antique art of Liège. (*Ph. Giraudon.*)
498 *Girl polishing dishes*, by André Barys. Flemish school, 18th c. Mus. des Arts dec. (*Ph. Mus. des Arts dec.*)
499 *Dictating a letter*, by Gabriel Metsu. Mus. de Montpellier. (*Ph. Giraudon.*)
500 Colour Plate: *The Apothecary*, by Pietro Longhi. Accademia, Venice. (*Ektachrome Arte e Colore.*)
501 Young Master of Arts and his escort. Chinese engraving. B.N. (*Ph. Pont Royal.*)
502 Preparing and drinking tea. Engraving B.N. (*Ph. Pont Royal.*)
503 Villager dressed for rain. Water colour from *The Streets of Pekin*, B.N. (*Ph. B.N.*)
504 Festival of the Lights. Engraving from *Recueil historique des principaux traits de la vie des empereurs chinois*. B.N. (*Ph. B.N.*)
505 Village school. Drawing from *La Vie d'un Chinois*. B.N. (*Ph. B.N.*)
506 Exchange of cups. Drawing from *La Vie d'un Chinois*. B.N. (*Ph. B.N.*)
507 Opium smoker in a Meos village. (*Ph. D. Darbois.*)
508 *India Dock, near London Bridge*, by Samuel Scott. 1757. (*Ph. Radio Times Hulton Pic. Lib.*)
509 Street in the City of London. 18th c. engraving. (*Ph. Radio Times Hulton Pic. Lib.*)
510 Town crier, London. (*Atlas-Photo.*)
511 Mr Justice in his library. (*Ph. Black Star. Rapho.*)
512 The stocks or *Hudibras in Tribulation*. Hogarth engraving. (*Ph. Radio Times Hulton Pic. Lib.*)
513 18th c. houses at Richmond, Surrey. (*Ph. Radio Times Hulton Pic. Lib.*)
514 Marriage à la Mode. Hogarth engraving. Lib. of Dec. Art. (*Ph. P. Brossé.*)
515 The game of whist. Gilray. (*Ph. Radio Times Hulton Pic. Lib.*)
516 Cowper Thornhill's race from Stilton to London, 1745. Engraving. (*Ph. Radio Times Hulton Pic. Lib.*)
517 Cock fight. Hogarth engraving. Lib. of Dec. Art. (*Ph. P. Brossé.*)
518 Boxing match. Engraving. Lib. of Dec. Art. (*Ph. P. Brossé.*)
519 *Reading the newspaper*, by Webb. (*Ph. Radio Times Hulton Pic. Lib.*)
520 An inn yard. Hogarth engraving. (*Ph. Radio Times Hulton Pic. Lib.*)
521 The election. Hogarth engraving. (*Ph. Radio Times Hulton Pic. Lib.*)
522 Butcher at Copenhagen. Engraving. Lib. of Dec. Art. (*Ph. P. Brossé.*)
523 Allegorical picture of northern trading by J.-M. Wagner. Breslau Mus. (*Ph. Marburg.*)
524 Danish peasants. 18th c. engraving. Lib. of Dec. Art. (*Ph. P. Brossé.*)
525 Interior of a farm at Sotesdal, Norway, in the 18th c. Lib. of Dec. Art. (*Ph. P. Brossé.*)
526 Norwegian peasant and his family. Mus. of Pop. Art and Folklore, Oslo. (*Ph. Giraudon.*)
527 Lapplander on skis. Engraving from a German work. Late 18th c. (*Ph. Doc. Franc.*)
528 Wintering in Nova Zembla, Spitzbergen. Drawing from a work of Th. De Bry. (*Ph. Doc. Franc.*)
529 Game of ball among the Lapps. From a work on Greenland. Copenhagen, 1741. (*Ph. Doc. Franc.*)
530 The stage coach arriving at Liège. French school, late 18th c. (*Ph. Bulloz.*)
531 The Carnival of 1781, Piazza Venezia, Rome. Rome Mus. (*Ph. Anderson. Giraudon.*)
532 Fashionable party in Venice. Fresco by Allessandro Longhi. Palazzo Stucky, Venice. (*Ph. Alinari. Giraudon.*)
533 *Reading in the park*, by J-B. Mallet. Detail. Doucet coll. (*Ph. Bulloz.*)
534 Colour Plate: Swiss tiled stove. Winterthur, 1765. Mus. of Dec. Art. (*Ektachrome Giraudon.*)
535 Early levée. Engraving by Moreau the younger. B.N. (*Ph. Doc. Franc.*)
536 *The Letter*, by J-B. Mallet. Detail. Mus. of Dec. Art. (*Ph. Mus. Dec. Art.*)
537 *Silence, or Do Not Wake Him.* Engraving by Laurent Cars after Greuze. Detail. (*Ph. Petit. Doc. Franc.*)
538 A visit from the doctor. 18th c. engraving. B.N. (*Ph. Doc. Franc.*)
539 The broomseller. Detail from series of prints of 18th-c. small tradesmen. B.N. (*Ph. Doc. Franc.*)
540 *Seamstresses getting up*, by Nicolas Lavreince. Detail. Mus. of Dec. Art. (*Ph. Mus. Dec. Art.*)
541 Vegetable stall. Engraving. B.N. (*Ph. Pont Royal.*)
542 Workshop of Sieur Jadot, cabinet maker. 1776. Engraving. B.N. (*Ph. Doc. Franc.*)
543 Enamelled snuff-box with portrait of Louis XVI. Picardi. 18th c. Mus. of Dec. Art. (*Ph. Giraudon.*)
544 Life at Secota, Virginia. 1585. Engraving from a work by Th. De Bry. (*Ph. Adenis. Doc. Franc.*)
545 Hunting buffalo in America. Engraving by Saint-Saveur. 18th c. B.N. (*Ph. B.N.*)
546 Layout of a fort in Florida. From a work by Th. De Bry. (*Ph. Adenis. Doc. Franc.*)
547 Red Indian family. Engraving from a travel book. (*Ph. U.S.I.S.*)
548 Portrait of present-day Indian chief. (*Ph. Zalewski. Rapho.*)
549 Portrait of the Pawnee Indian chief Ponca. 1858. (*Ph. U.S.I.S.*)
550 Pilgrim fathers going to church with drums. Commemoration ceremony in New England. (*Ph. U.S.I.S.*)
551 Old log cabin at Decatur, Illinois. (*Ph. U.S.I.S.*)
552 Quakers negotiating a treaty of friendship with Indians. Early 18th c. (*Ph. U.S.I.S.*)
553 House at Newburg, once George Washington's headquarters. Old engraving. (*Ph. U.S.I.S.*)

554 Reconstruction of a room at the Raleigh Tavern, frequented by Jefferson and Patrick Henry in the 18th c. (*Ph. U.S.I.S.*)
555 Cotton harvest. Engraving, B.N. (*Ph. Pont Royal.*)
556 Japanese house near Tokyo. (*Ph. Werner Bishof. Magnum.*)
557 Japanese welcoming a visitor. (*Pan Asia Photo News. Rapho.*)
558 Interior of modern Japanese house. (*Ph. Werner Bishof. Magnum.*)
559 Tea ceremony. (*Ph. Werner Bishof. Magnum.*)
560 Women cleaning house. Print from the *Book of the Green Houses*. Toyokuni I. Janette Ostier coll., Paris. (*Ph. Franceschi.*)
561 Old dressing-table and mirror. Janette Ostier coll., Paris. (*Ph. Michaelides.*)
562 Woman at her toilet. Shuncho print. 18th c. Janette Ostier coll., Paris. (*Ph. Michaelides.*)
563 Woman lacing her sandal. 18th c. Netsuke. Janette Ostier coll., Paris. (*Ph. Michaelides.*)
564 Child playing at horsemen. Surimono, 18th c. Janette Ostier coll., Paris. (*Ph. Franceschi.*)
565 Noodle seller. Surimono, 18th c. Janette Ostier coll., Paris. (*Ph. Franceschi.*)
566 The walk at night. Nagaye print of Harunobu. Janette Ostier coll., Paris. (*Ph. M. Poplin.*)
567 The geisha quarter. Print from the *Book of the Green Houses*. Toyokuni I. Janette Ostier coll., Paris. (*Ph. Franceschi.*)
568 Interior of a house in the geisha quarter. Print from the *Book of the Green Houses*. Janette Ostier coll., Paris. (*Ph. Franceschi.*)
569 Geisha getting ready to dance. (*Pan Asia Photo News. Rapho.*)
570 The theatre. Toyoharu print, 18th c. Janette Ostier coll., Paris. (*Ph. Franceschi.*)
571 *Nô* actor from the Kikugoro Kabuki company of Tokyo. (*Pan Asia Photo News. Rapho.*)
572 Japanese Bunraku puppets. (*Pan Asia Photo News. Rapho.*)
573 COLOUR PLATE: Interior of a palace. Painting by Moromasa. Early 18th c. Janette Ostier coll., Paris. (*Ektachrome Michaelides.*)
574 View of Anamooka. Engraving from *Cook's Third Voyage*. B.N. (*Ph. P. Brossé.*)
575 Village built on piles. Borneo. (*Ph. G. Bourdelon.*)
576 Native of Sandur island dancing. Engraving from *Cook's Third Voyage*. B.N. (*Ph. P. Brossé.*)
577 Night dance by women of Hapaee. Engraving from *Cook's Third Voyage*. B.N. (*Ph. P. Brossé.*)
578 View of the interior of a house at the edge of Nootka. Engraving from *Cook's Third Voyage*. B.N. (*Ph. P. Brossé.*)
579 Burial after a human sacrifice has taken place in the marshes of O-Taiti. Engraving from *Cook's Third Voyage*. B.N. (*Ph. P. Brossé.*)
580 *Café des Patriotes*, by Swebach des Fontaines. Mus. Carnavalet. (*Ph. Bulloz.*)
581 The freedom of the press. Popular engraving. 18th c. B.N. (*Ph. Giraudon.*)
582 Dr Guillotine trying on his uniform of a Garde Française. Anonymous gouache. 18th c. Boucault coll., Paris. (*Ph. Giraudon.*)
583 *The arrival of the stagecoach*, by L. Boilly. Detail. Louvre. (*Ph. Giraudon.*)
584 *Family scene*, by Combette. Year 9 of the Republic. Mus. de Tours. (*Ph. Bulloz.*)
585 Official reception. Engraving by Debucourt. Detail. (*Ph. Bulloz.*)
586 The cocoa seller. Engraving by Debucourt after a drawing by Vernet. (*Ph. Petit. Doc. Franc.*)
587 Students during a torchlight demonstration. Engraving from *Habits and customs of Germany*. B.N. (*Ph. P. Brossé.*)
588 Dance in a beer garden at Heidelberg. Engraving from *Habits and customs of Germany*. B.N. (*Ph. P. Brossé.*)
589 Travel memento of a German student. Drawing by J-A. Klein. Munich. 1819. Lib. of Dec. Art. (*Ph. P. Brossé.*)
590 The Main from the terrace of the White Swans Inn at Wurtzburg. Engraving. Mus. of Dec. Art. (*Ph. P. Brossé.*)
591 New Year's visit. Drawing by Lecomte. 1818. B.N. (*Ph. Pont Royal.*)
592 Spanish fiesta, from a film set. (*Ph. David Seymour. Magnum.*)
593 *Corrida*, by Goya. Real Academia de Bellas Artes de San Fernando, Madrid. (*Ph. Real Acad.*)
594 Andalusian street traders. Engraving. B.N. (*Ph. P. Brossé.*)
595 Dancing the bolero. Engraving B.N. (*Ph. P. Brossé.*)
596 Muletiers. Engraving from *Sketches of Spain and Spanish Characters*. c. 1830. B.N. (*Ph. P. Brossé.*)
597 Playing Mora. Engraving by James Godby. *Italian Scenery*. London, 1804. B.N. (*Ph. P. Brossé.*)
598 Neapolitans eating spaghetti. Engraving by James Godby. *Italian Scenery*. London, 1804. B.N. (*Ph. P. Brossé.*)
599 Austrian boys at a folk dancing school. (*Schmauss Bavaria. Atlas-Photo.*)
600 Black Forest peasants. Engraving, Mus. of Dec. Art. (*Ph. P. Brossé.*)
601 Peasants from the region of Baden. Engraving. B.N. (*Ph. P. Brossé.*)
602 Women from Augsburg. Engraving. Lib. of Dec. Art. (*Ph. P. Brossé.*)
603 COLOUR PLATE: *Wedding on the island of Föhr*, by Oluf Braren. Staatliche Hochschule für Bildende Künste, Hamburg. (*Agfacolor. J. Sello.*)
604 Interior at Pontivy, Brittany, 1804. Engraving from *Dress and Manners of French provinces*. B.N. (*Ph. P. Brossé.*)
605 Peasants from Quimperlé. Photograph of 1858. B.N. (*Reprint: P. Brossé.*)
606 Wedding at Batz. Engraving from *Dress and Manners of French provinces*. B.N. (*Ph. P. Brossé.*)
607 Traditional way of striking a bargain in Finistère. Engraving from *Dress and Manners of French provinces*. B.N. (*Ph. P. Brossé.*)
608 Couple on horseback returning from church. Swedish engraving. Lib. of Dec. Art. (*Ph. P. Brossé.*)
609 Swedish interior. Popular engraving. Lib. of Dec. Art. (*Ph. P. Brossé.*)
610 Two Dutch peasants from Marken island. (*Ph. J. Roubier. Rapho.*)
611 Sieve-makers at Zamorsk, Poland. 19th c. engraving. Lib. of Dec. Art. (*Ph. P. Brossé.*)
612 Frozen meat market. Engraving from *Habits and Customs of Russia*. Houbigant, 1821. B.N. (*Ph. P. Bossé.*)
613 Blessing of the waters. Engraving from *Habits and Customs of Russia*. Houbigant, 1821. B.N. (*Ph. P. Brossé.*)
614 Switchback on the ice. Engraving from *Habits and Customs of Russia*. Houbigant, 1821. B.N. (*Ph. P. Brossé.*)
615 Drinking scene. Engraving from *Habits and Customs of Russia*. Houbigant, 1821. B.N. (*Ph. P. Brossé.*)
616 Russian dandy in a barouche. Engraving, 1820. B.N. (*Ph. Pont Royal.*)
617 Wedding. Engraving from *Habits and Customs of Russia*. Houbigant, 1821. B.N. (*Ph. P. Brossé.*)
618 *What is your name, my pretty girl?* Illustration to a popular song. 19th c. Russian engraving. Mme Ehrenbourg and P-L. Duchartre. (*Ph. Mus. Pedagog.*)
619 Posting-house on the Kostroma Road at Yaroslaw. Engraving, 1849. (*Ph. Pont Royal.*)
620 *It's time the boy got married*. Illustration to a popular song. 19th c. Russian engraving. Mme Ehrenbourg and M. P-L. Duchartre. (*Ph. Mus. Pedagog.*)
621 '*What a bear*', *says the mother-in-law*. Illustration to a popular song. 19th c. Russian engraving. Mme Ehrenbourg and M. P-L. Duchartre. (*Ph. Mus. Pedagog.*)
622 Ukrainian dance. Illustration to a popular song. 19th c. Russian engraving. Mme Ehrenbourg and M. P-L. Duchartre. (*Ph. Mus. Pedagog.*)
623 *She'll be content to spin*. Illustration to a popular song. 19th c. Russian engraving. Mme Ehrenbourg and M. P-L. Duchartre. (*Ph. Mus. Pedagog.*)
624 Ivan the Terrible. White wood toy. Popular Russian art. 19th c. Mme Ehrenbourg and M. P-L. Duchartre. (*Ph. Mus. Pedagog.*)
625 Doll made of pine cone, moss and bark. Popular Russian art, 19th c. Mme Ehrenbourg and M. P-L. Duchartre. (*Ph. Mus. Pedagog.*)
626 The five floors of an apartment block. Drawing from a work of E. Texier. (*Ph. Pont Royal.*)
627 *Kitchen interior*, by Martin Drolling. Louvre. (*Ph. Giraudon.*)
628 Distributing presents. Engraving by Deveria. (*Ph. Bulloz.*)
629 Shopping. Detail from a series of engravings. 1840. B.N. (*Ph. Giraudon.*)
630 At the Concerts Musard. Engraving by Bouchot, 1838. (*Ph. Giraudon.*)
631 Throng at the Ambigu-Comique theatre. Engraving, 1830, after a painting by Boilly. (*Ph. Bulloz.*)
632 Railway from Paris to Saint-Germain in 1857. Engraving. Dollfuss coll. (*Ph. Giraudon.*)
633 COLOUR PLATE: Selling carpets in a big store. Stereoscopic colour photo. (*Yvan Christ coll.*)
634 Family store. Fashion lithograph. 1850. Mus. Carnavalet, Paris. (*Ph. Giraudon.*)
635 The dentist or *Life on the Third Floor*. Contemporary photo. (*Yvan Christ coll.*)
636 The restaurant or *Life on the Ground Floor*. Contemporary photo. (*Yvan Christ coll.*)
637 Saratoga in 1860. Contemporary photograph. (*Ringart coll.*)
638 American family celebrating Independence Day. Drawing by C. H. Brainard, 19th c. (*Ph. U.S.I.S.*)
639 *Market of black slaves, U.S.A.*, c. 1852, by Taylor. Yale Univ. Lib. (*Ph. U.S.I.S.*)
640 Californian saloon at the time of the gold rush, 1852. Engraving from *Illustrated London News*. (*Ph. Pont Royal.*)
641 Train arriving in the station. Film set for *Beloved Vagabond*. (*Twentieth Century Fox. Jakovski coll.*)
642 *Election time*, by George Caleb Flingham. Boatmen's National Bank of St Louis. (*Drefts Photo. Coll. Pont Royal.*)
643 Lincoln during an electoral campaign in Illinois, 1858. Engraving. (*Ph. U.S.I.S.*)
644 Pilgrims at Benares. (*Ph. Vitold de Golish.*)
645 Chariot for the feast of Jugannath. (*Ph. Ringart coll.*)
646 Fakirs. (*Ringart coll.*)
647 Two Saddbous, their bodies smeared with ashes, lying on thorns in the centre of Calcutta. (*Ph. Vitold de Golish.*)
648 Two men in the streets of Bombay. Detail of photograph. (*Ringart coll.*)
649 Little girl in a sari. (*Ph. Vitold de Golish.*)
650 Interior of a palace. (*Ph. G. Bourdelon.*)
651 Young woman standing by a marble honeycomb window. The Red Fort, Delhi. Mongol period. (*Ph. G. Bourdelon.*)
652 Indian husband and wife. (*Ph. Ringart coll.*)
653 Buffalo among temple ruins in village. Bijapur, South India. (*Ph. Vitold de Golish.*)
654 Women making offering to the *linga*. Bhubaneswar. (*Ph. Vitold de Golish.*)
655 Traditional burial of a holy man. Badami, Bijapur. (*Ph. Vitold de Golish.*)
656 Paddle-wheel steamer. Stereoscopic photo. (*Yvan Christ coll.*)
657 Suburban street in England. Contemporary photograph. (*Ringart coll.*)
658 Arrival of the Channel steamer at Boulogne. (*Radio Times Hulton Pic. Lib.*)

659 English hansom-cab. Detail of a photograph. (*Cossira coll.*)
660 Tea-time in an English family. From a film set. (*Ph. Black Star. Rapho.*)
661 English bachelor apartment. (*Ph. Pont Royal.*)
662 Dinner of the Dilettante Society at the Thatched House Club. Engraving by J-H. Le Keux after T. H. Shepherd. 19th c. B.N. (*Ph. B. Brossé.*)
663 Great Ardsley Main Colliery, England. Engraving. (*Ph. Radio Times Hulton Pic. Lib.*)
664 Giving out miners' lamps at dawn. Engraving, 1878. (*Ph. Radio Times Hulton Pic. Lib.*)
665 The slums. Engraving by Gustave Doré. (*Radio Times Hulton Pic. Lib.*)
666 Colour Plate: New York Elevated Rly. Late 19th c. (*Jakovski coll.*)
667 Statue of Chappe and his telegraph. Detail from an old photograph. (*Yvan Christ coll.*)
668 Stage-coach. Travel photo. (*Yvan Christ coll.*)
669 Railway station. Reproduction of a picture by A. Binet from the 1891 Salon. (*Jakovski coll.*)
670 Washroom and sleeping compartment of a sleeping car, 1875. (*Doc. Compagnie internationale des Wagons-Lits.*)
671 Restaurant car, *c.* 1885. (*Doc. Comp. Int. des Wagons-Lit.*)
672 German prince driving his own car. Photograph, 1907. (*Ringart coll.*)
673 Omnibus between Tizi-Ouzou and Fort-National, North Africa. Photograph. (*Cossira coll.*)
674 Fifth Avenue, New York, 1900. (*Cossira coll.*)
675 Parisian horse-drawn omnibus. Photograph. (*Jakovski coll.*)
676 Early tramways. Photograph. (*Jakovski coll.*)
677 New Renault motor bus. Paris. (*Jakovski coll.*)
678 Paris metro. Post-card. (*Yvan Christ coll.*)
679 Woman driving a horse-drawn taxi. Paris. Photograph. (*Yvan Christ coll.*)
680 Motor taxi rank in Berlin. Photograph. (*Ringart coll.*)
681 Bicycle. Engraving from a manufacturer's catalogue, France, 1897. (*J. Espagne coll.*)
682 Milk train arriving in a main goods yard. Photograph. (*Cossira coll.*)
683 Automotive fire-engine. Photograph, 1899. (*Jakovski coll.*)
684 First automatic horse-drawn roadsweeper. Photograph. (*Cossira coll.*)
685 Horse-drawn dustcart. Photograph. (*Cossira coll.*)
686 Water-cart in a big city. Photograph. (*Cossira coll.*)
687 Fashionable Berlin lady. Detail from a photograph, 1906. (*Ringart coll.*)
688 An English tourist in a Paris street. Detail from a photograph. (*Yvan Christ coll.*)
689 Model of button-boot. From a catalogue of 1914. (*Jakovski coll.*)
690 Fashionable women at Deauville, August 1910. Photograph. (*Cossira coll.*)
691 Tourists in Berlin. Photograph. (*Ringart coll.*)
692 The walk. Detail from a photograph. (*Ringart coll.*)
693 The newspaper-stand. Detail of a photograph. (*Yvan Christ coll.*)
694 Bootblack. Photograph. (*Doc. Pont Royal.*)
695 Cocoa-stall. Detail of a post-card. (*Yvan Christ coll.*)
696 Performing bears. (*Ph. Monde et Camera.*)
697 Street photographer. Detail from a post-card. (*Yvan Christ coll.*)
698 Early camera. Engraving from a manufacturer's catalogue. 1897. (*Jacques Espagne coll.*)
699 Women with sandwich-boards. Photograph. (*Cossira coll.*)
700 Paris food store. (*Ph. Monde et Camera.*)
701 Family photo. (*Yvan Christ coll.*)
702 Middle class bedroom. Photograph. (*Yvan Christ coll.*)
703 Middle class bathroom. Photograph. (*Yvan Christ coll.*)
704 Gas company advertisement. Detail of an engraving from a souvenir calendar for 1892. (*Doc. Pont Royal.*)
705 Sewing-machine, Engraving from a manufacturer's catalogue, 1897. (*Jacques Espagne coll.*)
706 Miss Blanche Bates, the actress, telephoning in her New York apartment. Photograph, 1902. (*Ringart coll.*)
707 Employment bureau. Post-card. (*Yvan Christ coll.*)
708 Nursemaids out with their charges. Detail from post-card. (*Yvan Christ coll.*)
709 Little girl having her bath. Photograph. (*Pierre Espagne coll.*)
710 Playing diabolo. Detail from a photograph. (*Ringart coll.*)
711 The first clockwork railways. Photograph. (*Pierre Espagne coll.*)
712 Coming out of the Lycée Condorcet, Paris. Painting by Jean Béraud, 1898. Mus. Carnavalet. (*Ph. Bulloz.*)
713 Girls going into school. Photograph. (*Cossira coll.*)
714 Students outside the Sorbonne, Paris. 1912. Photograph. (*Cossira coll.*)
715 Game of croquet. Detail of photograph. (*Yvan Christ coll.*)
716 Golf. Detail of photograph. (*Ringart coll.*)
717 Bathing belle. Photograph. 1900. (*Ringart coll.*)
718 View of a beach, 1900. Photograph. (*Ringart coll.*)
719 Early camping caravans. Photograph. (*Cossira coll.*)
720 M. Hémery in a Benz at the world speed championship. Photograph. (*Jakovski coll.*)
721 Shot-putting in a German stadium. Photograph. (*Ringart coll.*)
722 Cinema at Milan. Contemporary publicity hand-out. (*Jakovski coll.*)
723 Dancing in the streets, Bastille Day. Detail of photograph. (*Yvan Christ coll.*)
724 Meal-time in a foreman's family. Photograph. (*Pierre Espagne coll.*)
725 Reading the employment advertisements in a Copenhagen street. Engraving. Lib. of Dec. Art. (*Ph. P. Brossé.*)
726 Typewriter. Engraving from manufacturer's catalogue, 1897. (*Jacques Espagne coll.*)
727 Street demonstration. Post-card. (*Yvan Christ coll.*)
728 Mothers' Aid Day-Nursery. Photograph. (*Yvan Christ coll.*)
729 School canteen. Engraving from *l'Illustration*, October 1888. (*Ph. Fr. Inst. Nat. Pedagog.*)
730 Early mechanical threshing machines. Photograph. (*Jakovski coll.*)
731 Le Bourget airport, France. Photograph. Compagnie aérienne française. (*Ringart coll.*)
732 Rumanian peasants listening to the radio. Photograph. (*Ringart coll.*)
733 First television demonstration. Photograph. (*Ringart coll.*)
734 Colour Plate: *The Strong Man*, painting by Bombois. *c.* 1930. Mus. Nat. d'Art Moderne. (*Ektachrome Giraudon.*)
735 Demonstration of new dental techniques in London, 1931. (*Ph. Keystone.*)
736 Baby in an incubator. Photograph. (*Ringart coll.*)
737 X-ray examination. Photograph. (*Ringart coll.*)
738 Holiday camp, England. Photograph. (*Ringart coll.*)
739 Young Sokols playing soldiers. Photograph. (*Ringart coll.*)
740 English-style house-boat interior on the Dal Lake at Shrinagar, Kashmir. (*Ph. G. Bourdelon.*)
741 Kitchen of a New York apartment. Photograph. (*Ringart coll.*)
742 Suffragette meeting in China. Photograph. (*Ringart coll.*)
743 Tokyo bus conductresses. Photograph. (*Ringart coll.*)
744 Telephone exchange in Poland. Photograph. (*Cossira coll.*)
745 Fashion plate. Summer 1920. (*Jakovski coll.*)
746 Cycling costume, Atlantic City, U.S.A. Detail of photograph. (*Ringart coll.*)
747 English women's hockey team. Photograph, 1935. (*Ringart coll.*)
748 Production line in car factory. Photograph. (*Ringart coll.*)
749 Municipal canteen, New York, Photograph. (*Ringart coll.*)
750 Coalminer's house at Liévin. Photograph. (*Harlingue coll.*)
751 First paid holidays. Photograph. (*Yvan Christ coll.*)
752 Preparations for the 27th Grand Prix of the A.C.F at Montlhéry, 1935. Photograph. (*Cossira coll.*)
753 American football match between Harvard and Rhode Island at Cambridge, Mass. U.S.A. (*Ph. Keystone.*)
754 Denver, Colorado, U.S.A. seen from a jet aircraft. (*Ph. E. Hartmann. Magnum.*)
755 Multi-storey car park at Houston, U.S.A. (*Ph. H. Cartier-Bresson. Magnum.*)
756 Taxi caught in a traffic jam, Tokyo. (*Ph. Marc Riboud. Magnum.*)
757 Rush hour in New York. (*Ph. H. Cartier-Bresson. Magnum.*)
758 Bus queue in the U.S.A. (*Ph. H. Cartier-Bresson. Magnum.*)
759 Autoroute du Sud, leaving Paris. (*Ph. Pugnet. Rapho.*)
760 View of part of Brasilia. (*Ph. René Burri. Magnum.*)
761 Modern block of flats in Finland. (*Ph. Kryn Taconis. Magnum.*)
762 Garden city at Sceaux, France. (*Ph. Micheline Broutta.*)
763 Colour Plate: Times Square, New York, at night. (*Kodachrome H. Cartier-Bresson. Magnum.*)
764 Living-room in a modern flat. (*Ph. Persson. Rapho.*)
765 Corner of a modern living-room. (*Ph. Boucher. Coll. Maison et Jardin.*)
766 Jayne Mansfield's living-room, in Hollywood. (*Ph. Inge Morath. Magnum.*)
767 American child's room. (*Ph. Inge Morath. Magnum.*)
768 Modern sanitary installations. (*Doc. Formica.*)
769 Functional kitchen. (*Ph. Pierre Jahan.*)
770 Two-temperature refrigerator. (*Ph. Geischeidt. Black Star. Rapho.*)
771 Washing machine. (*Ph. Belzeaux. Rapho.*)
772 Washing and ironing machine. (*Ph. R. Crane. Black Star. Rapho.*)
773 Silverplated table setting. (*Ph. Kollar, Doc. Christofle.*)
774 Silverplated tea-pot. (*Ph. Kollar, Doc. Christofle.*)
775 Child eating its dinner, Pekin. (*Ph. D. Darbois.*)
776 Shopping in a supermarket, U.S.A. (*Ph. Marc Riboud. Magnum.*)
777 Self-service restaurant, U.S.A. (*Ph. H. Cartier-Bresson. Magnum.*)
778 Window-shopping in Paris. (*Ph. Ciccione. Rapho.*)
779 Escalator in a big Tokyo store. (*Ph. Marc Riboud. Magnum.*)
780 Children's clothing department in a multiple store. (*Ph. J. Verroust.*)
781 American models in Hollywood. (*Ph. Dennis Stock. Magnum.*)
782 News stand in an Italian street. (*Ph. Viollon. Rapho.*)
783 Children watching television. (*Ph. Claude Limot. Rapho.*)
784 Week-end traffic near New York. (*Ph. H. Cartier-Bresson. Magnum.*)
785 Open-air dancing in a summer holiday camp. (*Detail of a photograph by Marc Riboud. Magnum.*)

786 Camping site. (*Ph. Le Cuziat, Rapho.*)
787 Passengers on an air liner. (*Ph. Eric Hartmann. Magnum.*)
788 Group of tourists. (*Detail of ph. Sabine Weiss. Rapho.*)
789 Winter sports at Barèges. (*Ph. Yan. Rapho.*)
790 Broadway at night. (*Ph. Conzett and Huber. Rapho.*)
791 Sunday gardening in an American suburb. (*Ph. Black Star. Rapho.*)
792 Large American family. (*Ph. Cornell Capa. Magnum.*)
793 American picnic. (*Ph. H. Cartier-Bresson. Magnum.*)
794 Baseball players. (*Detail of a U.S.I.S. photograph.*)
795 Female clerical workers in national bank-note printing offices. Washington. (*Ph. H. Cartier-Bresson. Magnum.*)
796 Coffee-break. (*Ph. Cornell Capa. Magnum.*)
797 Bookshop window, U.S.A. (*Ph. H. Cartier-Bresson. Magnum.*)
798 Baby-care course using celluloid dolls, in U.S.A. (*Ph. H. Cartier-Bresson. Magnum.*)
799 Women's club at Miami, Florida. (*Ph. H. Cartier-Bresson. Magnum.*)
800 Amusement arcade with pin-tables at Las Vegas. (*Ph. H. Cartier-Bresson. Magnum.*)
801 Drive-in cinema, U.S.A. (*Ph. Marc Riboud. Magnum.*)
802 Coney Island beach. (*Ph. Belzeaux. Rapho.*)
803 Motel near Cape Canaveral, Florida. (*Ph. U.S.I.S.*)
804 Small shopkeeper in Turkestan. (*Ph. H. Cartier-Bresson. Magnum.*)
805 Queue of visitors outside Lenin's mausoleum in Red Square, Moscow. (*Ph. Cornell Capa. Magnum.*)
806 Delegation from Asiatic provinces visiting Moscow University. (*Ph. H. Cartier-Bresson. Magnum.*)
807 New blocks of flats on the riverside, Moscow. (*Ph. Cornell Capa. Magnum.*)
808 Subway station, Moscow. (*Ph. Cornell Capa. Magnum.*)
809 Moscow shoppers. (*Ph. H. Cartier-Bresson. Magnum.*)
810 Children on a collective farm and their teachers. Akmolensk district. (*Ph. Soviet Information Bureau.*)
811 Moscow fashion show. (*Detail of ph. H. Cartier-Bresson. Magnum.*)
812 Child's room. Furniture exhibition, Moscow 1959. (*Ph. Soviet Information Bureau.*)
813 Park of culture and rest. (*Ph. H. Cartier-Bresson. Magnum.*)
814 Holiday-makers at a seaside resort on the Black Sea. (*Ph. H. Cartier-Bresson. Magnum.*)
815 Engineers and forewomen of the new generation in China. (*Ph. D. Darbois.*)
816 Nursery school in Pekin. (*Ph. D. Darbois.*)
817 May Day parade, Pekin. (*Ph. D. Darbois.*)
818 May Day ball, Pekin. (*Ph. D. Darbois.*)
819 School for adult education in Nigeria. (*Ph. G. Rodger. Magnum.*)
820 Woman pedlar in the market at Kano, Nigeria. (*Detail of ph. G. Rodger. Magnum.*)
821 Indian labourer on the site of Brasilia. (*Ph. René Burri. Magnum.*)
822 Peruvians in traditional Inca costume posing for photographs in a square in Cuzco. (*Ph. Cornell Capa. Magnum.*)
823 Japanese schoolboys in uniform. (*Ph. D. Darbois.*)
824 Old-fashioned schoolroom in Africa. (*Ph. D. Darbois.*)
825 Students at a Buddhist school in Rangoon, Burma. (*Ph. Werner Bishof. Magnum.*)
826 Combine-harvesters. (*Ph. Zalewski. Rapho.*)
827 Surgical operation in an African hospital. (*Ph. D. Darbois.*)
828 Indian using an adze on the site of Brasilia. (*Ph. René Burri. Magnum.*)
829 Targui at the wheel of a truck in the Sahara. (*Ph. G. Rodger. Magnum.*)
830 COLOUR PLATE: Façade of a building by Le Corbusier at Chandigar, Pakistan. (*Kodachrome Marc Riboud. Magnum.*)
831 COLOUR PLATE: Workings at La Forminière diamond mines at Bakwanga, Kasai. (*Ektachrome Michel Huet.*)
832 First Communion procession led by a beadle, Paris. (*Detail of ph. P. Dubure. Rapho.*)
833 Traditional country wedding in France. (*Ph. Doisneau. Rapho.*)
834 Horse-drawn hearse in a small French village. (*Ph. H. Cartier-Bresson. Magnum.*)
835 Changing of the Guard at Copenhagen. (*Ph. H. Cartier-Bresson. Magnum.*)
836 Penitent in a Holy Week procession, Seville, Spain. (*Detail of ph. by A. Martin. Atlas Photo.*)
837 Gypsy camp at Epsom. (*Ph. P. Popper, Atlas.*)
838 Geishas in a Tokyo tea-house. (*Ph. Marc Riboud. Magnum.*)
839 Vietnamese woman worshipper in the streets of Saigon. (*Ph. D. Darbois.*)
840 Russian peasant woman on a pilgrimage to Zagorsk. (*Detail from a ph. A. E. Anderson. Rapho.*)
841 Postman in a Copenhagen street. (*Ph. H. Cartier-Bresson. Magnum.*)
842 Woman spinning at Oliena, Sardinia. (*Ph. G. Viollon.*)
843 Building an igloo, Baffinland. (*Ph. D. Darbois.*)
844 Old woman near Laghouat. (*Ph. M. Broutta.*)
845 Roadsweeper at Otavalo (Equador). (*Ph. F. Hébert-Stevens.*)
846 Cock fight in Burma. (*Ph. D. Darbois.*)
847 Witchcraft in a village near Luang-Prabang, Laos. (*Ph. D. Darbois.*)
848 Dayak smoking on the verandah of his house. Central Borneo. (*Ph. G. Bourdelon.*)
849 Girls dancing at Kordofan, Sudan. (*Ph. G. Rodger. Magnum.*)
850 A head-hunter. (*Ph. T Saulnier. Paris-Match.*)
851 Jivaros head-shrinkers. (*Ph. P. Allard.*)
852 Secretary working in individual booth in a New York office. (*Ph. H. Cartier-Bresson. Magnum.*)
853 Push-button kitchen, *Mrs America*, controlled by an electronic brain. Moscow exhibition. Summer 1959. (*Ph. U.S.I.S.*)
854 Relaxing treatment. (*Ph. Black Star. Rapho.*)
855 Electro-encephalography used on a child in the hospital of Vanderbilt Univ., Nashville, Tennessee. (*Ph. U.S.I.S.*)
856 Control and organisation room of atomic pile G2 at Marcoule, France. (*Ph. P. Jahan, from C.E.A.*)
857 Engineers wearing protective clothing in radioactivity research lab. at Dounreay, Scotland. (*Ph. Brit. Embassy.*)
858 Petroleum plant in the desert near Kuwait. (*Ph. G. Rodger. Magnum.*)
859 Supreme court and Chapel, Brasilia. (*Ph. René Burri. Magnum.*)
860 New reservoir under construction, Kuwait. (*Ph. G. Rodger. Magnum.*)
861 Detail of Parliament building, Brasilia. (*Ph. R. Burri. Magnum.*)
862 Pilot in training capsule for space flight. American experimental station. (*Ph. C. Capa. Magnum.*)
863 COLOUR PLATE: Parliament building and dome seen through the arches of the Supreme Court. (*Ektachrome R. Burri. Magnum.*)
864 Hiker on a road near Brasilia. (*Ph. R. Burri. Magnum.*)

JACKET ILLUSTRATIONS:—Design by Jacques Dubois.

On the front cover:

*The Baker's shop.* 15th c. miniature from *the Calendar of Charles of Angoulême.* MS. B.N. (*Ph. Pont Royal.*)

*Street in New York.* Detail of a 19th c. print. (*Jakovski coll.*)

*Aztec priest.* Detail from *Codex Borbonicus.* Palais Bourbon Lib., Paris. (*Ph. Pierre Espagne.*)

*Woman carrying offerings.* Egyptian statuette in coloured wood. 11th dynasty. Cairo Mus. (*Ph. Hassia.*)

*The Railway.* English colour print. B.N. (*Ektachrome B.N.*)

*Girl sitting juggling with balls of wool.* Attic red figure vase, Athens, 5th c. B.C. Exhibition *Domestic Life in Greece and Rome,* Louvre. (*Ph. Franceschi.*)

*The Bookseller.* Water colour from *The Streets of Pekin,* 18th c. B.N. (*Ph. B.N.*)

*Key.* Drawing based on an original. (*Doc. Jacques Dubois.*)

*Small Flemish town in the 15th c.* Detail from *the Madonna of the Screen of Rushes,* by the Master of Flémalle. Reproduced by courtesy of the trustees of the National Gallery, London. (*Ektachrome Ed. Skira.*)

On the back cover:

*Detail of Parliament building, Brasilia.* (*Ph. René Burri. Magnum.*)

*Illustration of a Russian popular song.* 19th c. engraving. Mme Ehrenbourg and M. P-L. Duchartre. (*Ph. Mus. Pédagogique, France.*)

*Village women near Douenza, Sudan.* (*Ph. Michel Huet.*)

*Man planting leeks.* German woodcut. B.N. From work by P. de Crescentiis. Spier, 1493. B.N. (*Ph. Pont Royal.*)

*Supple wooden spoon.* Brittany. 17th–18th c. Mus. des Arts et Traditions Populaires. Paris.

*Roman scales.* Bronze. Exhibition *Domestic Life in Greece and Rome,* Louvre. (*Ph. Franceschi.*)

*Vine-grower's bill-hook.* Mus. des Arts et Traditions Populaires, Paris. (*Ph. Sougez.*)

ENDPAPERS:

*Concentric clock.* Engraving from Dichiaratione di Horologia di Mantova. Mantua, 1547. (*Ph. Philippe Brossé.*)